CHINA'S
MEGATRENDS

Also by John Naisbitt

Megatrends

Global Paradox

Megatrends Asia

Mind Set!

Reinventing the Corporation (with Patricia Aburdene)

Megatrends 2000 (with Patricia Aburdene)

Megatrends for Women (with Patricia Aburdene)

Japan's Identity Crisis (with Shosaburo Kimura)

Megachallenges (Japanese language only)

High Tech High Touch (with Nana Naisbitt and Douglas Philips)

CHINA'S
MEGATRENDS

The 8 Pillars
of a New Society

JOHN AND DORIS
NAISBITT

HARPER
BUSINESS

An Imprint of HarperCollinsPublishers
www.harpercollins.com

HarperCollins books may be purchased for educational, business, or sales
promotional use. For information, please write: Special Markets Department,
HarperCollins Publishers, 10 East 53rd Street, New York, NY 10022.

FIRST EDITION

Designed by William Ruoto

Library of Congress Cataloging-in-Publication Data
Naisbitt, John.
    China's megatrends: the 8 pillars of a new society / John Naisbitt and
Doris Naisbitt.—1st ed.
        p.   cm.
    ISBN 978-0-06-185944-1
    1. Economic forecasting—China.   2. —Social prediction—China.
3. China—Economic conditions—21st century.   4. China—Social
conditions—21st century.   I. Naisbitt, Doris.   II. Title.
    HC427.95.N35 2010
    330.951—dc22   2009023554

10 11 12 13 14   WBG/RRD   10 9 8 7 6 5 4 3 2 1

For Lily, Jade, and Tao, our young friends,
who are growing up in a new China

Contents

Prologue: A New System on the Rise

For many years I carried a regret, the feeling I had missed one of the great opportunities in life. It was back in 1996 and the offer I received was made by one of the most powerful men of the time: Jiang Zemin, the president of China.

It was at a private meeting at the leadership compound in Beijing, in the same room where Mao had received his guests. The reason for Jiang Zemin's invitation was *Megatrends*, a book I had written in 1982 analyzing the economic, political, social, and cultural transition taking place in the United States. It was on the best-seller list of the *New York Times* for more than two years, mostly as number one, and became a huge global success. *Megatrends* also made its way to China, and to my surprise I was told that it must have sold at least 20 million copies in China alone—pirated copies, a common distribution system at the time. The members of the first generation after the Cultural Revolution had just graduated from colleges and universities and were hungry and eager to learn from the West. "You don't know how famous you are in China," were the very first words President Jiang said to me.

Before my visit to Beijing I had spent a few days in Taipei. This was a critical period in relations between the United States and China. President Clinton had deployed aircraft carriers in response to China's sending missiles into waters close to Taiwan. The two countries were teetering at the brink of a clash over Taiwan, and so it was not surprising that Taiwan was the elephant in the room during our two-hour conversation. Before very long, Taiwan became a subject of discussion. I had visited both China and Taiwan many times since 1967, and I had witnessed the huge changes that had taken place. I noticed the unspoken discomfort with how well Taiwan presented itself to the world and how modest China's presentation was in comparison. So I said, "President Jiang, Taiwan has a small story to tell, and tells it very well. China has a big story to tell, and does a terrible job in telling it."

Silence.

And then: "Why don't you tell it? We will give you all the support you need."

As tempting as that offer was, I could not accept it. I was too much engaged in other things. And—for whatever reason—I was not ready.

Ten years later, the offer came back, this time from China's new corporate world. It happened during the taping of a television program. I was having a dialogue with a Chinese businessman, Wang Wei, who had founded one of China's first mergers and acquisitions firms and was also head of the China Mergers & Acquisitions Association. He had studied and worked in New York and returned to China in 1992. As the dialogue was recorded, we had time between takes and soon became engaged in a lively conversation about China and its future. Wang Wei told me that he had read *Megatrends* in 1982 and that it had been a great influence on him.

A few days later I received an e-mail from him: "There are many books about China's past and China's rise and about China's political, economic, and cultural future. But what we need is an analysis as you did in *Megatrends*. Not even the Chinese know what is really going on in China and where it is headed. Why don't you find out and write about what China's megatrends are?"

This time I was ready, not only because ten more years of traveling

China extensively had increased my visits to China to a total of more than one hundred, and deepened my understanding of the country and its people, but also because this time I would not do it alone. Over the last decade I have been traveling in China with my wife, Doris. She was my German-language publisher before she became my wife in 2000. As it turned out, she was a perfect match in more ways than one. We travel the world together, do our research together, and share the excitement about what is happening in China. She was with me when we got to know Wang Wei, who has become a very good friend, a most reliable partner, a great supporter, and the initiator of this book.

Only a few months after our first conversations and his e-mail to me, together with another Chinese partner we founded the Naisbitt China Institute as an independent, stand-alone institute, strongly supported by Nankai University and Tianjin University of Finance and Economics (I am a professor at both universities). Our commitment was to step back from the western view and assumptions, and look at China as the Chinese look at their country; we would be open to its shortcomings, but would not judge China by our own values and standards.

At first we needed to collect as much information as possible about what was happening on the ground. We started intense meetings with our staff, as many as twenty-eight students and graduate students from two universities in Tianjin, led by Chinese entrepreneurs and academics. We briefed them about what we were looking for. First, and most important, they should collect only facts, things that have indeed been done—no plans, no declarations. Second, they had to get used to the principle that we did not frame the subjects; any frame would have given the research a certain direction, and thus we would have missed what we were hoping to find—things we did not know, things that would surprise us. This process was unusual compared with the Chinese way of thinking. A third challenge was to shorten and translate the media articles that were selected and make them into the database.

It was truly a pleasure to work with our team, and also to have met with students in other parts of China.

In parallel with this monitoring of local Chinese media, Doris and

I traveled around China, interviewing entrepreneurs, academics, politicians, artists, dissidents, and expatriates, always keeping our goal in mind: to tell the China's story from the inside out, not from the outside in as most recent books on China have done.

We were in search of China's megatrends. We were aware that we were looking at a country undergoing great and very complex change, with each region and each city moving at its own level and its own speed. We were looking for patterns, in which a series of single events would begin to make sense and form a picture of the new China, just as such events did in the United States in 1982, when I wrote *Megatrends*.

What we found was of much greater dimensions and importance than we had anticipated. We concentrated on the obvious shifts in the social, political, cultural, and economic life of the country, but it seemed that those shifts were only the result of something else—something overarching, which we could not define. Then, one afternoon in Beijing, it became clear to us, and we wondered why we had not seen it before. Whereas America in 1982 had been transforming within a system that was already well in place, China in 2009 is creating an entirely new social and economic system—and a political model, which may well prove that "the end of history" was just another pause along history's path.

John Naisbitt, May 2009

CHINA'S 8 PILLARS OF A NEW SOCIETY

1. Emancipation of the Mind

2. Balancing Top-Down and Bottom-Up

3. Framing the Forest and Letting
   the Trees Grow

4. Crossing the River by Feeling the Stones

5. Artistic and Intellectual Ferment

6. Joining the World

7. Freedom and Fairness

8. From Olympic Medals to Nobel Prizes

The concept of the 8 pillars and their selection and description are entirely the work and responsibility of the authors.

Introduction

Any speculation about China's future begins with an analysis of the first thirty years of the "reforms and opening up," as the Chinese call the period when the country began its evolution from a postwar communist society to a new form of governance and development, never seen before in modern history. Why has "autocratic" China succeeded while many other, democratically governed states have failed to make economic progress? Why is it that despite all efforts by westerners to push China toward western-style democratization, there is no similar outcry for such a shift in China?

In looking at China on its own terms and merits, it becomes clear that the constancy of the Communist Party has worked not against but for the well-being of the Chinese people. Long-term strategic planning could be carried out without the distractions and disruptions of elections that characterize western democracies. China was not torn by political rivalry and was not slowed down by abrupt changes in its course; rather, it was attuned to common goals from early on in its reforms. Top-down strategies were supported by bottom-up participation. And we found that China has reinvented itself as if it were a huge enterprise, resting on 8 Pillars that buttress its aims.

Those 8 Pillars, we believe, are the foundation of China's new socio-economic system.

Reinventing China

China in 1978: A visionary, decisive, assertive CEO takes over a very large, moribund company that is on the verge of collapse. The workforce is demoralized, patronized, and poorly educated. The CEO is determined to turn the run-down enterprise into a healthy, profitable, sustainable company, and to bring modest wealth to the people. And he has a clear strategy for achieving this goal.

First, he needs an effective team, a workforce that meets the demand of the enterprise. Subordinated thinking must change to emancipated thinking. The emancipation of minds will release energy and strengthen self-esteem. People will stand on their own feet to contribute to the process of transforming the company.

Second, he must engage both the leadership and the employees in creating an interplay between top-down orders and bottom-up demands. He must encourage the bottom to contribute to the process of forming and shaping the company. Harmony within the hierarchical order of the company will be sustainable if top-down goals and guidelines on the one hand, and bottom-up ideas, feedback, and demand on the other, do not collide but instead work together to strengthen the whole.

Third, he must shape the values and culture of the company, set clear goals, and communicate these goals. Only a profitable company can provide wealth for the people. He must set the big frames of reference and guiding principles within which people can move without instructions for every step. This will leave enough room for talented people to develop their skills, and it will allow creativity to unfold.

Fourth, he will need to build trust instead of fear. Failures in experimentation within the guidelines cannot be condemned, because only experimentation that allows mistakes will lead to innovations. Trial and error, changes, and adaptations must be possible at any time.

Fifth, creativity will be the key to further advancements of the society. Artistic and intellectual ferment needs to be welcomed and supported as a source of inspiration and liberation for the new company culture.

Sixth, as soon as the company establishes itself in its home market, it will be open for other markets, invest in other markets, and invite outsiders to transfer know-how into the company.

Seventh, everyone's behavior will have an impact on others. Success will arouse jealousy, and idleness will arouse complaints. Sooner or later more engaged and more talented workers will move up and make more money, while others, who are not so talented or diligent, will grumble about their stagnant position. The more freedom and fairness can be complementary, the greater the harmony in the company.

And eighth, after the company establishes a solid position in the market as a manufacturer, the next aim will be to move from imitation to innovation. In the process all previous steps are moved to higher levels, upgrading the quality of work and the inventiveness of the enterprise—and increasing revenues, with profitability enhancing the lives of the workers and their families.

China in 2009: The company has changed from an almost bankrupt state into a very profitable enterprise, the third largest of its kind in the world. It has made clever moves in its challenges and crisis, and its economic success is now recognized around the globe.

Deng's Cat

This description of how to transform a company is not far from how the CEOs Deng Xiaoping, Jiang Zemin, and Hu Jintao have moved China from being a primitive, dispirited country to being the third largest economy in the world, with undiminished momentum. The eight steps described above are similar to the 8 Pillars that have structured the transformation of China and that form the core of this book.

China is creating an entirely new social and economic society with a "company culture" that serves the needs of the enterprise and its people on its own path to modernity and prosperity. Deng, the father of modern China, early on developed a Chinese approach for how to turn a moribund China around. This has caused some dispute, in and outside China, about his political alignment. The misunderstanding lies in the interpretation of his most famous aphorism: "It doesn't matter if the cat is black or white, so long as it catches mice."

To Deng Xiaoping the question was not whether communism or capitalism would be best for the enterprise; the real question was what works and what doesn't work to enable the country to achieve its potential for the future.

So the question whether China is a capitalist country with a communist coat or a communist country with capitalist coat is the wrong question. It is not either-or; nor is it both of them. And China definitely is not a communist country that is slowly peeling off one communist layer after the other in preparation for slipping into the capitalist coat held by the West.

Despite China's embrace of the bicolored economic cat, and despite the country's opening up and reforms, the color of the *political* cat was never in question, and no western-style democracy was ever on the rise. Deng Xiaoping underlined this in 1992, when he said that "the Chinese people should hold on to the basic foundation of the Party without swaying for a hundred years." Within this huge frame China has developed concepts for the best ways to handle its multiple challenges.

Westerners like to focus on what China's "reforms and opening up" mean in terms of western thinking—with the conviction that the western model is the best form of government. That approach will lead to disappointment and unrealistic expectations. The real answer lies not in ideology but in performance. Gideon Rachman, chief commentator on foreign affairs for the *Financial Times*, quoted Deng Xiaoping's translator, Zhang Wei-Wei, who remarked, "The Chinese believe in performance legitimacy. If the government governs well, it is perceived as legitimate."

Bursting Old Frames

It is not easy to describe the new system that China is creating, partly because, as with other entities that have evolved, it takes a while before a new system finds a name. China's leadership most often calls its approach "socialism with Chinese characteristics." Others call it "Chinese capitalism" or a "socialist market economy."

We agree with Thomas Kuhn: "You cannot understand a new paradigm by using the vocabulary of the old paradigm." The more the new paradigm unfolds, the more an adequate vocabulary will emerge.

Just as new vocabulary arises from new thinking, the self-conception of the Communist Party is changing. The claim of leadership remains, but ideological control is increasingly replaced by laws and rules, adapted to international standards.

Chinese leaders soon discovered that to be successful on the path to modernization—to enable the shift from a planned economy to a market economy—they had to embrace decentralization. But decentralization, by definition, places more power in the hands of the people. China, often thought of as a monolith, is actually decentralizing power more than any other country in the world.

At the provincial level, in local governments and city councils, we see a gradual handover of governance directly to the people. The periphery is more and more becoming the center. No other country has implemented pilot projects on such a wide scale. China's leadership creates the broad concept, and enables the people to organize the evolution of the new China. Laws and regulations are often tested in so-called trial zones, and if they succeed in practice, they become national. China's early special economic zones were a huge experimental laboratory for institutional and jurisdictional change.

China has created space for both private enterprise and profitable state-owned enterprises. It also continues to provide a nourishing environment for entrepreneurs, where new talent can unfold and flourish. But its highest goal is a harmonious society and governance that is based on trust: the people trusting the leadership to create the opportunities for a better life, and the leadership trusting the people to be the driving force in the process. China's new model is based on a balance between top-down and bottom-up forces, which, in a combined effort, improve the standard of living and create wealth for the people.

Two Diametric Systems: The American Eagle Meets the Kung Fu Panda

There is increasing competition between western and eastern societies and values. America, as the leader of the West, is wounded. China, the newly emerging leader of the East, has a long way to go until it can economically challenge its western counterpart, but its direction is firmly set. All signs are pointing to a continuing global shift from West to East.

China can increasingly set economic and political rules. Western countries need the Chinese market to keep up their growth and are competing with one another for an advantage in entering the Chinese markets. Nevertheless, the West still claims the right and the moral duty to turn Chinese politics in the direction of establishing a western democracy.

In the political sphere the West continues to claim that democracy is the world's best way of governing. But from what we have seen in China, we have to question whether modern western democracy is the only acceptable form of government. Can what the West calls an "autocratic government" successfully increase the wealth and political stability of a quarter of the world's population? Is it possible that capitalism and big government can fit together in ways that westerners cannot easily envision? For many countries in the third world today, China is beginning to offer a tempting counter-model—one that could, over time, constitute a real challenge for the western democratic way of governing.

"What," wrote the correspondent Howard W. French in an essay on China's "new paradigm" in the *International Herald Tribune* in March 2007, "if sure-footed bureaucrats—chosen purely on the basis of merit, rigorously trained and ideologically vetted—were allowed to implement and execute, free of harassment from a meddlesome congress?

Might that not be the explanation, for example, for the extraordinary marshalling of resources here to create world-class infrastructure, majestic cities, airports, highways and dams rising in record time out of the economic rubble of the proletarian cultural revolution?"

Any admission that China is changing for the better, that it seeks its own compromises and even allows some forms of a pluralistic society, would for many westerners be a frightening challenge to the role of the West as the custodian of the global moral high ground. The opening up of China not only widens the latitude of the Chinese leadership but also shakes the political range of the reform elite. Europe and the United States are facing a new player, which is economically strong, politically stable, and unhesitant to represent its own values in the world.

While the American eagle, which once flew unchallenged at impressive heights, is struggling to regain its position, on the other side of the globe a once clumsy panda, well trained in martial arts, is on the rise.

China Is Rising. So What?

In his July 4, 2009, column in the *New York Times*, David Brooks wrote, "These days it's impossible to think about America and its future role in the world without also thinking about China."

If America is called the country of unlimited possibilities, and Europe is the union obsessed about regulating everything from working conditions to bananas, then China can be called the country of strategic advancement. The opening up of China was part of a strategic plan to use foreign support and technology transfer to increase its own might through economic development. To reach the goal of changing from the "workshop of the world" to the innovator of new technologies for the world, China has protected Chinese companies by limiting foreign shareholdings, and has strengthened Chinese corporations by allowing a fierce, Darwinian competition among them.

In the last thirty years the strategic planning of the Chinese leadership has catapulted the once backward, underdeveloped country into one that has beaten Germany as export champion of the world, and has replaced it as the world's third largest economy. And this planning has moved China into the powerful position of determining the political and economic conditions under which western companies will gain access to its enormous market.

Unlike the European Union, which in 2000 grandly announced that it would "become the most competitive, knowledge-based economy in the world by 2010" but never managed to implement necessary reforms to reach that target, and unlike Japan, which seems entangled in its own ties with the past, China has not only met but exceeded its goals.

What if a single country could produce most goods of the highest quality and put them on the global market for an unbeatable price? The Nobel laureate Paul Samuelson predicts that China could become such a country. Not only is China changing to match global trading conditions; it is changing the conditions of global trade.

The West Is a Lecturing Society; China Is a Learning Society

How did the West and western companies get into such a defensive situation? The West gladly embraced Francis Fukuyama's 1989 essay and his 1992 book *The End of History*, in which he wrote that the model of the western democracy may well be the final stage of humanity's social and cultural evolution and the ultimate form of governing. His theory was also supported by humanism, which argues for a universal morality based on the human condition we all share. This led to "missionary thinking" and to a sense of being required to bless all nations with these western values. But what is considered "support" to reach the level of western evolution is often received as lecturing.

China, on the other hand, is well aware that it has come only part of its way and therefore still needs to correct, improve, and add. This belief has sustained China as a learning society, open to any theory or practice that can serve its goals. That is one of China's strongest assets. When Deng Xiaoping visited the United States in 1979, he was taken to a Ford plant outside Atlanta. Ford made more cars in that one factory in one month than all of China produced in a year. During that visit Deng said, "We want to learn from you." And China did.

Frank Sieren, a correspondent for *Die Zeit* in Beijing, painted this future scenario: picture a Chinese car for about $5,000, with four doors, navigation system, and air bags—paid for at the cashier at Wal-Mart. No fancy presentation, no showrooms, and a slim distribution system—delivery each Friday in the parking lot.

Although all this leads to an optimistic economic outlook, China will have to face and solve indisputable internal problems:

"Economic progress is realized at an excessively high cost of resources and environment. There is an imbalance in development between urban and rural areas, among regions, and between the economy and society. It has become more difficult to bring about a steady growth of agriculture and continue to increase farmers' incomes. There are still many problems affecting people's immediate interests in areas such as employment, social security, income distribution, education, public health, housing, work safety, administration of justice and public order; and some low-income people live a difficult life. More efforts are needed to promote ideological and ethical progress. The governance capability of the Party falls somewhat short of the need to deal with the situations and tasks. In-depth investigations and studies have yet to be conducted on some major practical issues related to reforms, development and stability. Some primary Party cadres are not honest and upright, their formalism and bureaucratism are quite conspicuous, and extravagance, waste, corruption, and other undesirable behaviours are still serious problems."

What sounds as if it were taken from a western commentary is in fact taken word-for-word from President Hu Jintao's speech at the Seventeenth National Congress in Beijing in October 2007.

The West is still far ahead of China. But China is already an equal competitor in the global marketplace and is on the way to creating a political counter-model to western modern democracy, fitting to Chinese history and society—just as America created a model fitting to its history and society more than 200 years ago. We will identify the 8 Pillars on which the new Chinese system rests.

Pillar 1

Emancipation of the Mind

The dimension of Deng Xiaoping's call for emancipating the minds of the people can be captured only in the context of the time: almost 1 billion people divided in a class struggle had to be united in the common goal of transforming the country. The destructive forces of the Cultural Revolution had to be turned into constructive energy for building a new China. The transformation had to start with allowing people to reclaim their own thinking. The liberation of minds from indoctrination to emancipation was the first and most important pillar of the transformation of China.

"Cast off the shackles that bind our spirit."

China in May 1978: A tiny giant of a man, Deng Xiaoping, makes the first, indispensable step in China's journey to modernity and a market economy as he calls upon his people: "We need to bring about a great emancipation in our way of thinking."

Deng understood that a top-down centralized society with little space for personal contribution was not fertile ground for a market economy. The emancipation of minds was necessary for a successful economic reform characterized by decentralization. At the time, China looked much like an old-fashioned company that had been run by a dictatorial president, definite about his own ideas, deaf to criticism, and adamant against any change. China's people were like incapacitated employees gagged for decades who would have to learn to think independently. Decentralization and emancipation had to go hand in hand.

In the years between 1949 and 1976, the Great Leap Forward and the Cultural Revolution had melded the most populous nation on earth into a huge gray mass: hungry, isolated, and indoctrinated, with any work carried on outside the state structure illegal. Education and knowledge were condemned, universities were closed, and national college entrance examinations were suspended. This was Mao's version of a "race to the bottom."

How did people make it through those years? Many books have been written about how deep the wounds from these days are and how much they are still hurting. But in many of our conversations it was surprising to us how little bitterness there is. This might well be part of the Chinese people's ability to adapt to circumstances that cannot be changed, and of their much more forward-looking attitude toward life. They feel it is more useful to put energy into their future well-being than to dwell in the past. Many of our successful Chinese acquaintances were sent to rural parts of China for "reeducation" during the Cultural Revolution; and although moving people like chess pieces, and taking them away from their family life, jobs, schools, and universities, seems quite dismaying to us, most of them found something good in it.

A Good Idea at the Time

"That's just how it was," said our friend Wang Wei, one of China's very successful businessmen. In 1976, Wang—the tall, handsome older son of an average Chinese urban family—was seventeen years old and full of energy. Like 12 million other students, he was sent to the countryside between 1966 and 1976; he was told to leave school to work in a small village in the mountains of Liaoning province, in northeastern China. It was not exactly what he had been dreaming of, but he made the best of it, he worked hard, and it paid off. A talent for organizing and leadership qualities were needed even under those circumstances. Wang Wei was soon promoted, and after working in the fields and raising sheep he became the leader of a production team of almost 1,000 farmers.

In this countrywide reeducation program President Jiang Zemin worked as an assembly line worker at an automobile plant in Shanghai. Chen Kaige, China's famous filmmaker, was sent to work in a rubber plantation in Yunnan, just one year after he had entered high school in Beijing. The vice president of Nanjing University was removed from his job as head of the sociology department to work in construction as a hod carrier—a terrible job (as John knows from his own experience in Utah). Asked how he felt about carrying bricks and mortar up ladders to bricklayers, the vice president said, "It seemed like a good idea at the time."

In 1978 the concept of a good idea changed.

To turn around the moribund enterprise, China, Deng had to promote emancipation instead of indoctrination. At the beginning of this process, eighteen bold farmers—who, in desperation, had overcome their own indoctrinated thinking—initiated the first big step in reforms. We tell their story in the chapter on Pillar 2. Deng Xiaoping's reinventing process needed initiatives from the ground to improve productivity. That's why he supported the proposal of the farmers for a change in agriculture. Very soon the spirit of emancipation could be found in many areas. Gradual but widespread educational reforms were started. Science, art, and society itself started to experiment with increased individual freedom. Artists were no longer driven by remittance work, stuck in traditional calligraphy or propaganda art. It was the dawn of new values and a new detachment from the masses. Just as in the Renaissance, Chinese artists started to focus on their own work and ideas and painted what was important to them and important for China in their eyes. They were more than willing to march at the front of the emancipation parade.

But it was not only artists who moved to the front of the parade. People from all walks of life came forward, including simple people from the countryside.

Freedom Has Many Faces

"Freedom for Chinese is not directly connected with the circumstances they live in," Wang Yukun, director of the Center for Chinese Enterprise Thinking, Tsinghua University, and a former Fulbright scholar, explained to us. "When I grew up in Shandong, times for our family were not good at all. But my mother, born in 1920, worked harder than a man and carried the full responsibility to feed her six children because our father barely made enough money to keep him alone alive, but never lost her freedom of spirit. She was illiterate, but she held on to her goal to enable a good education for her children. She fought for this wish throughout the years of poverty and deprivation; she broke with the tradition of the oldest son working on the farm instead of continuing school; she insisted on higher education for my elder sister, against the common thinking that any investment in a daughter would be of benefit for the future husband's family. All of my mother's decisions were made in peace of mind, the certainty that no one and no system could get hold of the freedom in her spirit. 'Only outside the field,' she kept telling us, 'will you be able to see the mud on your feet.'

"We all made it out of the mud," Yukun said, "and so did China."

Deng Xiaoping encouraged the whole nation "to step out of the field to see the mud on their feet."

Deng's call for emancipating minds was a call for looking at the Chinese reality without ideologically colored glasses. Calling for the emancipation of minds and, in the official language, "seeking the truth from facts" marked the dawn of a new era for China's people. Also, this call entailed an impressive balancing act for China's political leaders. To trust the people and let loose the rigid grip of doctrinarism released huge energy. The energy of 1 billion people could, like atomic power, work for the construction or the destruction of a new China. Without a certain degree of confidence and peace of mind about what he was doing, Deng would not have had that initial thrust, and what followed would not and could not have happened. In 1978, 165,000 young Chinese graduated from a university; in 2007 the number of graduates had risen to 4.5 million.

Very early on, in 1977, when Deng as education minister reopened the door to higher education, Wang Wei, Wang Yukun, Chen Kaige, and thousands of others seized the opportunity to make the most of their talents. A thirst for knowledge swept through China and narrowed social and cultural gaps nationwide. When colleges and universities resumed their regular teaching programs, when engineers and technicians were reassigned to their former duties, and especially when Deng Xiaoping called science and technology the "number one kind of productivity," the demand for a wide diversity of publications soared. The idea that "everybody has an equal right to higher education" soon aroused China's hunger for information and knowledge. From a baseline of several hundred periodicals in 1978, the number increased to almost 10,000 by 2007. Before the "opening up" only about 1,000 book titles were published annually. Today more than 250,000 titles are published each year. China now produces the most publications in the world per year: more than 3 billion copies of magazines and 6 billion copies of books annually, according to official figures.

A few years ago, as we strolled through the largest bookstore in Shanghai (seven floors, each the size of a football field) we were blown away by the endless rows of books and magazines. Not only were Chinese of all ages looking and buying; many were sitting on the stairs or on the floor, copying pages out of books they probably couldn't afford to buy.

Pulling Yourself Up by Your Bootstraps

People who report about China come from different societies and have different backgrounds. Most journalists report on China with reference to their own country: how China differs; how far China is advanced or how far behind it is. This creates various angles for stories. The speech President Hu Jintao gave at the Seventeenth Party Congress in 2007 was a very good summery of China's position, goals, and problems. The call for further emancipation of the mind and the continuing of reforms and opening up in economic, cultural, and political life was at the center of the speech. Anyone can download it from the Internet. But just as Barack Obama's speeches are interpreted differently by Democrats and Republicans, what stands behind Hu's words leaves room for interpretation.

To get the best reading, the context of the past and the present are as important as the words themselves. We, like many others, keep reminding ourselves that ours is a western base and that our personal view is not necessarily in harmony with the Chinese view. Any fair appraisal needs to be made as much as possible within the Chinese context. Our western background very much determined our first judgment about the situation of a Chinese couple.

It was in the year 2000. We left our hotel in Shanghai and walked a few steps, around a corner. It was as if we were stepping into a different world. Not more than about fifty yards away from the five-star Ritz-Carlton was a little store. "Store" is actually too grand a word. It was a little kiosk, with an addition in the back that had some blue-red-and-white striped material stretched over a metal rack to make a kind of tent. We learned later that this addition, approximately four square yards, was the home of the couple who in the front part sold snacks and drinks to migrant construction workers working in the buildings that were being erected on practically every street. What to western eyes would seem unbearable living conditions was already progress for the couple. They had left their work on a farm and felt that they now had a much better life. We continued to visit that little kiosk, speaking with the couple through Michelle Wan, a good friend from the Ritz-Carlton who became our interpreter and reporter when we wanted to know how the two shopkeepers were doing.

You will not find them there today. They slowly made their way up, first with the kiosk near the hotel, which already allowed a better education for their "left behind" child; then they opened another little kiosk; and a little later they hired someone to help them. They no longer slept in the tent behind their goods; they now had a modest apartment. And then one day they were gone; they had opened a "real store" in a different neighborhood.

Detatching and Letting Go

Thirty years earlier such an initiative would have been unthinkable. "Emancipating minds" was the starting point, opening the door for people to think for themselves and make their own decisions. Nevertheless the Chinese self-concept still differs from that of westerners. The Chinese see themselves more as part of a network than as individuals, and they welcome a strong, cautious leadership that ensures a good performance for all. To run China as an enterprise fits that concept very well. Chinese gain power and self-confidence in the family, in a group, in the network in which they are integrated.

Our friend Zhang Haihua explained to us that much of Chinese thinking has its roots in Chinese agricultural history. For thousands of years, Chinese lived in villages near their fields, and the survival and well-being of individuals depended on how much they supported both the village and the fields. Reinforced by Confucius, the concept was extended to loyalty to the country and the government, and it included respect for and obedience to teachers and superiors.

The first reforms took place in agriculture, where today 40 percent of the Chinese still work, and this will probably be the last area where emancipating minds will be complete.

Emancipation Takes Time

China started its modernization from a point where the West was more than 100 years ago. But the West tends to measure China's economic and political progress against the values and standards developed over a century or more. Chinese look at China from the background of their own history. People experience a great deal of joy and optimism about their current and future living conditions. Westerners would consider the current conditions backward, but this is only because we are looking at them through American or European eyes.

Emancipation takes time. If you think of modern democracy, the West started the process more than 200 years ago. But in Switzerland it was not until in February 1971 that women were first fully allowed to vote. In America racial segregation continued well into the 1960s. India, the biggest "democracy," still has a caste system that is profoundly undemocratic.

There are violations of human rights in China, and every violation against human rights should be condemned. But on the other hand, no nation has achieved more on certain basic human rights in such a short time. Article 3 of the United Nations Human Rights Declaration says that everyone has the right to life, liberty, and security of person. Under the government of the Communist Party of China, more than 400 million people came out of poverty, starvation, and a fight for survival. China has a literacy rate of 90.9 percent; life expectancy at birth is 73 years; and the per capita GDP is $5,962. India has a literacy rate of 61 percent, life expectancy of 69 years, and a per capita GDP of $2,762. (GDPs are on a price power parity basis. Source: IMF.)

The Revival of the Chinese Entrepreneurial Gene

Life, liberty, and security certainly imply creating a stable economic base. Deng's call for emancipating minds was the spark that reawakened the Chinese entrepreneurial gene, which had been dormant for a long time. This liberation eased the great pressure during the comprehensive social transition, and it increasingly helped the Chinese to deal with change. It carried China through a proactive fight against poverty and backwardness. It set up a completely new framework for and attitude toward doing business on every scale, from very small to very large.

China's transformation to a market economy required changes on all fronts. China was like a company in which everything was obsolete—from the buildings to the management, from bookkeeping to the workforce to equipment—and all operations were a disorganized mess.

In a well-run enterprise, employees are encouraged to develop entrepreneurial thinking, adding to the economic potential of the company. The emancipation of minds opened the eyes of the people to all kinds of business opportunities. Some of these opportunities were unusual, as our examples will show, and at the beginning many were only partly legal. But eventually they all contributed to the whole and served the common goal. As chaotic as the process sometimes was, it had the right mixture of control and freedom, and it led to an explosion of private businesses. By the year 2008 two-thirds of China's economy was in the private sector.

A New Generation in Old Structures

By 1992 China was aware that it needed to accelerate progress in its science and technology sector, or further development would come to a halt. A strategy needed to be set in a national plan for the following year. Two diametrically opposed strategies were suggested to President Jiang Zemin, as related by Robert Lawrence Kuhn in his biography of Jiang, *The Man Who Changed China.*

One strategy was presented by Zhu Rongji, the vice president; the other was presented by Dr. Song Jian, who was in charge of science and technology. Song advocated a bold approach: to establish national-level, high-tech industrial parks, modeled after the high-tech parks around Boston in the United States, with favorable policies to encourage the creation of new, innovative companies.

Zhu wanted to go in the opposite direction, with a renewed commitment to revitalize China's state-owned enterprises (SOEs), for which he was responsible. "We have so many large state-owned enterprises, they should be the place to develop China's advanced science and technology; they have the critical mass necessary for advanced research and development."

Song responded, "In the seniority-based hierarchy of state-owned enterprises, how could young people ever get a chance to do anything original, to challenge accepted ways and norms? Young people would never be respected, no matter how good their ideas are."

Jiang had not entered the discussion, but he listened and made some notes. Finally he spoke: "I agree with the proposal of Comrade Song Jian."

This was a further unfolding of emancipated thinking within the government, and an example of Jiang's context-oriented leadership. The comfortable way would been to keep young, bright people in old structures to solve a problem, but he understood the constraints this way would impose, and instead saw the opportunity of giving people the freedom to create their own dynamic start-ups.

Cutting Brittle Branches

In 1997, Jiang took another important step. China's SOEs still employed more than 100 million people. The SOEs were competing against one another, not so much for customers as for permission to declare bankruptcy, the only way to get aid for the workers from the government. But too many bankruptcies would cause too much unemployment and endanger stability. Jiang supported a strategy promoted by Zhu Rongji, in which healthy enterprises would carry a sick one—a strategy that only rarely brought down both.

And it was Jiang who introduced a concept that seemed totally contrary to the tenets of a presumably communist economy: privatization. The state, Jiang asserted, would withdraw from certain sectors while keeping control of key industries. In Jiang's opinion, private shareholding was the best hope for China's SOE assets.

There has been very little talk in the West about leadership skills within China's Communist Party, although the results should speak for themselves. Jiang Zemin kept the context in mind, and in making his decisions he focused on the goal rather than on his own ego. This style of leadership was characteristic of Jiang Zemin, but it can also be seen on many levels and in many functions of Chinese society.

Bold Steps

In the spring of 2007, John spoke to an assembly of CEOs of big SOEs. As always, he expressed strong support for free trade, a low level of regulations, and an entrepreneurial-friendly environment. He had not been asked beforehand what he was going to say or not say, and to our surprise he was often interrupted by applause.

In the lively discussion that followed, one of the CEOs asked John, "Do you think all SOEs should be privatized?" For a moment John hesitated, and then he said just one word: "Yes." Another moment of silence, and then strong applause, though not from everyone.

After this forum of CEOs Wang Wei told us, "Most of them already knew that the market economy would definitely be built up on private ownership, but they would still want the confirmation from someone they learned from many years ago." As Wei said, most of the audience members had read *Megatrends* years ago and had been inspired by it. They had come to hear John and also, as Wei put it, to pay their respects to him. And it was touching when many of them lined up after the event to get their original copies of *Megatrends* signed.

One CEO told us what Wang Wei told the audience at the end of the talk: "John's books *Megatrends* and *Megatrends Asia* set a milestone, especially for the Chinese. However, with the booming Chinese picture, the megatrends would be enhanced. That is why John's new work on China is important and that is why I, as a deal maker, have to do my work to merge John's mind with the Chinese reality."

China's SOEs still account for about half of China's basic industrial GDP, and further privatization will not happen overnight; it will be a gradual process. But as the history of China's reforms shows, bold moves have been made when they seemed necessary. What will be the mix, the best balance, between state-owned and privately owned enterprises?

The Evolution of the Banking System

China's SOEs are somewhat like California's redwood trees; they grow best in a certain climate, surmount all others in height, and, if healthy, are a source of valuable timber.

One bastion of China's SOEs is the banking industry: almost all banks are state-owned. But this sector, like many others, has undergone an emancipation process. What it has accomplished is astonishing. The process was not an economic miracle but a clever strategy, and reforms at the right time transformed the Industrial and Commercial Bank of China (ICBC) from an inflexible, sedate communist bank to the brightest star in the firmament of international finance. As of February 10, 2006, ICBC was ten times larger than Citibank. By the spring of 2008, two years after the its initial public offering (IPO), the biggest in global history, ICBC had a stock exchange value of $232 billion and ranked as by far the world's biggest bank.

But in the process of development, the central bankers have acted with some care. First, small, shareholding banks were allowed to test collaboration with foreign banks. In this process Citigroup, in January 2005, was permitted to buy 5 percent of the Shanghai Pudong Development Bank. A year before, HSBC had bought 8 percent of the Bank of Shanghai. In the following months China's central bankers agreed to a maximum of 15 percent that a western bank could hold in a Chinese bank.

We got to know the governor of China's central bank, Dai Xianglong, two years later, when he was mayor of Tianjin. Vice Mayor Cui Jin Du of Tianjin had reported to Dai that the Naisbitt China Institute had made it a mission to find out what was really going on in China.

Mayor Dai, who was acclaimed as the best central banker in the world after the financial crisis of 1997, gave us a very warm welcome and a grand lunch. Chinese grand lunches have a certain rhythm: special dishes, artfully arranged on little plates, one after another, are served top-down in hierarchical order. These are ten or more courses. As the meal proceeds, toasts are addressed from one person to another, tiny wineglasses are raised to cheer the person toasted, and after some nice words, each person takes a sip of the wine. If you sipping seriously, and the party is big enough, you can become quite happy. We had to hold back at lunch, but we had fun just the same. Mayor Dai is a charming and amusing man. We wished some of the journalists who criticize China so self-righteously and condescendingly would also write about the cosmopolitanism and *savoir-vivre* of some top-ranking Chinese politicians.

Mayor Dai brought his twenty-five-year-old copy of *Megatrends* with him to have it signed. This is worth mentioning because it shows how the members of China's elite, at a time when the West did not at all think of China as a future player on the global stage, were interested in western theories and commentaries. Ever since the reforms and the opening up, the Communist Party of China has been working step-by-step to achieve its economic and political goals, seizing on any western knowledge that would serve these goals, and increasingly leaving the path of dogmatic communist directives.

This was the case with some early experimental side movements in the banking sector. Before the Asian financial crisis, the Beijing Bank Control had approved the first Chinese private shareholding bank, Minsheng Bank. But its radius of operation remained limited. Jing Shuping, the CEO of Minsheng Bank, is convinced that state bankers do not understand the consumer's mentality. They think of ordinary people more as supplicants than clients. China has the third highest savings rate in the world, and by 2007 about 150 million Chinese held stock or bonds. This is a lot of money waiting to be well treated.

Some voices in the press keep demanding a faster opening up of the banking system. *Caijng*, an influential economic magazine, has pointed out that banking as a state monopoly can lead only to a dead end. Further reforms will not stop, and the emancipation of the banking system will continue. By 2008 three of the five biggest banks in the world were already Chinese. The CEO of ICBC, Jiang Jianqing, sees the future of his bank in Internet banking and electronic money transfers and believes that e-banking will become one of the strongest forces driving future growth.

In the first decade of the twenty-first century one of the main goals of the Chinese government has been to connect China more strongly with Africa. In 2007 ICBC bought 20 percent of Standard Bank, the biggest bank in Africa. At the time, this was China's largest foreign investment. Many of China's investors are interested in Africa, and Africa could certainly benefit from their investments. China's practice of making improvements in infrastructure as a trade for access to natural resources is one contribution, and in the long run the Chinese social-economic model itself may help pull millions of Africans out of the mud. Many African leaders are aware that only thirty years ago, China was as poor as Malawi. If Africa could achieve even half of China's economic success, the continent would be transformed.

A Smart Strategy

China's SOEs have had their problems. In China's centrally planned economy, their assets had lain idle. They were buried in bookkeeping; no one took responsibility for them and no one cared. But the new market mechanisms changed the picture. Goods produced with no market demand would have to be accounted for as bad assets and written off right away, causing a huge drop in viability. Such a restructuring process is very painful and costly, but the Chinese leadership had a smart, creative solution: the Chinese government would "invite" global players to help handle nonperforming assets.

In other words, the government shifted a great amount of the debt into state-run asset management firms and engaged western banks as waste deposits. Those bad assets are largely coming out from so-called market transformation cost. Ironically, ten years later, the subprime crisis developed in the United States because of similar bad assets. By 2000 China had already cleaned up its act in many areas, but there were still a tremendous number of nonperforming assets. Once more, China enterprise showed cleverness in overcoming this hurdle.

At the end of November 2001, a foreign investment consortium under the leadership of Morgan Stanley was allowed to buy a package of bad assets against shares in Chinese companies, $100 million in debt, with a paper value of $1.2 billion. In 2003, Deutsche Bank bought such a package with a value of about $400 million.

This continuous process of emancipating minds and allowing entrepreneurial talent to take incremental steps strengthened the private sector and transformed some SOEs into successful private businesses. From the beginning of the reforms in the late 1970s, the position of private businesses went through two phases: first, from illegal to complementary; second, from complementary to integral to the socialist market economy. In March 1999 the new approach and the new role of private businesses were put into China's constitution. In the following June the China Security Regulatory Commission, which governs the country's stock markets, cleared the way for private enterprises to list B shares dominated by foreign currency.

In the first steps of China's IPOs, listing a private company was like walking through freshly poured concrete. In the case of Clever Software Group, which was based in Beijing and went public in 1999, the concrete shoe involved taking the controlling stake in Heilongjiang's Acheng and Steel Company. This company was located in the heart of China's so-called rust belt in the northeastern region, which was populated by moribund SEOs. The "acquisition" gave Clever Software Group access to investors' funds, and also made it easier to secure financing from state banks. "We landed ourselves in a completely different industry," said an executive. Clever Software's frustration was not unique; according to estimates, between 1997 and 1998 twenty-two private enterprises had to acquire "backdoor listings" by taking controlling stakes in listed state companies.

Mergers & Acquisitions

This was the environment in 1997, when our colleague Wang Wei established his new company, China M&A Management, a boutique advisory firm. His story is typical of people in his generation, who used the reforms and opening up to make the most of their brains and talents.

After Wang Wei finished his studies at Northeast University of Finance and Economics in Dalian in 1985, he earned an MBA from the graduate school run by the central bank and got an assignment as an economist in the Bank of China. He was young, talented, and promising, and it took only four months until he had a chance to prove his worth. He was sent to Tokyo, where he worked for six months in bond trading in Nomura Securities. He also took the American Graduate Record Examination, which evaluates verbal reasoning, quantitative reasoning, critical thinking, and analytical writing. This led to invitations to enroll at five American universities. But the Bank of China did not allow him to leave and urged him to stay on for another year, until 1987. That year he left China to go to the United States.

"When I arrived in New York," he told us, "all I had in my pocket was $20. I got a job as a research assistant with $600 monthly salary and worked periodically with Chemical Bank. This provided me with a modest living so that I could stay in New York for a year. Then Robert Visek, vice president in charge of the country risk analysis department, became my mentor. He had visited the Bank of China and knew that I had published a book, *Country Risk Analysis*, in 1987. I got an internship in the World Bank in Washington in summer 1988, so my wife, Wang Jay, could come to the States as well."

Twenty years later, after Wei had told him about this book, Robert Visek, looking back, said that Wang Wei's initial chances for success were very low and that even the strongest optimists could not have foreseen how impressive China's progress would be.

With Visek's encouragement Wang Wei continued his studies, earned a PhD in economics, and got a job offer from Goldman Sachs. One of Wei's friends in those days, Er-Fei Liu, whom he helped at the time, today is chairman of Merrill Lynch Asia. During all his years of study, Wang Wei had never gone back to China. Finally, in spring 1992, he decided to take a trip home before he starting his new job. "I spent three weeks in Beijing, Shenzhen, and Hainan and found myself in the epicenters of the emerging China. Everyone was excited, energized, and creative; everyone wanted to do business in almost every field. During my stay I had a chance to have conversations with the governor of the central bank. Not surprisingly, he talked about how much China needed a total reform and said that the financial fields would be in the center. If I could return, I would be the first PhD recipient to return from the United States after the 1989 event. At that moment my fate was clear. In America I could make a career, but in China I could make a real difference."

From Slaughtering Cattle to Cash Cows

Like many of China's bright people, Wei returned to China with no smaller wish than "to make history." As the executive vice president of China Southern Securities between 1992 and 1996, he gained more experience and conducted IPOs for more than thirty Chinese companies, all of them state-owned. And he gained the insight that "the state-owned sector was rotten to the root and most deals became rubbish shares."

This was the right time, and it implied a challenging goal, so in 1997 he started his company, China M&A Management. "I realized that the private sector was the future. I wanted to privatize China through mergers and acquisitions," he said in an interview with *Asiaweek* in 2000. His goal—transforming lame state ventures into champions of the new market—can be taken as a metaphor for change in China: "What I do is to change state companies into shareholding companies. I don't necessarily change the ownership, but I change the way they operate."

In the bigger picture, just like a well-run enterprise, China keeps changing the way it operates. It shook off obsolete structures and tried out new business and management models. And it "shook off the doctrines that bound its spirits." It transformed itself from a poor, backward enterprise into a flourishing enterprise, the third biggest of its kind in the world. And there is no sign that China is anywhere near the end of its transformation.

Feelings toward and opinions about China are perhaps more diverse and diametrical than those about any other country in the world. Although everyone is aware of China and its growing importance, many opinions continue to be based on prejudice and ignorance. Honest confrontation is necessary in several matters, but we don't feel entitled to lecture a leadership that has led millions out of poverty, has the support of the vast majority of its people, and is well aware of what needs to be done to continue the transition. In keeping silent silence about the dark days of the past, China is not alone. It took Europe several decades to digest World War II and discuss this war openly. China will discuss its own past when it is ready to do so.

At the beginning of this chapter we wrote that thirty years ago China was a hungry country. Thirty years after the beginning of the "emancipation of the mind," China is still a hungry country. But today China's hunger is for sustaining economic success, for further social advancement, and for a stronger voice in the global community.

Achievement as Legitimation

China's land area is only one-third arable and two-thirds mountains and deserts. The country suffers from a lack of water, and what water it has is is unequally distributed. It has fifty-five national minorities and roughly 2,000 local dialects. It has a high level of urbanization, which is predicted to reach 65 percent by the middle of the twenty-first century; but today 43 percent of the workers are still in agriculture, contributing only 11 percent to China's GDP. China is becoming an aging society: the total population over age sixty will reach 300 million in just fifteen years.

How can such a country be united? Who can manage 1.3 billion people and achieve an overall goal of modest wealth?

China's leadership was never elected in the western democratic way; rather, it drew its legitimacy from results. China's leadership is strongly driven by context. The leaders believe in the power of the right process, adapt well to change, process information through interaction, align themselves through engagement, and implement their ideas through the people.

And one of the first things Deng, the father of China's reinvention, made clear was that only emancipated people could contribute to the process.

Who Decides?

"Emancipate" derives from the Latin *emancipare*, which referred to releasing a son or a slave out of *mancipium*, or being under someone's rule, into freedom. Emancipation implies freedom to have an opinion, to make decisions, and to choose between several options without coercion.

Of course it often happens that one person's free choice is diametrically opposed to someone else's. A certain choice might be good in your eyes and bad in our eyes or vice versa. Who decides? The Chinese believe that we should decide for ourselves and they should decide for themselves.

But this is not how most people in the West look at China. Westerners tend to argue for a universal morality and for converting others to this standard. Where does westerners' need to lecture come from? Sociologists tell us that cultures can have two different views of "the truth." Some cultures, called universalistic, believe that certain "truths" or values are self-evident and are part of the basic human condition. The West is one of these cultures. Other cultures are what is called "particularistic": they believe that what is right for me is right for me and what is right for you is right for you. In other words, the members of each particular society determine what is best for them on the basis of their own needs.

Most individualistic countries tend to be universalistic and most group-oriented societies tend to be particularistic. The United States as the flag carrier of individual freedom in the world, and Europe as flag carrier for humanism, therefore feel the responsibility to admonish those countries and societies that do not live up to the universal values by which all individuals should abide. However, if you are from a group-oriented society, where loyalty is first to the group and then to the individual, you of course would believe that your way is the right way for you and that others should stay out of your affairs—especially in times of crisis.

For some time China acted no differently from an enterprise in crisis. When a company is run-down and on the brink of collapse, it cannot afford to vote on how to get out of the mess. Decisions have to be made quickly, and with the long term in view. Survival of the company has to take priority over individuals' interests and benefits. Those who would prefer to fight against the company's culture and goals would have to choose: leave or adjust. Only over time, as the enterprise stabilizes and reestablishes itself, would collaborators enjoy more freedom and choice. But all emancipation stops when the survival of enterprise is endangered. As we have seen since September 11, freedom can be curtailed even in the United States.

The Call of the West

China has a long way to go in several regards, including human rights, judicial and environmental responsibility, and freedom of speech. But possible threats come from the economic side. How can the leadership weather the economic and financial crisis? Can it keep up growth and hold down unemployment? Can it fight corruption up and down the hierarchical chain? Enterprises are judged not against other enterprises by evaluating company cultures, management style, and leadership skills, but by their own economic performance.

Elizabeth J. Perry, professor of government and director of the F-Yenching Institute, in a speech at Harvard University, said, "We have a limited understanding of what keeps the current Chinese state structure together and what allows the political system to act as effectively as it does." China is creating its own new society, its own political system. It started its march by borrowing from Marxism-Leninism, but soon adapted those doctrines to its own ideas and needs. It picked up parts of capitalism as useful tools to reach economic goals, but did not let go of its political base.

China is like a biracial child that, after it has undergone a significant emancipation process, starts to disconnect from its parents—communism and capitalism—using the strength it gained from both sides to start walking on its own feet.

President Hu Jintao called the emancipation of the mind "a magic instrument for developing socialism with Chinese characteristics," and assured his people that China would stay on this path. "We must continue to emancipate our minds," he said, "seek truth from facts, keep up with the times, make bold changes and innovations, stay away from rigidity or stagnation, fear no risks, never be confused by any interference." The calls of the West for democratic capitalism fade away, leaving no echo.

Hu Jintao's China

Even if the Chinese rhetoric sounds a little stiff to western ears, the content is clear. To continue emancipating minds is a further loosening of control, seeking the truth from facts rather than embellishing reality, holding on to reforms, and—something seldom heard from western politicians—fearing no risk.

Although Mao is still honored for his role in reestablishing China, the mistake of the Cultural Revolution is no longer denied. In his report to the Seventeenth Party Congress in October 2008, President Hu looked back to the beginning and reviewed the run-up to the emancipation of minds. He listed three main advances that Deng Xiaoping and his supporters had made following the "precarious situation left by the Cultural Revolution (1966–1976)":

1. A "scientific appraisal" of Mao Zedong's thought thoroughly repudiated the erroneous theory and practice of class struggle.

2. Deng persisted in the "emancipation the mind and seeking truth from facts."

3. A historic political decision was made to "shift the focus of the work of the Party and the state to economic development and introducing reforms and opening up."

China is still catching up with the western world. As an editorial in the *China Daily* put it in 2007: "We will have to press ahead on that road if we want to achieve more. It is important to keep in mind that the past 30 years were not only about the economy. It was the emancipation of the mind that made all the achievements possible. While we appreciate the good looking numbers today, let us not lose the determination to blaze new trails."

Walking New Trails

China's media are also increasingly walking along new trails. The more emancipated minds are, the less they accept paternalism and censorship, even if these are self-imposed. Although the media are still in government hands, an opening up, a much greater diversity, a more critical view, and more reporting about what is going on in the country can be observed. We noticed the difference, compared with the past, during John's book tour for *Mind Set!* in autumn 2006.

During some previous visits to China, John would occasionally be interviewed by an official party newspaper, such as *People's Daily*, usually by an old warhorse of a reporter, and it was all pretty boring. Even when his publisher at the time, Foreign Language Press, was pushing *Megatrends Asia* in the early 1990s, nothing became very exciting. However, during the book tour for *Mind Set!* in 2006 his publisher, Citic Press, arranged dozens of interviews. In both Beijing and Shanghai, there were six to ten interviews a day for a week. And almost all the interviewers were in their twenties. The number of periodicals had multiplied dramatically, many of the interviewers were bilingual, many of them were women, and—most important—the interviewers had things they really were allowed to write about.

For the leadership, achieving total freedom of speech and press is a balancing act between top-down and bottom-up (we write more about this in Pillar 2). And it is also a question of perspective. Where does protection end and where does repression begin? Again, the Chinese understanding of protection and control differs from that of the West. A movie by Michael Moore about a Chinese president would cross the line, going beyond what is tolerated. The consideration of *mianzi*—

saving or losing face—is deeply ingrained in the Chinese soul and is a key to both censorship and self-censorship. There are things you just don't write about in China.

"The biggest potential threat to the Party comes from the educated urban middle class," wrote Geoff Dyer in his article "Stirring in the Suburbs" in the *Financial Times* on July 21, 2008. "If company executives, lawyers and university professors start challenging the political status quo, the Party's hold will become much less secure."

Correct. But the party knows this. After all, the policies of the Communist Party of China (CPC) created the environment that supports entrepreneurship, and the party was thus an agent in the development of a middle class. "To stop reforms and opening up will only lead to a blind alley," said Hu Jintao at the Seventeenth Party Congress. "In accordance with the overall landscape of China's socialist cause with Chinese characteristics, we shall push forward the economic, political, cultural, and social constructions."

A More Human Touch in Politics

The enterprise of China is no longer run the old-fashioned, dictatorial way. The CEO, board members, and management are not untouchable; nor is each word out of their mouths a law. The picture in the West is that there are the Chinese people and there is China's Communist Party leadership. What is forgotten is that the leaders are Chinese, too—human beings of flesh and blood, who sometimes, just like westerners, love wine and hate sea cucumbers.

There is an opening up also in the style of communication between politicians and citizens, including visiting foreigners. In 2000, when we started traveling in China together, meetings with higher-ranking Chinese officials still followed a certain protocol. These meetings would take place in a huge reception room with big armchairs lined up along the walls. The principals would be seated at the head of the room; the rest of the group would be seated along the sides, in hierarchical order. All the principals wore small, colorful bouquets of flowers on their chests. Then, in a more or less stiff atmosphere, the conversation would begin.

In 2007, Wang Wei introduced us to one of the people with a great share in Tianjin's transition to a global financial city: Cui Jin Du, its deputy mayor, who matches the picture of an engaged western businessman much more than the stereotype of a stiff Chinese bureaucrat. From the first moment, we felt very comfortable in his company. We got to know him not in an official meeting room, but in a traditional restaurant, famous for its special Chinese dumplings.

We learned that Mayor Cui, like Wang Wei, was one of the first young men to pass the difficult national exam in 1978 and become a college student. Four years later, with a degree in finance in his pocket, Cui entered the government as a junior staff member. After climbing up the government bureaucracy step-by-step, he was finally promoted to chief financial controller of Tianjin and became deputy mayor in 2002. Cui Jin Du is an eyewitness to and a pioneer in Tianjin's rapid growth during the past thirty years. He also is a good example of how the emancipation of minds released the talents and energy of a whole generation and allowed its members to grow. Reforms and opening up created the environment, but the skills, passion, and hard work of people like Cui Jin Du are turning a heavily industrial, polluted city of 12 million people into a global financial center.

What especially impressed Wang Wei and his colleagues about Mayor Cui was that he began using the Internet long ago and loves to communicate on the Web. Considering his working hours, that seems very reasonable to us. During two years of preparations for Tianjin's first International Private Equity Forum, which was attended by more than 5,000 CEOs and became an annual event, Cui would send most of his e-mails to Wang Wei, who organized the event, between ten P.M. and three A.M.

Not only is China changing on the surface; it faces change at all social levels and in all political hierarchies. After the earthquake in Szechuan, Premier Wen Jiabao became China's grandfather figure, loved because of his emphasis on and commitment to the people. Evidently, not only Barack Obama has discovered that the Internet is a handy public relations tool. Premier Wen Jiabao had a public Web chat in February 2009, and since then, communicating on the Web has become a new preference for some of China's high-ranking officials.

Shaping an Authentic China

Besides providing the freedom to have opinions, make decisions, and choose between several options without coercion, emancipation is also a necessary condition for authenticity.

Authenticity means that someone's acts are not driven by external influences; rather they originate in the person's own self. We can borrow from the art world and note that almost all painters start by copying. Painting reality, moving into abstraction, and even developing their own strokes will start with looking at what someone else does better, someone to learn from.

Ironically, much of the political and economic value system of the People's Republic has to be considered western in origin. Neither Marx nor Lenin was Chinese. And the market economy certainly did not grow on Chinese soil. But throughout its history, China has successfully implemented acquisitions from other nations: Buddhism, Marxism-Leninism, communism, capitalism, the market economy, western management theories, and western technologies. "Learn controlling from the Japanese, boldness from the Koreans, accuracy from the Germans, marketing strategies from the Americans," says the CEO of Chery, Yin Tongyao. It seems that an aspect of Chinese talent is to form a whole out of seemingly incompatible parts.

But the time will soon come when not the best copied but the most authentic Chinese product, service, and perhaps even way of thinking will be appreciated most. Authenticity and talent still need foreign confirmation if they are to be accepted in China. The filmmaker Chen Kaige, who was one of the students and graduates of Beijing's

movie academy after it opened its doors again, was not fully established in his home country until he received awards from the western
film industry.

Emancipating the mind also means creating your own role
models—for art, entrepreneurism, science, or any other field. Instead of
turning to the West, the Chinese are increasingly looking inward for
inspiration. China is gaining self-confidence, and self-confidence will
encourage creativity. In the end, creativity will lead to a shaking off
China's dependence on the opinions of, and on confirmation by, the
western world.

The CEO of a healthy, profitable company is not very vulnerable.
Results dampen criticism. The more the new Chinese system evolves,
and the stronger its outlines become, the less vulnerable the political
leadership will feel. But if we take into account how big a transformation the huge political "apparatus" of China has undergone, and how
the emancipation of the party proceeds, we would have to be optimistic
about the future.

The Wondrous Metamorphosis

The world-famous classical pianist Lang Lang says that because of all his
touring, he doesn't often get back to his hometown, Beijing; but it is his
favorite place to be. That has not always been the case. When he was a
kid, he says, "It was a closed society then, with suspicions of everything
from the West, but this has totally changed. It's as though its mind has
been opened."

Not only have China's minds been opened, but in a joint effort between the leadership and the people, the old-fashioned dictatorially run
enterprise of China has become a modern twenty-first-century endeavor. Hierarchies have flattened; decision making has been delegated
to all levels, increasingly drawing the people into in the continuing
process of modernization. China's emancipation of minds started with a
change in the mind-set of its leaders and gradually led to a transformation of the society.

When China moved from centuries of dynastic rule, it embarked on a primitive political process. Mao early on turned to the West and borrowed a political system that, as history showed, would never mature in China. Ideology became more important than people. To use a metaphor from nature, the system got stuck at the stage of a cocoon; it never changed, but held China in its grip for more than thirty years. In the political spring under Deng Xiaoping, the metamorphosis began. A Chinese proverb says that what for a caterpillar is the end of life, for a wise man is a butterfly.

Sometimes it's hard to say good-bye. And many times it takes courage to say good-bye. But there is no beginning without a good-bye.

When will the time come for China to make the bold step toward full political emancipation, shed the cocoon, and let the butterfly fly?

In 1978 China's Communist Party unsealed the rigid grip of the cocoon, which for decades had shut off the outside world. The miraculous metamorphosis began. But why is China still hiding behind the picture of the caterpillar when the picture of a butterfly is not only much more attractive but also more accurate? Why does it keep the communist caterpillar, if there is a Chinese butterfly? Why is China's Communist Party still called the Communist Party? How communist is the butterfly?

"Communism" comes from the Latin word *communis*—together. The concept of a commune working together fits well with China as a group-focused society. But communism has been defined in two ways.

According to one definition, communism is "a socioeconomic structure and political ideology that promotes the establishment of an egalitarian, classless, stateless society, based on common ownership and control of the means of production and property in general." Most of the world is familiar with this concept.

But there is a second type sometimes called "pure communism," which refers to a classless, stateless, oppression-free society where decisions on what to produce and what policies to pursue are made democratically, allowing every member of society to participate in the decision-making process in the political and economic spheres of life.

Let the Butterfly Fly

China's Communist Party under Mao chose to follow the first definition. China established a classless society rigidly held under the carapace. But like the caterpillar in nature, the Chinese matured. Unlike their comrades in the Soviet Union, they decided that this carapace was too tight and not practical to develop the country and satisfy the needs of the people. The inflexible Soviet Union broke up not because its Communist Party changed course or name, but because the system could not meet the demands of the people.

The Chinese leadership was too smart and too realistic to be reined in by an outdated ideology, when "seeking the truth from facts" showed that it did not work. As Deng claimed, human insights should be based on practical experience: if a theory does not work, drop it.

But China's leadership hesitates to admit that it has stepped out of its ideological father's footsteps and is now walking on its own, leaving obstructive communist ideas behind, and selecting what works for China and what does not. The leadership of China's Communist Party is supported by the people not because it calls itself communist, but for what it has achieved. China has ventured out and succeeded, despite all teething troubles and despite all condemnation by the West. It has brought great progress to its country and its people. If it continues the chosen path and matures its own system as we describe it in Pillar 2, China is on the way toward creating an alternative to the democracy of the West. China is called not the People's Communist Republic of China but the People's Republic of China. China's party has much stronger ties to the people than to communism; it is much more a people's party than a communist party.

China's goal is an oppression-free society where decisions are made in a top-down, bottom-up process that allows all members of society to participate in the decision making in the political, economic, and cultural spheres of life. China is picking the raisins out of the communist cake.

The last steps toward full political emancipation will be to let the butterfly fly and to call it what it is: a butterfly.

"Cut off the shackles that bind your spirit," was Deng's call to the people of China. China has liberated the minds of the people, and it has developed self-confidence—without which there is no self-criticism. Much of the criticism is done publicly; more delicate matters are still dealt with behind closed doors. But the commitment to operate "in the sunshine" has been made. China's leaders are not perfect, but they are not blind.

Emancipation of the mind has loosened control and given more freedom to the individual. Emancipation of the mind has gone down the social ladder to the lowest-ranking groups, upgrading their self-image, allowing them to see the value of their contributions to the whole, encouraging them to claim their role in society. The direction of China's future is set. Emancipation will continue on all levels.

In our process of analyzing what is really going on in China, the pillars we describe in this book slowly appeared. The 8 Pillars are the support structures for China's reforms, and all follow from Pillar 1, emancipation of the mind. Without the liberation of the people to make individual contributions to the whole, the structures would have collapsed. Only the people can do it. From artists to entrepreneurs, people have been freed to think and act for themselves, to determine their own steps toward the modernization of China. Indoctrination is built on fear; emancipation is built trust. The leaders of China continue to press on with the emancipation process of the new system so that they and the people can contribute to China's future.

Emancipation of the mind was China's springtime, when blossoms started to bloom. Summer will see the fruits ripen, and in autumn the harvest begins.

Pillar 2

Balancing Top-Down and Bottom-Up

The evolving Chinese dynamic of top-down government directives and bottom-up citizen initiatives is shaping a new model we call "vertical democracy."

The most important, most delicate, and most critical pillar on which the sustainability of the new Chinese society rests is balancing its top-down and bottom-up forces. Keeping the equilibrium is the key to China's sustainability, and it is the key to understanding China's political self-concept.

What Does Freedom Mean to a Chinese?

For Americans, freedom means the opportunity to determine how they live, unfettered by arbitrary actions of others. This view is shared in most of the western world, where the rights of the individual are a major pillar of society. But freedom means different things to different people.

Chinese thinking is very much influenced by two fundamental requirements: social order and harmony. Social order and harmony were central to the teachings of Confucius, who believed that only order could provide true freedom. This concept also prevails in team sports, where rules set the conditions for freedom in playing. In the same way, an orderly society establishes the context within which people can act freely. In the Chinese way of thinking, order does not oppress people but defines room to maneuver.

From this perspective, what the West understands as freedom of choice by the individual, with limited social and legal contexts established by each society, leads to continuing preoccupation with who is right and who is wrong. Indeed, many people in the West believe that contention and discord lead to breakthroughs, new ideas, and innovation. But conflict and disharmony, especially in such serious matters as governance, do not fit the Chinese mentality.

China's Vertical Democracy

When westerners think about a free, democratic society, they think about a horizontal structure, in which individuals have an equal vote and periodically elect their leaders. Most western democracies have this model in mind. But what if there is a totally different way to look at freedom and democracy, one that comes from a different cultural heritage and from different ways of looking at society and the world? What if this is a vertical, rather than a horizontal, model of democracy?

The Chinese believe that we are all born connected, and every individual is part of a whole. Harmony with others is the key to living in traditional Chinese society. Personal accountability is not as important as the quality of your relationships with the people around you. In this picture, politics is run not by rival parties or politicians but by consensus in a top-down, bottom-up process.

In such a highly decentralized society, the leadership frames a broad concept for the society as a whole that incorporates bottom-up ideas, initiatives, and demands. Top-down and bottom-up initiatives are then established and encouraged to adjust flexibly as conditions and circumstances require, all in the context of an overarching common goal set by the leadership. This creates a vertical structure, with a constant flow of ideas and experiences up and down the hierarchy. China is in the early stages of creating, within this structure, a democratic model that fits Chinese history and thinking. Although this vertical democratic process certainly has its weaknesses—which we will explore—its major strength is that it releases politicians from election-driven thinking and permits long-term strategic planning.

In the eyes of the West, justification for governing a country stands or falls on who is elected; in the eyes of the Chinese, justification for governance rests more on accomplishments. On this criterion the Chinese government has unquestionably performed well.

The Chinese leadership holds on to the Communist Party, and the Communist Party of China (CPC) holds on to its command and control in governing the country—but the concept of what command and control mean has changed radically over the last thirty years. The party has changed from an arbitrary top-down autocracy to a functioning one-party leadership with strong bottom-up participation, a vertically organized democratic society with increasing transparency in making and executing decisions. As President Hu has said, "Power must be exercised in the sunshine to ensure that it is exercised correctly."

China's Views and Values

For millennia China was a feudalistic autocracy, ruled strictly top-down. Bottom-up forces were suppressed, and only after reforms began in 1978 did the political status of the people undergo a fundamental change. With the beginning of the emancipation of minds, opinions slowly started to diversify, and bottom-up voices began to make themselves heard. Questioning the political and economic structures, which themselves were in the early stages of modification and development, became thinkable, at least to a modest degree. But the leadership of the party was still unquestioned.

In an interview with the *New York Times* in 2001, Jiang Zemin said that if the multiethnic developing country had not had a strong leadership that rallied 1.2 billion people behind the cause of modernization, "the country would have fallen apart like a heap of loose sand." One can argue about whether it is better to be a loose grain of sand than part of a coherent whole, but it is indisputable that without Deng Xiaoping's firm framing of the common goal, the speed, progress, and success of the Chinese "economic miracle" would not have been possible.

Regardless of any interpretation, "The People" are in the center of China's political system: People's Republic of China, National People's Congress, Standing National Congress of the National People's Congress, Supreme People's Court. And, in one of the most memorable moments in John's life, President Jiang Zemin during a long personal meeting recited Lincoln's Gettysburg Address by heart, ending with: ". . . of the people, by the people, for the people." But the question remained how China understands the role of the people in its political system.

What does "of the people, by the people, for the people" mean for China?

Jiang Zemin answered this question in September 2000, in an interview with Mike Wallace for CBS Television. Wallace had asked him, "Why is it that Americans can elect their national leader, but you apparently don't trust the Chinese people to elect your national leaders?"

"I am also an elected leader, though we have different electoral systems," Jiang responded. "Each country should have its own system, because our two countries have different cultures and historic traditions, and different levels of education and economic development."

Wallace's next question was why China is a one-party state. Jiang replied, "Why must we have opposition parties? You are trying to apply the American values and the American political system to the whole world. But that is not very wise. Let me be frank," Jiang continued, "China and the United States differ greatly in terms of our values. You Americans always use your values in making judgments about the political situation in other countries. We want to learn from the West about science and technology and how to manage the economy, but this must be combined with specific conditions here. That's how we have made great progress in the last twenty years."

The First Bottom-Up Initiative

Deng's speech of 1978, "Emancipate the Minds, Seek the Truth from Facts, Unite and Look Forward," became the party's new manifesto and changed its mission almost overnight from class struggle to economic development. In parallel with the economic modernization of China, Chinese society experienced a gradual loosening and an increase in freedom. There was a shift in the mind-set of the political leaders. If they had not understood the important role of bottom-up participation, the first initiative in this direction would have been turned down, and we would have never heard what eighteen farmers in a remote village had dared to do.

This first bottom-up initiative was driven by desperation and courage. It was, as it turned out, a significant push toward changes in economic thinking, a bottom-up rebellion in an extremely backward, isolated village. During Mao's era a system called *da-guo-fan*, or "under one big pot," had been seen as the guarantee that the needs of the people would be satisfied: everyone should get the same amount of food regardless of the value of his work in creating it. But instead of giving everyone enough, this system gave everyone almost nothing. Living conditions finally became so bad that in Xiaogang village of Fengyang county in Anhui province, a group of eighteen destitute farmers decided to take action and fight for a better life. At any risk.

On an evening in October 1978, the impoverished group met secretly, dipped their fingertips in red ink, and sealed a pioneering paper. "If we are successful we will not ask the country for any money or grain. If we are not [successful] we cadres are willing to risk imprisonment or the death penalty. . . ." This agreement is now at the National Museum of China in Beijing.

The farmers agreed to split up the commune's cropland into eighteen individual plots and allocate them among its member households. Working independently, each household and each family would cultivate its plot on its own and keep the crop. This was a revolutionary and dangerous step, because during the Cultural Revolution farmers, many of whom owned less than one acre of land, had been persecuted, dispossessed, and even killed as bourgeois "landlords." The agreement in Xiangang village was an act against all rules of the commune system that had tied down farmers and farming for decades.

This bold act gained early support from Wan Li, the first secretary of the Anhui Provincial Party Committee, and its success came to the attention of Deng Xiaoping and changed the course of Chinese history. In December 1978 the Third Plenary Session of the Eleventh Central Committee opened the path to reform by agreeing to "shift the focus of all Party work toward socialist modernization and construction." Deng restored family farms, allowed market distribution, and praised consumer goods. Bottom-up initiatives and energy, once released, would support and implement the goals set and outlined by the Communist Party.

The Maturing of Vertical Democracy

In retrospect it seems there could not have been a better way to lead a country of such enormous dimensions out of poverty and guide it into modernization. Had China established a western-style horizontal democracy, energy would have gone into competing for elections, and a vast array of candidates would have presented innumerable programs for solving China's problems to people who had practically no history of democratic decision making. This is what happened during the early days of reform in the Soviet Union under President Gorbachev. In China, such action could have easily resulted in chaos, the opposite of the harmony and order that the country longed for. Instead of splitting the society into different parties and factions in the name of democratic reform, the Chinese made adjustments within the one-party system. By paying heed to bottom-up initiatives and maintaining a central decision-making body at the top, the Chinese were able to undertake a gigantic transition in an astonishingly peaceful manner.

In the last thirty years, 400 million Chinese people have been lifted out of poverty and the struggle for survival. Change happened gradually, with many ups and downs. One major action that had an enormous impact was a government directive of 1984 that permitted farmers to move from the countryside and settle in the cities. This was a reaction against the years when such migration was a crime. As a result, during the last decade 250 million Chinese migrant workers, one-third of them women, left their villages for jobs in cities; this has been the largest-scale migration in history. The migrants work in factories, as house cleaners, in restaurants, at construction sites, as garbage collectors, and in child care. There is hardly a sector where they are not found.

Migrant workers are often badly educated, but full of hope and very inventive when it comes to changing their destiny and moving up the job ladder. They practice learning by doing, often exaggerating their credentials to get a job. Most Chinese are ambitious, willing to work hard, and always looking forward. We were not surprised when we read in *China Daily* that 76 percent of the Chinese believe the world will be better in five years.

Building on what the Chinese Communist Party has achieved, and often overachieved, most of the Chinese trust the government to continue the path to modest wealth while adding new goals to further improve living conditions and focus more strongly on environmental considerations. Throughout this process, the Chinese leadership has never adopted the western idea that leaders need to have the brightest ideas and be content experts. The Chinese prefer "context leadership," in which a leader sets a frame and leaves it to the people to work out the details. Progress is evolutionary—an interplay between top-down framing and bottom-up growth (see Pillar 3).

"It is impossible for democracy here to be exactly the same as democracy practiced in the Western world, as would be preferred by people in the West," Jiang Zemin said during his interview with the *New York Times*. President Hu corroborated this thinking in his speech at the Seventeenth National Congress in October 2007, saying, "We must always put people first," and, "We must expand the citizens' orderly participation in political affairs at each level and in every field." The development of a vertical democracy will, over time, further strengthen the bottom-up forces. This was reconfirmed by Premier Wen Jiabao at an executive meeting of the State Council in January 2008, when he paraphrased Lincoln's Gettysburg Address: "The government is of the people, for the people, and responsible to the people."

The Increasing Power of Bottom-Up

China has provided a stable political and social environment. In any country, the peaceful transfer of political leadership is a marker of stability. The smoothly negotiated transfer from Deng Xiaoping to Jiang Zemin to Hu Jintao has gone practically unnoticed by most people in the West, but political stability is a basic requirement for the continuing shift of more and more power to bottom-up forces. In the vertical Chinese structure a decision is much more the responsibility of collective leadership than of the individual politician, and this naturally lessens the pressure on any one person. In addition, decision-making processes have increasingly included the opinions of ordinary people.

- All around China various arrangements are being created for tapping into the opinions of ordinary citizens. In Shaanxi province, an online project recently asked people in a small town for their opinions and suggestions regarding education, housing, farmers, tourism, environmental protection, traffic, Medicare, law and order, and so on. In early returns the five topics of greatest interest were "housing" (7,938 votes), "people's livelihood" (6,924 votes), "education" (6,745 votes), "Medicare" (6,596 votes), and "traffic" (6, 386 votes). And more than 30,000 suggestions were received.

- China is giving a louder voice to women. Under the headline "Will the Participation of Women Enhance the Society?" the *Jiamusi Daily* reported the results of a survey of women conducted in the city of Jiamusi. The results showed that women's participation in the city's social development had noticeably strengthened. In order of preference, the women checked off these considerations: (1) "want to take part in the advancement of social activities"; (2) "hope that their rights will be respected"; (3) "want to enter politics"; (4) "hope to raise the level of social security"; and (5) "hope to expand educational opportunities."

- In early 2008, the Macheng City Association of Women Entrepreneurs was established in Hubei province. Sixty women became members, pledging to enhance the quality of life, to guide members to operate in accordance with the law, to be honest and trustworthy, and to strengthen exchanges between enterprises.

China's bottom-up initiatives have developed rapidly throughout the entire society. As we shall see in the next chapters, practically no area has been left untouched by this development. By putting the welfare of the nation over that of individuals, China has transformed itself in one generation in a way that other countries have needed three or four generations to achieve.

Since his election as party leader in November 2002 Hu Jintao has invited the complete politburo to attend "study-meetings." Experts are invited to speak about law, democracy, financial crises, social changes, revolutions, and religion. In one such speech, He Weifang of Beijing University offered a seven-point program for the country: "reducing the dominance of the Party in the political system, strengthening the authority of the National People's Congress, giving more freedom to assemble and demonstrate, clearing out the nuisance of bureaucracy, protecting private ownership, changing the property rights of farmers, and increasing the stability of law." The senior leadership of the country is studying all possibilities to ensure that China continues its development. The necessity of reform in the legal system, for example, is something the leadership is well aware of. President Hu, in his speech at the Seventeenth Congress, said, "We must implement the rule of law as a fundamental principle and by speeding up the building of a socialist country under the rule of law."

The Hard Battle against Corruption

In the efforts to improve the rule of law, implementing the law is often the stronger challenge. For China, a subject near the top of this agenda is corruption. We have had many open discussions with Chinese leaders about corruption, which they consider one of the biggest challenges they face, especially at the local level.

There is, as everyone knows, a lot of large-scale development and construction in China; and, as is always the case in such a situation, there is a lot of money floating around. This of course was true when the Pudong district of Shanghai was about to be built. The "godfather" of Pudong, Minister Zhao Qizheng, from the very beginning paid a great deal of attention to this painful phenomenon. He used to say, "When the high rise goes up, some cadres will fall."

To prevent government officials from reaping profits for themselves, the Pudong government laid down and executed a set of rules that came to be known as the "three high-tension lines." No official was allowed to: (1) make decisions on projects without open bidding, appraisals, and contracting that would keep the processes open, fair, and impartial; (2) single-handedly set the price of land or decide on preferential treatment for a certain project; or (3) use his or her power to reap profits for relatives or friends. Two additional hard-and-fast rules became known as "firewalls." No leader of a development company was allowed to: make arbitrary decisions regarding loans, or act arbitrarily as a capital guarantor for someone else's bank loan without the approval of the company's board of directors or the agreement of the supervisory board.

As Zhao Qizheng writes in his case study *Shanghai Pudong Miracle*, "Clean government is an important aspect of the investment environment."

On a smaller scale, we have talked with various officials about creating a "chop index." All applications demand "chops": stamps by the various officials whose approval is needed. Each chop carries the temptation of an official who may seek a little side benefit. Reduce the number of chops, and you reduce the number of temptations. A chop index would quickly tell you if the number of chops for any given process has been reduced.

"House Cleaning" was the title of an article appearing in *China Daily* on March 3, 2008. It reported that Huang Songyou, a vice president of the Supreme People's Court, had been removed; and that Zhu Zhigang, a member of the National People's Congress (NPC) standing committee and deputy director of its financial and economic affairs committee, had resigned and that two other NPC delegates had also submitted their resignations. The reasons differed, but all had to do with financial irregularities.

In March 2009 an editorial in *China Daily* demanded "no mercy for the corrupt" and said that if corrupt officials were shown undeserved leniency during sentencing, it would shake the confidence of the general public. The editorial also demanded a greater knowledge of the law by government employees. One should remember that in October 2007 Liu Zhihua, a former vice mayor of Beijing, was sentenced to death for taking bribes.

Another news article, in January 2009, pointed out that identifying corrupt officials is only dealing with symptoms. Without effective ways to find and eliminate the root cause, the symptom will emerge again. *China Daily* recently reported that many corrupt officials who have fled abroad transferred their illegal fortunes to other countries through their spouses or children, who had already migrated overseas. An effective preventive mechanism has yet to be put into place. What slows down the efforts to devise such a mechanism is the absolute power in the hands of top officials in governments at various levels in China. To let such officials implement checks on their own use of power is like "letting a bird build a cage to put itself in." That is why the task of developing such a mechanism will eventually need to be taken up under the strict framework of the law.

"Opening Up" the Chinese Way

Wu Bangguo, chairman of the standing committee of the National People's Congress, in a speech of March 2009 to the 3,000 deputies, said, "China will actively draw on the fruits from the entire human civilization, including achievements made in the political sphere, but it can by no means indiscriminately copy the western system." China's vertical democratization will continue, but it will bear the signature of the Chinese need for order and harmony. Wu noted, "We will not have multiparty rule, or the separation of legislative and judicial powers." He pointed out three main differences between China and the West in this respect:

- China's system already includes multi-interest cooperation under the leadership of the CPC, but it is not a western multiparty system.

- The system of the People's Congress is not meant to be a western system of the separation of powers.

- Deputies to the People's Congress are broadly representative, but do not represent a single party or group as members of western parliaments do.

The CPC has begun to permit greater diversity within its ranks. For example, entrepreneurs, the former condemned capitalists, have joined the decision-making process; at one time this would have been unthinkable. President Hu has noted, "We must select and recommend a greater number of outstanding non-CPC persons for leading positions."

When it comes to single cases, many stereotypes are meaningless. An admittedly atypical party member is Chen Ailian, owner and chairwoman of Wanfeng Auto Holding Group, the largest manufacturer of aluminum alloy wheels in Asia and one of the top suppliers of auto parts in the country. Her story not only epitomizes the boom in the private economy but also indicates the rising political status of the private sector—she is an elected delegate to the Party Congress and has been a member of the CPC since 1995. In an interview with *China Daily* in October 2007, she said that she had not been surprised when she was elected: "Like workers, farmers, intellectuals, cadres and soldiers, pri-

vate entrepreneurs are also builders of socialism with Chinese characteristics."

Bottom-Up Social Innovation

Trust cannot be demanded, ordered, or bought. Central and local governments and all political institutions are increasingly working on gaining the trust of the people by listening to their problems and including
their voices and opinions in the top-down decision process. In the last
decade the Internet started to play an increasing role as a communications tool with regard to approval or disapproval of any government
plan or action. In the chapter on Pillar 4, "Crossing the River by Feeling the Stones," we write about the Internet as a tool of the information
flow in the vertical democracy. In China as in other countries, Internet
communities of all kinds are organized quickly and have immediate access to any information, which in some critical blogs is hidden behind
stories about dogs, recipes, or holiday greetings.

The government, for its part, is increasingly open to bottom-up
voices from different levels. Debates within the council are no longer
about ideological dogma, but about the various demands of social forces.
Communist Party secretaries are addressing and dealing with the growing problems of migrant workers, rural unemployment, and an underdeveloped social network. There are many signs of change in many fields.

City politicians are facing a young, well-educated people who want to
make independent decisions with little governmental intervention. When
President Hu says, "We must reduce government intervention and mi-
cromanagement of operations," he can be understood in only one way: as
saying that the leadership is well aware of the need to pull farther out of
the life of the Chinese people.

Party intellectuals are thinking about reforms in the educational system and are aware that education is a number one priority. China's
school system is rather rigid; there is too much respect, with too little
individual assertiveness; too much demand for memorization, with
too little emphasis on creativity. President Hu has said, "We must give

priority to education and turn China into a country rich in human recourses."

Representatives of the farmers are demanding higher subsidies and the government has strengthened its efforts to promote rural economic and regional development. Improving education is also high on the list of priorities in rural areas. But there is much more to do to narrow the gap between urban and rural standards.

In 2004 Premier Wen, as part of the new government, promised to rescind all taxes on farmers' land. Never before had China leased land to famers free; such leases had always entailed paying dues to the central government. Skepticism was widespread, but Wen kept his promise. Since 2005 farmers have used their land without paying a tax. Agriculture in China still accounts for about 10 percent of the Chinese GDP, compared with 1.2 percent in the United States and 0.9 percent in Germany. The number of people involved is huge: 43 percent of China's population works in agriculture.

In recent years, with the advantage of being adjacent to farmland, Hongsheng town in Fujin city has been developing a project called "Build the Farm and the City Together." There is broad cooperation involving large cross-regional agricultural machinery, the promotion of agricultural science and technology, the development of the livestock industry, new rural construction, culture, education, and health—all of which has increased the scale of agriculture in the town and brought substantial benefits to the farmers. The town and the farmers exchange personnel so as to learn from each other. The *Jiamusi Daily* says the model of "Build the Farm and the City Together" works with a minimum of input to produce the maximum output, and contributes importantly to China's growing economy.

Shaping the Vertical Democracy

Possibilities for further strengthening the bottom-up forces have grown dramatically. President Hu has noted, "Citizens will have more extensive democratic rights." As we have described, when China started its transformation to a market economy, there was no detailed plan for how this would happen; instead, it evolved in a top-down, bottom-up process. The party communicated the concept but did not organize the evolution. The Chinese people shared the creation of the new China, contributing their ideas and their work. Building on the synergies of this model, the vertical model of Chinese democracy will slowly evolve. One of the steps along the way will be increasing transparency.

The village of Shuangxi in Zhangzhou City has established a program called "Sunshine Village Affairs." It means something like "Let the daylight in so we can see what is going on." The goal is "zero distance between villagers and village affairs." To start with, three to five village representatives are elected by villagers in every district to make up a monitoring group that supervises the day-to-day management of village affairs. The program is meant to support the farmers in "their right to know and their right to manage and supervise, which advances stability, harmony, and development in the villages."

Another sign of strengthening the bottom-up process is the increasing number of protests. An example is what happened in the East China Maglev Project.

"East China Maglev Project Suspended Amid Radiation Concerns"

In one of China's many new suburbs, Xinzhuang, at the end of Shanghai's first subway line, residents protested against what might otherwise be seen as a project in the public interest—the construction of a high-speed magnetic levitation train route linking the eastern districts of Shanghai and Hangzhou. The 35 billion-RMB ($4.5 billion) maglev project was approved by the central government in March 2006. German technology would accelerate the train to a maximum speed of 450 kilometers (about 280 miles) per hour. The high-tech wonder was supposed to be operating by 2010, when Shanghai will host the World Expo.

But when the project was announced by the local governments in January 2007, it caused outrage instead of enthusiasm. The residents along the route started to fight it. Petitioners were deployed, knocking at the doors of government officials every day; thousands of complaints were sent out online; and the local government was put under extreme pressure. The government of Minhang, a mostly residential district in which housing development is the main source of local government revenue, received more than 5,000 petitioners on a single day in March.

In January 2007 thousands of protesters thronged People's Square in Shanghai, in front of the city hall, to protest against the plan. To circumvent government regulations barring protests, they described the demonstration as a walk, which everyone happened to take at the same time. And they succeeded.

The *Financial Times* reported in its July 21, 2008, issue: "The project has been suspended in line with the arrangements of the municipal government," according to a spokesman of the local government of Minhang district in the city's southern suburbs. "The ongoing concerns from residents living along the proposed route [were] the major reason for the suspension," an official of the Shanghai Municipal People's Congress confirmed. "The government is working on the issue," he said on condition of anonymity. The petitioners had apparently succeeded in persuading the government to think twice.

The High Art of Building Bridger

In the charter of the CPC of October 22, 2007, one passage reads: "China is in the beginning of socialism and will stay there for a long time." We often realize that whereas the West thinks in decades, at most, the Chinese have always thought in dynasties. Even today they think in terms of generations of leadership in the development of modern China. There is a long way to go, but if China's people continue to "feel the stones as they cross the river," they will stay patient on the way.

"We have reached a relatively comfortable standard of living for the people as a whole," said President Hu, "but the trend of a growing gap in income distribution has not been thoroughly reversed. There are still a considerable number of impoverished and low-income people in both rural and urban areas. It has become more difficult to accommodate the interests of all sides. Efforts to balance the development have yielded remarkable results, but the foundation of agriculture remains weak."

China's Communist Party has to handle and balance the forces of exploding capitalism and entrepreneurial creativity on one side, and poverty, poor education, and backwardness on the other side. The dynamics of economic development are changing social conditions at an accelerating speed. What took three or four generations in other countries is now happening within one generation in China.

Because of the complexity of the transformation, it is astonishing that collisions between top-down and bottom-up forces could, in most cases, be cushioned. One reason is the political reality that people know there is no alternative to the CPC: the political risks would be too high. The CPC, on the other hand, knows that it cannot overstretch the patience of the people and cannot ignore its obligations to them.

On a Knife's Edge

The German journalist Georg Blume wrote in an essay on China, "China without the CPC would currently only promise chaos. Party cliques, local mafia networks and violent gangs would fight for power. Charismatic sects could lure parts of the population and provoke uprisings. There are enough examples of such horror scenarios to be found in Chinese history." He continued, "The truth is that there has never been an outcry for elections, not even after the student revolt in 1989." What happened in 1989 was indeed the most dangerous period in the process of creating a new society. The events leading up to the tragedy go back some time.

At the end of the 1980s, inflation got out of hand and an outburst of protests rippled throughout the country. The Chinese people were claiming their share in progress and improvements and were no longer willing to wait for top-down adjustments.

To understand the genesis of the problem, one has to go back to 1984, when China was still in the experimental stages of reform and a "two-track pricing system" had been installed. Its purpose had been to support state-owned enterprises (SOEs) by setting prices for them. These prices were much lower than the market-driven prices of private companies and collectives. The unintended consequence was that the system opened a door for buying and selling this advantage. Goods started to go through several hands, gradually doubling their price as they were moved illegally from SOEs to the free market. The prices of goods and materials of all kinds actually became market-driven and moved totally out of the control of the government. Instead of allowing the SOEs to recover and improve their situation, the new system served the resellers, including government officials who were supposed to prevent any such corruption of the system. An estimated 70 percent of the margins of SOEs is believed to have flowed into private pockets in 1988.

It is not a surprise that this misuse of official positions for personal gain led to an acute sense of unfairness among the people. Hatred of officials and their relatives who had participated in this large-scale corruption started to rise and spread. China's *Economic Daily* warned that "officials who resell commodities are bringing calamity upon the country."

In an effort to change course and restore the balance between top-down and bottom-up forces, the government decided to go farther into the free market. It loosened control, ended the two-track pricing system, and allowed prices to be set by the market. This wasn't an entirely top-down decision. The bold step followed a survey revealing that the majority of the Chinese people would support such a decision and that they were willing to accept a lower standard of living for a while to make it happen. The move was also backed by the advice of the Nobel laureate Milton Friedman, who had come to China and strongly advocated economic freedom and free markets.

Prices were decontrolled in March 1988. In the following month, prices rose 95 percent and inflation was out of control. Fearing for their economic survival, people began to buy everything in unreasonable amounts, contributing to further panic and a shortage of durables and, soon, consumer products. In May 1988 the news agency Xinhua tried to calm the increasingly angry masses: "China's price reform is a courageous act. We must take certain risks, but the Central Committee has confidence that this will be done properly and will come out all right."

But in August 1988 the supply situation had become so bad that the Shanghai municipal government began to distribute food and fuel. Soon shortages in even such common goods as cooking pots were so severe that people could buy a new item only by trading in an old one. In the cities, construction came to a halt and huge numbers of construction workers lost their jobs. Returning to their villages, they found even worse conditions. Desperately looking for a way to survive, they went back to the cities. Conditions in the big cities were not any better for highly educated academics, and many university professors had to take side jobs. One can easily imagine how students lost confidence in a promising future for the country and for themselves.

In October 1988, the policy of removing price controls was declared a failure. But even the step of admitting this mistake did not renew the people's faith in China's leadership. The Chinese people had lost confidence in reforms, and the government had lost what had carried reforms though trial and error: the people's trust in an eventual victory. The progress of ten years of reforms was at the brink of collapse.

During 1989, China's economic growth rate fell to its lowest level since 1978. Sources of financing dried up, consumer spending fell, factories had to close, unemployment rose, and money stopped circulating—a critical factor in discontent and organized protests. By the second half of 1989, the number of privately registered small businesses (ge-ti-hu) would have decreased by 3 million. Privately administered big enterprises decreased from 200,000 to 90,600.

A wave of frustration swept through the country, and the scapegoat was the CPC: the political leadership and its role in people's lives. Opposition grew rapidly, waiting for something to ignite the fire. The death of the liberal reformer Hu Yaobang, who had resigned a year before from his position as general secretary of the CPC, because of his tolerance for "bourgeois liberalization," finally drove the bottom-up opposition to uncontrolled outbursts, demonstrations, and the tragedy of Tiananmen Square.

At their height, demonstrations against the government involved nearly 1 million Chinese workers and students who were united in protesting the continuing role of the CPC in public life. During the demonstrations, signs reading "Hello Mr. Democracy" in Chinese and English were held up, profoundly embarrassing the party as having failed not only in front of its people, but also in front of the world, which was watching through the reporting of international media.

But the cry for democracy, which was widely supported in the West, did not rise because of a political desire for free elections; it arose from deep frustration and disappointment with the economic reality of China's reforms, the opening up, and—mostly—the continuing corruption. Top-down and bottom-up forces were out of balance. At any time, the protests against the government and against the role of the CPC could have led to a cessation of reforms, a reimposition of oppressive government, and even civil war. Taking all that into account, and looking back at the events in Tiananmen Square, we should be surprised not at what did happen, but at what did *not* happen.

China did not have a civil war, did not reverse its economic reforms, and did not again lock itself away from the outside world. Whether by instinct or through strategic planning, Deng took all the steps to ensure that economic reforms would not come to a halt. In a New Year's editorial of 1990, *People's Daily* wrote, "We must sustain stability. Even if we have to develop at a slow pace for ten years, China will achieve fundamental change at the end."

All the leadership's energy was put into restoring the balance between holding on to the CPC and cautiously allowing further economic reforms. Balance was eventually restored, and the country made the transition from an overheated economy to stable growth. Reform, once again, became the main focus of continued development.

The Asian Games of the year 1990 were the first large-scale international sports event to be held in the People's Republic of China, and the beginning of the continuation of reforms. During these games, Deng announced the development of Pudong, the backward district of Shanghai across the Huangpu River. In the same year, the Shanghai stock exchange was opened. The person responsible for beating the gong fainted in excitement and fell to the floor.

Although on one hand confidence in the government's ability to calm the situation was growing, on the other hand a debate about the direction of reforms started again and resulted in the question whether this was capitalism or communism. Again, Deng—who earlier had announced his retirement—intervened. He began with a series of unsigned articles titled "Calming the Huangpu." "China should hold on to liberal thinking, should be willing to take risk, carry on reform, and not be constrained by a debate [about] whether it was called communist or capitalist," he wrote.

But calming took time, until Deng started his famous "southern tour" in spring 1992 and, in a series of "viewpoints," set guidelines for the direction of China's continuing reforms: "The important key is economic development." By the time the Fourteenth National Congress of the Communist Party was convened in October 1992, Deng's strong words and his southern tour had brought the party into line again. The question whether this was communism or capitalism faded away, and a new theoretical approach was written into the party's bylaws: "socialism with Chinese characteristics."

In the years to come, China will reach a point where it deals with this part of its history, and the West will reach a point where it does not measure the existing China against the China of 1989, holding on to the iconic picture of the student and the tank. The West takes this image as a symbol of China's political situation, and the CPC does too little to correct that impression and thus feeds the westerners' claim that there is an outcry for western-style democracy in China. The West blames China, which started its march to freedom and civil society only thirty years ago, and forgets that from the beginning of free trade under Johan de Witt, it took Europe three centuries to establish a democratic market economy. It took America almost 200 years to get rid of slavery and apartheid. It is not only the Chinese who have blood on their hands.

Time to Update the Picture

The West is still thinking of China's past, and westerners seem to have a lot of resentment and not much motivation to reframe the picture. But how would the West react if China continually pointed out how democratically elected western politicians often make promises that they do not keep? What if China questioned the credibility and honesty of coalitions between parties in western Europe that a few weeks before were accusing each other of incompetence and misjudgment? What if the western model of liberal democracy is not the "end of history" and not the final form of human governance?

China's leadership has achieved remarkable results, which even harsh critics are beginning to concede. All signs, as we have pointed out, are in the direction of further liberation and stronger bottom-up participation. A vertical democracy moves in a firmer frame, but loses much less energy in rivalries, political gesturing, and quarrels; and it fulfills the Chinese desire for harmony and stability. The vertical democratic model is not driven by short-term considerations; it does not have to bend to special interests, voter backlash.

Western Democracy Is Not Essential for Economic Prosperity

Since the fall of the Soviet Union, many have believed that democracy coupled with capitalism is the winner as the most successful model for national development. Now China's model of a vertical democracy, however imperfect and by far not in its final stage, is shaping up to become another option. One place in the world that has already demonstrated that increasing wealth and political stability can be compatible with both a western and a Chinese model is Hong Kong. Twelve years ago, when Hong Kong was handed back to China, and the talk was of "one country and two systems," the western fear was that Hong Kong would become more and more like the mainland. We now see that the mainland is becoming more and more like Hong Kong.

Hong Kong is called the freest economy in the world, but it cannot be called democratic in the western sense, although, apart from foreign politics and military, it enjoys many privileges. It still holds on to its own legal system, its own currency, left-side traffic, and its own immigration policy.

Throughout the more than 100 years Great Britain was in charge, the British never installed democratic institutions in Hong Kong. There has never been a representative of Hong Kong in the British House of Commons, not even in 1980 when Great Britain was negotiating Hong Kong's return to the mainland. And even the last of Britain's Hong Kong governors, Chris Patten, was appointed by the Queen. But Britain never attempted to give Hong Kong's people a western democracy—and they never really demanded it.

Even each year on the first of July, the anniversary of the hand-back to China, when the democracy movement makes its voice heard in the streets of Hong Kong, the people of Hong Kong have more interest in the freedom to use their talents, make money, and the opportunity to buy goods of their choice. And maybe to lose money in the famous horse races at the Hong Kong Jockey Club. During the Chinese-English negotiations about the hand-back, Deng Xiaoping said: "Hong Kong can hold on to horse races and dancing nights," which in fact meant it could hold on to its political and economic system. The bets in Hong Kong still are the only legal bets allowed to the gambling-loving Chinese. There is nothing like a state lottery or casinos. Whoever has witnessed the crowds and the unbelievable amounts of their bets knows that economic wealth without a western democratic political model can be enjoyed very much.

It seems that capitalism and a one-party system can work together. And, on the other hand, democracy does not guarantee economic success, as we can see from many countries in Latin America.

Step-by-Step toward Democracy

At the opening of the Party Congress in 2007, President Hu deepened China's will for political restructuring. Hu also echoed his speech at

Yale in 2006, when he said that China would not embrace western-style democracy, but would be open to any tested experience buttressing democracy. "Comparatively speaking, democracy is the best form of government in human history," Yu Keping, deputy chief of the Central Compilation and Translation Bureau, wrote in an article titled "Democracy Is a Lovely Thing," published in the *Study Times*, a newspaper sponsored by the CPC Central Committee's Party School.

Experiments are already in place. In 200 townships in Sichuan and Hubei, experimental elections for party chiefs are being held. One of the elected leaders, Chen Guohua, became the Communist Party chief of Longxing township in Chongqing municipality. He won a landslide victory, promising to quadruple the local GDP within three years. But now he has to deliver, and prove progress in an annual performance review. If even one-third of the people express no confidence, he will be removed from his seat. Politicians are able to set frames top-down to reach goals, but the frames will be judged bottom-up.

Hubei and Sichuan townships are only two areas where village elections have taken place in the last decade. Cheng Li, director of the Thornton China Center of the Brookings Institution, said that such elections have taken place in 680,000 Chinese villages. Every five years all eligible voters in China, probably around 900 million, directly elect representatives for the people's congress at the township and country levels. Those representatives then elect government leaders, approve budgets, and endorse policy at their respective levels and elect representatives to higher levels.

The power of the base is not only strengthened by a stronger participation in the political decision making. Since the Communist Party took over in 1949, information regarding severe disasters, especially death tolls, was kept under tight control. In 2005 the government issued a directive ordering transparency in the death toll in natural disasters. After the 2008 earthquake in Sichuan, the provincial government released detailed information: 68,712 people died, 17,921 are missing, and more than 3,500 students were killed or are missing. As *People's Daily* reports, the publishing of such figures empowers the base to demand better safety in school buildings and psychological treatment for survivors. It also helps to create more efficiency in organizing the reconstruction. Statistics, which were published in the following year, showed what had been achieved in that year: tidier, safer schools; new condos; and evenly paved roads.

In China's top-down, bottom-up vertical democracy the leadership is driven not so much by individuals as by consensus leadership—you do not find counterparts of Roosevelt, Bush, or Obama in the same way you find them in the West. Instead, one speaks of the party leadership, not of, say, Jiang or Hu. In China, individual knowledge and charisma are *not* the preferred leadership style. The preferred style is the ability of a leader to set a context in which the group can be successful.

In many conversations with our friend Stephen Rhinesmith, author of *Leading in Times of Crisis* and other books on management and leadership, we discussed the similarities between China's vertical democracy and enterprise leadership. There are many parallels between how Steve describes context leadership and how the Chinese leadership runs China. He notes: "Context-oriented CEOs focus more on the environment in which decisions are made than on having the answers themselves. They create the values and purpose of the enterprise and build an effective executive team; they engage their leadership and their people and set a culture and climate in which people's ideas can make a difference; and they have an especially strong belief in the power of the right social processes to produce the best decisions and a commitment to implement them."

Any CEO who could present a turnaround as successful, dramatic, and transforming as China's would be highly praised. Not so in the political parallel. In a cover story on democracy in *Time* magazine of January 12, 2009, the headline read: "Most Asian Nations Now Hold Elections. Yet True Democracy Still Eludes the Region." The West still claims the right to decide what constitutes a *true* democracy for any country in the world.

But for countries that judge the model of a vertical democracy against results achieved, the Chinese model is very likely to be serviceable. This model can pull a moribund country out of backwardness and poverty and turn it into a viable member of the geopolitical world.

China's vertical democracy is based on the interplay between top-down and bottom-up forces. The trouble with understanding how democracy works in China is that the West never hears about the bottom-up forces and the power these forces have within the system. Everyone in China knows how the initiative of eighteen farmers in a remote village changed the country's overarching rural policy almost overnight.

From this first step in agriculture the power of the bottom-up forces has increased, and it will continue to increase gradually. The direction of the relationship between top-down and bottom-up forces is set to create a system that is built on trust: the government trusting its people and the people trusting the government. It is a model that fits Chinese history, Chinese thinking, and the Chinese people's strong desire for a harmonious and stable society. And as the party's tolerance of diversity grows, fewer people will stand against it.

Western democracy was not built in one generation; it matured over several hundred years. China has made giant steps in only one generation. It will move on and strengthen the equilibrium between the top-down and bottom-up forces during the years to come.

Our belief is that the world, and the Chinese people, will be better off if the West supports the gradual evolution of vertical democracy and economic development in China, rather than focusing on the difficulties that China faces as its reforms mature.

Pillar 3

Framing the Forest and Letting the Trees Grow

In the vertical democracy that China is creating, the vision and the goals are being shaped in a top-down, bottom-up process. The government frames the policies and priorities within which citizens create their own roles and their own contributions to the whole, forming a structure that allows and benefits from diversity while sustaining order and harmony.

Thirty years ago China was like a huge forest in which all the trees had to be alike. Any plant that disturbed the uniformity had been cut down or torn out. But this kind of uniform forest proved to be unsustainable. Deng Xiaoping realized this, and his call for emancipating minds and allowing variety to take root was indispensable for China's survival and development.

Part of the balancing act was to reforest gradually, waiting to see what grew and what didn't grow, and letting the plants and trees in the forest, over time, organize themselves.

It would not work to try to change a pine forest to a rain forest. But that's what the West calls for when it looks at China. It wants China to be its kind of forest.

"China's political and legal system has never been disposed to become a Western-bourgeoisie-liberal model," Harro von Senger, an expert on Chinese law at the Swiss Institute for Comparative Law, writes in his book *Supraplanning*. He notes that China's political model for the twenty-first century continues to be the traditional pyramid.

Deng's call for emancipating the mind did not mean cutting off all the roots or changing the habitat of the forest from one day to another. Nor did it mean peeling off the hierarchical relationships which had been established throughout China's history and in which the Chinese felt comfortable. But the hierarchies in the slowly developing vertical democracy more and more look like a reactangle rather than a triangle.

New Frames

What has been true of China for centuries remains true today. Moving within a frame is not intrinsically negative. We all move within frames, including those we create for ourselves. But a vertically organized democracy will develop different frames, which work within the context of balancing top-down and bottom-up forces.

In the first years after reforms began, the Chinese people started to embrace freedom, and began to experience the responsibility that came with it. Framing a forest in which people could plant new trees and play with ideas to create initiatives was essential. But at the same time, Deng Xiaoping held on to the larger forest, socialism—the grand political frame within which new economic frames were contained. For westerners this might seem contradictory, but from a Chinese perspective balancing contradictions is a common, familiar way of thinking.

One overall economic frame was to reach "modest wealth" by the year 2010, but no detailed definitions of single steps were given. Increasing economic freedom created room for the people to engage in and benefit from the process, and it maintained momentum and enthusiasm to transform China into a modern society.

To silence ideological debates, Deng reaffirmed China's adherence to the banner of socialism and proclaimed its commitment to building "socialism with Chinese characteristics." This was nevertheless a radical change, and Mao's condemnation of capitalism may have still been sounding in many Chinese ears.

Until 1976 all Chinese businesses were under government ownership and control. People understood themselves to be part of a state project, sharing one class and one identity. From administration to state-owned enterprises (SOEs) to agricultural collectives, the Chinese people's mind-set was to receive orders and act within a very small top-down frame. As we have seen, the first step in reinventing China was the emancipation of minds. Only when people could think for themselves would they be able to create personal goals that would advance society. But these goals had to be in line with the large goal, framed by the Communist Party of China (CPC): "bringing down poverty and fighting backwardness." The political line of the CPC set the frame within which the Chinese people could operate. The overwhelming focus of reforms was economic development.

This was in sharp contrast to perestroika in the Soviet Union. Gorbachev's ambition to reform the Soviet Union stretched from economics to culture, agriculture, education, social welfare, and politics but did not involve framing a context. Instead of guiding the people by creating manageable frames within which they could take single steps, he started a process that was top-down and top-heavy, and it all came tumbling down and led to the fall of the Soviet Union.

Deng's view of reform was much more realistic. He could not do it all at once, and he could not do it alone. In a countrywide discussion about "practical experience as the only criterion for truth," Deng changed the situation from a radical class struggle to a joint modernization process. After blinding dogmatism was removed and replaced by "seeking the truth from facts," the picture that became visible was grim. The forest and the trees were in poor condition, malnourished and discouraged by the conditions of the years before Deng's takeover. The call for emancipating minds gave people the initial energy to step out of the fields and see the mud on their feet. People in most parts of the country were destitute; efficiency in any area of work was extremely low. As we said in previous chapters, agriculture, organized in collectives, was in a disastrous condition, SOEs were moribund, private companies were nonexistent, and technology was decades behind the rest of the world. No wonder that, at the Chinese People's Political Consultative Conference in March 1978, Deng's wake-up call included these principles: "Science and technology are the primary productive force" and "Intellectuals, too, are part of the workers' class."

With Deng's new framework for and attitude toward business and education, young people streamed in to take the exams for higher education. What a change of perspective! In the past, their future had offered nothing but blending in with the proletariat.

Deng's advance into a market economy was not undisputed. More than once Mao had called Deng a "capitalist roader." But capitalism was not the first loan from the West. Marxism was as much "western" as capitalism was. Maybe Deng's openness to the modern West resulted from his years in France, where he had first encountered Marxism. But most likely the cause was his own sense of reality, which allowed him to develop a subtle intuition for capitalism. His spirit was too big for him to be just a "capitalist roader" or just walk in westerners' footsteps. Instead, he was looking for what would serve China on its path to modernity. At some point it had become clear to him that centralization would suffocate reforms.

Moving within Chinese Patterns of Thinking

To develop goals and strategies, the CPC had introduced a concept of "main contradictions" in the mid-1930s. Every big shift in the history of modern China was initiated by the introduction of a new main contradiction. Within that context, Deng, who was about to guide China through the biggest transformation in its history, in 1978 introduced a new main contradiction to support this goal.

"The main contradiction in the Chinese society is the contradiction between the growing material and cultural needs of the people and the backward social production." This main contradiction, which became the new political frame, was written in the charter of the CPC at the beginning of Deng's era and is still valid today. It allowed balancing socialist principles with the materialistic demands of modernization.

Deng's first step had been "to release the production forces" and to turn toward a market economy. This resulted in a shift from central planning to decentralization and a market economy. And while the decentralization of China was loosening the central grip, the new socialist "built-up" frame, in which every Chinese could have a share, united China in a new common goal.

For the Chinese the contradiction represents an objective description of current reality that will need to be attended to. The basic assignment of the "socialist buildup" is to "keep liberating the productive forces and realize the socialist modernization step by step." The goals of fighting poverty and backwardness were articulated in the constitution of 1978. They were embodied in a three-step strategy, or three frames.

1980–1990: *double the GDP*

1990–2000: *double the GDP*

2000–2050: *complete the modernization of the country*

In a horizontal democracy any goal that exceeds a term of office is problematic in two ways. First, it is quite an advantage to be able to promise things you cannot be held responsible for, given the time allotted. This is especially true of environmental goals for, say, 2020 or 2050. Second, even sincere, meaningful promises can be invalidated by the next person or party elected. By contrast, the continuity of the CPC is much more a guarantee of its obligation to keep its promises.

By checking the record of promises we can see that China's goals were achieved and sometimes overachieved. According to the IMF, China's GDP rose from $309.3 billion in 1980 to about $1.2 trillion in 2000. Per capita income has risen from $251.4 in 1980 to $ 2,371.8 in 2000. There is no doubt that the CPC will hold on to the goal of constant improvement of China's economic development.

President Hu has said repeatedly, "Economic development still is the central task." Therefore, the CPC's understanding of economic results and of the well-being of the people is its justification for staying in power.

China's Goal Orientation

If a CEO has created an effective team and runs the company well, there will be little pressure for a change in leadership. Engaging both the leadership and the employees at large in the process of modernization and enhancement will allow delegating responsibility at all levels. President Hu Jintao addressed the relevant needs in his speech at the Seventeenth Party Congress:

- Reduce government intervention in microeconomic operations.

- Enhance China's capacity for independent innovation.

- Adapt the growing enthusiasm of the people for participation in public affairs.

- Expand the citizens' orderly participation in political affairs at each level and in every field.

The charters of the CPC for 2002 and 2007 both say: "The strategic goals for economic and cultural development are to stabilize the achieved level of modest wealth and to develop a society with modest wealth on a higher level that will bring advantages to more than a billion people, until the 100-year anniversary of the Party (2021)." Since China makes up roughly one-fifth of the world's population and is the world's third largest economy, it makes sense to find out how China thinks about this goal, rather than speculate from a western point of view about how China's politics can be interpreted.

The overarching frame expressed as "The socialist case will be crowned with victory" was set and has remained untouched, but within that frame the country changed dramatically.

From the very beginning of the reforms, Deng united genius, political instinct, and strategic planning. To a great degree China owes its rise to the giant spirit of this little man. Starting at the beginnings, one can trace how the 8 Pillars came about, though never named as such. In most cases a significant part of reform was resting on Pillar 2, described in the previous chapter: maintaining a balance between top-down and bottom-up forces.

Campaign Pledges and Strategic Goals

In the run-up to every election in a western horizontal democracy, politicians compete to set the most attractive goals; the same is true of the European Union (EU). In 2000 the EU made a pledge that Europe would become "the most dynamic knowledge-driven economy in the world by 2010."

Compare that fading pledge with the change China has undergone since Deng, in 1979, made it clear that the goal for China was to become an industrial power by the year 2000. He knew that economic progress was the only way to deal with poverty and backwardness. In contrast, the EU was out of touch with the people's parade, and it did not follow up and create an economic environment in which Europe's entrepreneurs could achieve what its politicians had promised.

In China's vertical democracy, goals are not campaign pledges but realistic intentions to be achieved in a top-down, bottom-up collaboration.

In the vertical democracy China is creating, goals are set top-down but have been nurtured bottom-up, and in many cases they have been tested before being implemented. China's goals exist in a context of creating and maintaining a harmonious society. What will China need in the next decades? How should China adapt to external influences? How can China stay competitive in borderless markets? All framing will be in this context, and for that reason people will relate to it and will see it not as constraining but as guiding.

Within the overarching goals people "balance the position in the group and maintain conformity" while developing and achieving individual goals, engaged in the process of modernization and creating modest wealth.

Flexible Frames

Despite the early progress in agricultural reforms, agriculture has become somewhat stagnant. In our discussions with people from the countryside we found that one reason why there has not been faster progress or more mechanized farming is the size of individual farmers' plots of land, and the limited possibility of voluntarily combining some of them. An important step toward reframing agriculture was taken in the fall of 2008. For the first time, farmers were allowed to lease their land-use rights. Until then, rural people had ownership of the produce of their land, but not of the land itself. Therefore, they were barred from trading land-use rights. But under the new policy, farmers can now subcontract, lease, or exchange the land they farm.

Such land transfers had already been taking place informally, so this is another case of bottom-up practices emerging and them being adopted nationally by the government. This new frame is essential in the effort to bridge the yawning gap between urban China and rural China.

In reaching goals and following strategies, the Chinese have always been ingenious. A proverb well known in China is based on a story of a decisive battle at the end of the Han dynasty prior to the Three Kingdoms in the third century. The story sheds light on many facets of China's strategic planning, its artful tactical maneuvers to reach its goals, and its readiness to exploit and benefit from the most favorable factors.

Master Sun's Martial Arts in Management

The combined forces of the southern warlords Sun Quan and Liu Bei engaged in a huge battle with Cao Cao, a northern warlord. The two armies settled down on opposite sides of the Yangtze River, at the narrows of the Red Cliffs. Taking advantage of a heavy mist before the battle, Zhuge Liang, Liu Bei's primary strategist, sent twenty boats packed full of straw off toward the other side of the river. Fearing an attack, Cao Cao's army shot thousands of arrows at the boats. At that point the boats were retrieved and pulled back to the other shore. According to the legend, in this way more than 100,000 arrows were obtained. Zhung Liang used this ingenious trick to obtain a wealth of ammunition from the enemy, and the underlying concept has been used until this day.

Letting the trees grow gave freedom to set goals. "Borrowing arrows" was an artful start at reaching them. In August 1978, the First Machinery Industry Ministry, which was in charge of the automobile industry in China, invited General Motors, Ford Toyota, Nissan, Renault, Citroën, Mercedes-Benz, Volkswagen, and some other companies to come to China. Joint ventures were the name of the new frame. The Chinese interpretation of this concept was "mutually shouldering risk."

One of the first international automakers to venture into China was Volkswagen. First contacts date to the year 1978, when the Chinese government, under Deng Xiaoping's new policy of economic reform, approached foreign enterprises to use capital and technology from abroad to accelerate industrialization in the country and to gain an international competitive edge. The boat was in the river and arrows started flying. In the following decades the Chinese slowly pulled one arrow after the other out of the joint venture boats.

In retrospect, this seems like a time when new "economic frames" were enough to encourage a variety of "trees" to "grow," but that was true only of strongly entrepreneurial people. The majority of people who were not in agriculture were workers at SOEs, which were as big as redwood trees but in a weak condition. Mentally, their workforces lingered in completely different frames.

Western journalists who, early on, were allowed to visit SOEs reported that conditions were backward and relaxed. A Japanese journalist who visited a steel plant in Chongqing in 1979 was amazed that one piece of equipment, still being used, was a 140-year-old British-made steamroller. A journalist from the *Washington Post* who had moved heaven and earth to visit a state-run silk factory in Guilin reported: "As in most factories in China, workers at this Guilin silk factory are not putting much effort into their work. This relaxed work attitude is going to be a major obstacle to the modernization of this most populous nation on earth."

Reinventing an old-fashioned enterprise is a capital-intense project. And capital was something that China lacked. Mao's autocratic policy had ruled out foreign investment. To turn this policy around, Deng again made a careful and clever move. To avoid too much disturbance if his model for inviting foreign investment failed, he limited the application of the new frame to certain areas, until its utility or uselessness was proved.

He designated four areas on China's south coast as "special economic zones." They would be allowed to import foreign goods and know-how and export Chinese products. This new frame opened the door for urgently needed foreign investment. China utilized foreign capital in three major categories:

- Foreign loans, export credits, and issuance of bonds overseas.

- Direct foreign investment including Chinese–foreign equity joint ventures, wholly foreign-owned enterprises, and Chinese- and foreign-owned cooperative development projects.

- International leasing, compensation trade, processing and assembly, issuance of stock overseas.

From 1979 to 2007 foreign capital utilized by China in real terms totaled $882.7 billion, including $691.9 billion of direct foreign investment. In 2007, foreign investment remained strong, and foreign capital utilized in real terms for the year totaled $78.3 billion, of which $74.8 billion was direct foreign investment, according to official figures.

China Frames Special Economic Zones

Beginning in 1980, China initially established five special economic zones: Shenzhen, Zhuhai, Shantou in Guandong province, Xiamen in Fujian province, and Hainan province. It has also opened fourteen coastal cities and set up fifteen bonded zones, fifty-four state economic and technological development zones, and fifty-three new high-tech industrial development zones in large and medium-size cities. All together, these have allowed Chinese entrepreneurs and scientists to operate with astonishing freedom and support.

One of the coastal open cities is our hometown in China: Tianjin. It is one of the four municipalities that have provincial status, reporting directly to the central government. It is also the city where we established the Naisbitt China Institute. We were welcomed to Tianjin in 2006 by Mayor Dai Xianglong, a former governor of China's central bank, who is now head of China's state pension plan. When he came to Tianjin in 2005, he had a mission. His goal was to turn Tianjin into the economic center of the Bo Hai Sea rim and an international port metropolis, a whole new city by the sea. Tianjin was set to become China's third new economic powerhouse, after Shenzhen and Shanghai Pudong.

The Bo Hai rim is among the three most important economic regions in China. Shanghai and Hong Kong were dominant in the last two decades, but now foreign investment and development seem to be moving toward Tianjing and its Binhai district. President Hu said in 2007, "The Binhai New Area in Tianjin will play a major role in reform, opening up, and independent innovation."

Mayor Dai Xianglong's appointment to Tianjin was good news for high-profile foreign investment, such as Airbus's first A320 aircraft assembly plant in Tianjin, and also for the emergence of Tianjin as a financial center. Bohai Bank was the first national bank to be approved in a decade. There are also plans to set up China's third stock exchange. A vibrant financial sector will be important in stimulating the growth of a service economy.

We put our bet on Tianjin. In 2006, when Mayor Dai gave us a warm welcome, we were also taken on a tour to Binhai. All we saw confirmed that we should base our institute in Tianjin. And Mayor Dai and Vice Mayor Cui have been very supportive in the setting up of the Naisbitt China Institute, along with Dr. Chen Zongsheng, the deputy secretary-general of the Tianjin municipal government. Dr. Chen is an outstanding example of of the professors who have left academe to become government officials—a trend in China. He was a highly respected scholar who had published more than twenty books on economics and had developed models for measuring the degree to which China's economy was drawn from the private sector. As early as 2000, he calculated that the economy had become a 65 percent market economy, a revelation that received widespread attention. He told us he went from being a scholar to being a government official because he wanted a new challenge, a chance to put his theories into practice and to learn more from working in the greater society.

Mayor Cui has also teamed up with the entrepreneur Wang Wei and the Asian Business School to create the Finance Museum of China in Tianjin, along the lines of the Museum of American Finance in New York and the Bank of England Museum in London. The museum features exhibits about the evolution of currencies from shells to gold coins and the earliest notes to the present, the twenty major events that have driven the development of finance in China, and a hall of fame of twenty key figures in that development. The museum occupies a handsome new building in downtown Tianjin and was opened to the public during the summer of 2009. Branches are planned for Beijing and Shanghai. The sponsors say there is "demand and a need to upgrade financial education to create a better understanding of financial innovation and support harmonious development."

Old and New China

We often talk about the changes in Tianjin with Zhang Haihua, a friend who was born there. We asked her what Tianjin was like in the years when she was growing up. She describes it as a rather small city of 8 million, heavily industrial, with the biggest port of northern China just fifty kilometers (about thirty-one miles) away.

Haihua's father, in the tradition of Mao's China, worked as a Communist Party leader for a state-owned radio manufacturing company called, of all names, Red Star. Shortly after Deng started his reforms, her mother was appointed as a member of the Tianjin Economic Development Area (TEDA). Previously, the mother had worked at an import-export company, earning fifty RMB (about five dollars) per month for twenty-five years. "I still remember when my mother took me to visit the area where the TEDA was about to be built. There was nothing. It was just another poor patch of land," Haihua remembers; "but my mother turned to me and said, 'One day this will area become one of the most important economic landmarks of China.'"

Her prediction came true; the GDP of the TEDA region surpassed the entire Tianjin city region a few years ago. Even today, landfills abound, with billions in investments pouring in.

Twenty-five years ago Deng Xiaoping stood in that same area on the saline ground of Tianjin city and pronounced, "There are tremendous hopes hiding in development zones." What makes TEDA stand out to-day is that, unlike Shenzhen and Guangdong, it began with a strategy of seeking a new kind of economic development, which emphasized recycling and sustainability. This northern port city of Tianjin has water shortages and briny water, which were the main deterrents to TEDA's industrial development. There are now three wastewater treatment plants that produce more than 120 million tons of clean water each year.

In collaboration with the State Oceanic Administration, a seawater desalination facility is being built. When completed, it will produce 100,000 tons of desalinated water every day, of which more than 80 percent will be dedicated for residential use in neighboring communities. The TEDA also has an integrated "eco-industry" program for a sustainable energy supply. In every link of the production chain, from raw materials to industrial products, there is control of emissions and an enhancement of energy usage. This is part of a "three-R" campaign to reduce, reuse, and recycle.

In the past twenty years, the area has attracted internationally known companies—including Motorola from the United States, Toyota from Japan, and Samsung from South Korea—that have invested in modern manufacturing facilities.

All this was still far in the future when Haihua's mother, even though she was earning good money in her new "golden bowl" job, felt that there was more to achieve. There was a "gold mine mood" in Tianjin, which had once had a proletarian tone. "Have you jumped into the ocean?" people would say to each other, meaning: Have you taken the big step and left your state company yet? Haihua's mother jumped, started her own business, and quickly had a very good income. But although all this happened within the new frame of a freer, market-oriented society, and although people were encouraged to set up small local or household enterprises, some leftover ideology was still in their bones.

Haihua remembers how embarrassed she felt when her mother insisted on driving a car through the campus of Beijing University, where she was a student, instead of using a bicycle, as everybody else did. And her mother did feel rather guilty to be making money, so much so that she gave drivers apartments and excessive bonuses.

Sha-zi Gua-zi

"One should not let the trees grow into heaven," was a saying in Austria, referring to people who made too much money too fast. In China trees that grew too high didn't scrape heaven but did scratch Marx's ideological firmament. Deng had declared that the new market economy was "an instrument applicable in any system to optimize division of goods and improve productivity." But what if this instrument was violating an essential Marxist rule? As it happened, a man called Sha-zi—which means fool in Chinese—caused a severe headache and a problem hard to solve in the early days of reframing. Wu Xiaobo tells the story in his book *Emerging China*.

In 1979 Sha-zi made a living by roasting *gua-zi*, melon seeds. They were as delicious as his brand name, Sha-zi Gua-zi, was appealing. And thus something happened that, "Marx forbid," should never have happened. He hired twelve people to meet the demand, and so he quickly moved from running a small enterprise to being a despicable person exploiting the masses. We read in Marx's *Das Kapital*: "If an employee hires more than eight people he can no longer be considered a small enterprise but instead should be thought of someone who is exploiting the masses." Sha-zi Gua-zi melon seeds could not have cared less. By 1982, Sha-zi was selling 9,000 kilos (more than 18,000 pounds) of *gua-zi* per day, and exploiting 105 workers. What kind of fool!

Deng fended off the critics—"Wait and see"—and encouraged further growth. By 1985, nearly 12 million private enterprises were registered, many with far more than eight employees. Chinese peasants never lacked intelligence, even though their talents had been bound for thirty years in tight ideological frames.

Old Iron to New Money

Also in *Emerging China*, Wu Xiaobo—a former visiting scholar at Harvard—tells the story of Lu Guanqiu, a farmer in Xiaoshan province who was seen riding his old bicycle up and down the streets for many years. Nobody seemed to notice that he was collecting any scrap metal he could find. In the fall of 1978, Lu must have had an idea about how to make the best use of all this old material. Considering the small number of cars in China at that time, his idea showed considerable foresight. Out of the material he had collected over the years, he began to make spare automobile parts, concentrating on those that wore out fastest. To find clients, he would put up a little booth in front of trade fairs, where at the time only SOEs were permitted to offer their goods. He set his prices 20 percent lower than the lowest price of any of the companies inside. In 1993 his little company became the first "township and village" enterprise to be listed on the Chinese stock exchange.

In some regions officials developed a policy called "one eye open, one shut." This involved a very generous interpretation of the official business frame when such generosity was to the benefit of small communities. Peddlers guided by fishing boats along the coastline had started to bring cloth, electronics, and hardware from the special economic zones. Soon small markets began to spring up, and itinerant peddlers bought the goods and sold them in the countryside. And then there is the story of a party secretary, Wu Renbao, who secretly set up a little workshop making hardware. Whenever officials came by, he and his employees pretended to be working in the fields. But as soon as the officials turned their backs, the ostensible farmers would go back to their benches and make hardware.

What happened in the following decades would, had it happened in Germany or Kentucky, probably have been praised as an entrepreneurial masterpiece and a new social and economic model. One step at a time, Wu Renbao moved from undercover hardware production in the fields to running a factory producing aerosols for fertilizers. He then used the gains from the factory to build a trading park. Over the years his business grew into a holding company with revenues of 2.6 billion euros in 2005.

He made all longtime residents of his community shareholders, with free housing, benefits, and incentives. Thousands of migrant workers have found work in Huaxi, officially the wealthiest village in China, and are paid many times what they would earn in farming. In 2006 the German magazine *Stern* featured a story about the economic rise of this village, titled "The Good Guy of Huaxi."

Zhu Rongji

If Deng Xiaoping can be called the reinventor of China, Zhu Rongji can be described as cleaning up its act. He arrived in Beijing as vice premier in 1991, recommended by Deng, and was put in charge of the economy. On one hand, the economy really started to take off; on the other hand, supply and demand continued to be out of balance, the financial system was chaotic, and the reform of SOEs was not making any significant progress. Changing economic and social conditions had necessitated a reframing adapted to free-market conditions.

Zhu initiated a national unified tax reform that revived the finances of the central government. He moved ahead with a reform of the exchange rate that made Chinese products suddenly cheaper and China a more attractive place for foreign investment; and he started a gradual, selective privatization process for SOEs.

A small county seat in Shandong had gone farther than any other in reforming SOEs, and the magic word in the success of this local government was: sell. The framing directive of the Central Committee said, "Some state-owned small enterprises can be leased out or sold to collectives or to individuals for managing." The head of this county seat declared, "From today onward, we are changing the relationship. From now on it is: You register, I record. You make money, I levy taxes. You get rich, I am happy. You break the law, I punish. You go bankrupt, I commiserate." As a result, through different methods, this county sold 272 state-owned or collective operations to individuals.

In January 1997 a survey showed that SOEs had reached a point where they would either change or die. The main reason was that ownership was not clearly delineated; it was too uniform. Divisions between government and private enterprise were unclear, and the ownership of assets was not well specified. In June 1997 the Asian financial crisis brought many Asian countries to the verge of collapse. Within four months the currencies of Thailand, Malaysia, the Philippines, and Indonesia lost almost 50 percent of their value. South Korea's currency, the won, lost 50 percent in just two months. Although China was not directly affected, the Chinese stock market fell and consumers stopped buying. Individually operated enterprises fell into a sharp decline, and some went out of business. But, unexpectedly, China's grim economy allowed what was overdue: the marketization of China's state-owned companies surged ahead.

In September 1997, at the Fifteenth National Congress, Jiang Zemin raised the idea of a "mixed ownership" system. It was the start of a third great epoch of "thought liberation," a new frame in which China's "redwood trees" were seen in a new way: "grasping the big ones and letting the little ones go."

In 1999, the Party Congress adopted amendments clarifying that the private sector was an important component of the socialist market economy. Reframing China's economy from centrally planned to a socialist market system was a complex interplay of top-down and bottom-up, letting go and holding back, trial and error, and "one eye open, one eye shut" policies—a huge shift from condemning capitalism to having two-thirds of the economy in private hands. Many of the once moribund SOEs actually became highly profitable. In October 2007 Hu Jintao renewed China's aim: "Oriented toward modernization, the world, and the future."

China's Twenty-First-Century Frame

Changes in economic framing have been continual in the thirty years of China's reforms. The most recent announcement, at the party's Seventeenth Congress in the fall of 2007, officially confirmed the shift from focusing on economic growth to enhancing the quality of living and the recovery of the environment.

Hu declared, "We must promote cultural development and notably enhance the cultural and ethical quality of the whole nation." The model that had made China the star of global economic growth was in effect declared obsolete and unsustainable. A new model was being put into place: "a scientific growth development model."

Henceforth, economic development in China must incorporate sustainable standards regarding the environment, energy, and the use of natural resources. Hu: "China is advancing toward an industrialized, information-based, urbanized, market-oriented, and international country."

Beijing set aside nearly 6 percent of its GDP for research and development in 2008. Hu said, "We will develop a modern industrial system, integrate IT application with industrialization, and we will upgrade new and high-technology industries and develop information, biotechnology, new materials, aerospace, marine, and other industries."

In other words, China will enter domains that are now in westerners' hands. Expect the growth of many new industries related to bioenergy, pollution-control technology, and waste treatment, matched by innovative practices in traditional farming and manufacturing. Concerns about energy use, environmental consequences, and sustainable use of natural resources must now be built into all economic development. Hu emphasized: "We must build a resource-conserving and environment-friendly society."

Empty promises? It does not seem so. With a growing social imbalance and increasing environmental damage, the Chinese have found that misuse of power and corruption leads to discontent, the strongest threat to the goal of creating a harmonious society. Hu said, "Scientific development and social harmony are integral to each other and neither is possible without the other." The increasingly open discussions about economic, environmental, cultural, social, and political considerations are a consequence of a growing self-confidence on the part of both the Chinese people and the Chinese leadership.

Earlier, Jiang Zemin announced some ideological frames at the Sixteenth Party Congress in 2002. Known as the "three represents," these were very large frames. A simplified version is:

1. The party must represent the development of China's advanced productive forces.

2. The party must always represent the development of China's culture.

3. The party must always represent the fundamental interests of the majority of the people of China.

These are frames to live by, but perhaps too general for guidance. The government's emphasis has moved to Hu's "scientific development concept" as the guiding ideology.

Balancing Release and Control

One frame that took quite long to widen was freedom of speech and freedom of the press. In a society where being connected is of more value than being an individual, the harmony of the whole is of great importance. Anything that would disturb this harmony would be silenced for the benefit of the whole. For many years, the fear of disharmony explained a great deal of the restrictions on the media, but things have changed. The more emancipated the people and the government have become, the more the attitude toward criticism is changing. There is now bottom-up participation in uniting goals for a new society.

But publishing is still strictly in Chinese hands—a fact that even Rupert Murdoch, despite his efforts in all directions, could not change. "We were driving against a wall in China" was his summary in a press conference in September 2006, after his fight for a slice of China's gigantic media cake had gone on for ten years. Neither a tough nor a soft strategy had worked at the end. China is not alone in having a heavy hand in the local media. Even the United States has strong restrictions regarding foreign ownership of multiple media. Murdoch, an Australian, took American citizenship. But in more regards than one, he might switch to China after all.

To the great pleasure of the global tabloid press, which in his own empire Murdoch can orchestrate so well, he may be able to tiptoe into a closer relationship with China through a private door. He married Deng Wendi, who was born in Jiangsu and grew up as the daughter of a Guangzhou factory manager, spoke no English until in her teens, and ten years later had an MBA from Yale. She is "the epitome of modern China: smart, hard working, quick thinking and ambitious," as *China Daily*'s correspondent Patrick Whitely wrote.

Murdoch's lust for China does not come as a surprise. China has the largest potential consumer market in the world for the media. In 2007 the number of daily newspapers exceeded 1,000. Compared with about 1,500 in the United States and 650 in Germany, this is not very many, but the number keeps increasing. Why should China hand that market over to foreign companies? China's much more clever strategy is to send out its time-tested straw boats, lean back, keep learning, and then pull out one arrow after another.

China's Scientific Outlook on Development

A new phrase, "a scientific outlook on development," has been frequently used by China's mass media in recent years. It refers to a new frame in the governing concept of the new generation of central authorities headed by Hu Jintao, and it is a key to understanding China's development and future trends. The core rules of the "scientific outlook on development" are:

- Put the people first.

- Balanced, sustainable development is the basic requirement.

- Planning with consideration for all concerned is a fundamental approach.

In rather stiff official language, this becomes: "We must pursue a scientific approach in development which should be comprehensive, balanced, and sustainable. It requires us to promote not only economic development but also political, cultural, social, and ecological development; to coordinate and give full consideration to all aspects, regions, and links in our development; to conserve resources and protect the environment for better living and development space for future generations; to focus on improving people's livelihoods and promoting social justice; and to ensure that the fruits of development are shared among all China's 1.3 billion people."

China's economic, social, and political frames need to be adapted, continually, to the changing needs of the people and to changing global conditions.

The people's approval of China's leadership will depend very much on how the leaders adapt old frames and create new frames that match the demands of this century.

Political Framing:

The maturing of China's vertical democracy will happen in parallel with the democratization of the CPC. The key is to develop, strengthen, and broaden electoral law without the consequences of disruptions and partitions of election-driven behavior. If the one-party system is offering enough pluralism to the Chinese people, who, except the Chinese, has the right to demand a change? How long will China's Communist Party hold on to the caterpillar before it lets the butterfly fly? Time will tell.

Military Framing:

China has never been a colonial power, and it shows no sign of territorial ambitions. In his speech at the Party Congress, President Hu described the main duty of national defense as "to safeguard China's sovereignty, security, and territorial integrity and to help maintain world peace." With the change in Taiwanese politics under Ma, the chance of a "peaceful national unification" seems more likely than ever. China is too smart not to use the synergies of "one country, two systems."

Economic Framing:

The goal for the twenty-first century is set: to change China from workshop of the world to innovator of the world. The biggest challenge, apart from maintaining growth, will be to implement the announced environmental considerations.

Cultural Framing:

There is a new appreciation of the old and a strong consciousness of the new. In the artistic world individuals express their own feelings, and these feelings are based on a new self-awareness, which often differs from the uniting social framework. Artists have detached themselves from old rules and values and are open to fantasy and imagination, all within the frame of the emancipation of the mind.

Pillar 4

Crossing the River by Feeling the Stones

The metaphor of crossing the river by feeling the stones reflects the attitude of the Chinese leadership at the beginning of the journey to a new China. In place of inflexible directions and goals, this mind-set allowed the country to feel its way, to allow trial and error, not to fear risk, to experiment, and to find the best way by "seeking the truth from facts."

When we start a journey toward a certain goal we do not know what setbacks and opportunities we will encounter along the way. We have to learn from the process. This is the essential idea behind Deng Xiaoping's famous aphorism "crossing the river by feeling the stones."

The goal is to one day stand at the other side of the river. You have never crossed this river before. But you know that there are stones in the riverbed, and you trust that they will give your feet support and direction. On some stones you will stop for a while to gather energy to get beyond where you are in your journey. Other stones will force you to alter your course. Sometimes you may reach a dead end and will need to back up and start again.

Pillar 4 is built on Deng's aphorism for China's efforts to reach its goals. China steps into new territory and will continue to strive to reach the other side of the river in building a new social economic system and

a harmonious society. China has learned as it went along—learned what
works and what doesn't work. It has been experimenting; it has stumbled; it has failed. But it has kept moving and has always kept its focus
on its goal: to get safely to the other side.

Whoever is interested in China and its history very soon comes across
the word "supraplanning," which has been translated as "strategy." Supraplanning at the highest level sets a grand, farsighted goal. It sets the
big frame, but it does not meticulously determine the single steps in
detail.

Supraplanning is an integral part of Chinese thinking. Cleverness and
smart maneuvering are highly valued and widely praised as wisdom. In
the battle at the Red Cliff, Liu Bei—general, warlord, and later emperor of Shu Han, during the Three Kingdoms era of China—used a
nonviolent, smart tactical maneuver to capture his enemy's ammunition
(we write about this in the chapter on Pillar 3). He operated at the
middle level of supraplanning, and, as part of the whole concept, took
one of the steps toward the final victory.

Crossing the river by feeling the stones is working within the context
of this thinking. The goal is clearly defined. To get to the other side of
the river China uses strategic planning and tactical maneuvers, leaving
space to act and space to react to changing circumstances, as the route
to the other shore evolves.

If we look at China's thirty years of reforms within this frame, it
does not come as a surprise that no other country has used the method
of trial and error so intensively for its development. And the method of
trial and error, in turn, has been combined with another aspect of traditional Chinese thinking, the idea that "all insight arises from practical experience."

From the very beginning China has used pilot projects to find out
what works and doesn't work. Legal norms, insurance, institutions, education models, investment models, and even cultural interests are tested
and must prove their value before they are adopted countrywide. This is
true even for the question of how the traditional Peking culture will be
maintained.

In harmony with President Hu's announcement of a goal to "promote Chinese culture and build the common spiritual home for the Chinese nation," the Ministry of Education is doing pilot testing of traditional Peking culture in ten provinces. Well-known themes of Peking opera such as "fight with wisdom" and "fight for history" are being taught in music classes at ten junior high schools and ten primary schools in each of ten provinces and municipalities. The project will promote traditional Peking opera, and if all goes well, the ministry will eventually expand the program throughout the country.

In this regard we were pleased to read in *China Daily* that the Peking opera *Red Cliff* was restaged at the National Center for the Performing Arts. "To cater to the tastes of young people," the commentator wrote, "some major scenes, including 'Borrowing Arrows by Scarecrow-Soldiers on Boats' [which we describe in Pillar 3], have been revised to make them more lyrical." We want to see it as soon as we can, but we are afraid we still won't understand the highly stylized acting.

The Chinese are not expecting their government to copy the Swedish welfare system, but tension is likely to develop if current problems are not addressed and taken care of by the leadership. The task of central and local government has enlarged from dealing with economic problems to improving the quality of life, culturally and environmentally, especially in rural areas.

When migration started and millions began working away from their homes, the goal was to make money, more money than ever possible at home. But as the country moved to higher goals, so did the people.

To emphasize the rising demands of people in the countryside, the Ministry of Commerce undertook a project to offer villagers the same shopping environment that urbanites have. The "Thousands of Rural Villages Project" was initiated in 2006 in Heilongjiang province.

Fujin, a major city in Heilongjiang province, funds the transformation of the shops in the rural areas, and elects one shop as a model for enjoyable shopping in each town. Those shops are set up as if they were part of a chain, with a unified format, unified standards of service, unified distribution, and unified training in management. This experiment greatly improved the way the shops are run and, according to the

Jiamusi Daily, "has fundamentally stopped fake and shoddy products from entering the market." The ministry is now expanding its "Thousands of Rural Villages Project" to other provinces throughout China.

President Hu addressed the needs of the rural population in his speech at the Party Congress: "We must promote a balanced development among regions and improve the pattern of land development."

China is making strong efforts toward improving standards of production and design. But although it is catching up and adapting to the demands of the twenty-first century, it cannot abandon the historical context in which it operates. Changing a mind-set is much harder than changing the technology of a production line.

Signposts for the Economy

When, as early as 1979, the central government received a request from Guandong and Fujian provinces to "move ahead of others," Deng responded with a new concept, the "special economic zone." The official announcement said, "On August 13, the State Council issued its provisions on some issues concerning foreign trade development to increase foreign exchange revenue, which proposed to expand the foreign trade authority of local governments and enterprises, and encouraged the establishment of more export-oriented special zones."

His tactics for testing what works and what doesn't work turned certain regions into huge economic laboratories. To start, Deng chose three small fishing villages on the South China Sea. One of them was Shenzhen, on the border with Hong Kong. In 1979 Shenzhen had 20,000 inhabitants, and nobody at that time could have imagined the Shenzhen of today, with more than 10 million people, one of the most modern cities in the world. It can easily be reached by train from Hong Kong, but a Chinese visa is still needed to cross the border.

Deng's concept "Let some cities get rich first" was a breakthrough. The founding and success of the special economic zones was one of the first big stones in crossing the river; the zones became solid rocks in China's economy, and symbols of reform.

These experimental zones had more flexible market policies and offered preferential terms to foreign investors, favorable taxes, and management of foreign exchange in order to encourage the building of factories to manufacture and export consumer goods. In the late 1980s, another figure, now universally familiar, became more visible on the political stage: Jiang Zemin. His role in structuring the special economic zones (SEZs) was to maintain a balance between economic progress and social stability.

In 1990 Deng Xiaoping announced the decision to develop Pudong, about which we wrote in the chapter on Pillar 2. Pudong is located on the east bank of the Huangpu River, which divides Shanghai into two parts. Whereas Paris and London, for example, developed both sides of the rivers Seine and Thames, respectively, in a balanced way, Shanghai had not done anything similar. The west bank, called Puxi in Chinese, began to prosper in the beginning of the twentieth century, but the east bank had remained farmland with some outdated factory buildings and residential houses. In 1990 this land was designated to become the "dragon head" of Chinese economic growth.

Henry Kissinger, during a visit to Shanghai in 1997, admitted that when China announced the plan to develop Pudong, he thought it was nothing more than a slogan. By 2001 Jiang Zemin, a former mayor of Shanghai, described Pudong as "a microcosm of Shanghai's modernization and the symbol of Chinese reform and opening up." Many visitors now consider Shanghai one of the most exciting cities in the world. Pudong's GDP alone grew from 6 billion RMB in 1990 to 271 billion RMB in 2007.

China's Visionary People

Westerners admire Pudong, but many can't imagine how it came about in "communist-run China." In 2000, the year we began traveling in China together, we had the opportunity to meet the "godfather of Pudong," Zhao Qizheng. Our meeting began in the traditional way; we sat in huge armchairs lined up along the walls of a large room, all of us wearing little bouquets on our chests. But what started formally quickly turned into a lively conversation. Zhao Qizheng, at that time minister of the Information Office of the State Council, to our surprise spoke German as well as English, and had many memories of his time in Germany, where he had worked as an engineer—and of Austria, where he went skiing and enjoyed Austrian wine and music.

Zhao had majored in nuclear physics in 1963, and he devoted the first twenty years of his career to scientific research, design, and production. This period included his work in Germany, where he gained his knowledge of the language. His view of the world is very open. In his book *Shanghai Pudong Miracle* he writes, "Learning to use international language to carry on a dialogue with the international community, overcoming the cultural gaps to solve difficult issues, and finally making restitution for past economic behavior by following common rules in international trade—this is how we should liaise with the world."

From 1991 to 1998, when Zhao was Shanghai's vice mayor and the first governor of the Shanghai Pudong New Area, he had a leading role in boosting Shanghai and "putting it on the fast track," as Deng Xiaoping had wished in 1990. Under the heading "Mapping Out Pudong's Development" Zhao Qizheng wrote:

"The building of a new city requires the wisdom of all sides and a long-term plan. It is like making a beautiful dress out of a piece of high-quality material. One has to carefully design it before cutting. If you were in too much of a rush, you might make a mistake. Then, if you sewed several gold buttons on it, it would be of no help. On the contrary, you would only invite mockery. That is what we bore in mind when we set out to develop Pudong. We sat down and mapped the plan with great care.

"Building the infrastructure is like building a football field. After we have built the field, we need to have famous football teams from China and abroad come and compete on the field to the cheers of thousands of spectators. So it was an important tenet—or we might say secret—of ours in the development of Pudong that infrastructure buildings should serve as function building. In other words, in planning such a project, we must bear in mind not only the project as such but also its functions after the project is completed."

Over the years, Zhao Qizheng witnessed the admiration for Pudong, but he also worried about China's rise. His analysis of the motive behind the "China threat" is realistic: "The West is concerned and even worried about China's rise, fearing it might cause a dent in the West-dominated international order and thus challenge their hegemony."

Pudong's further development goes hand in hand with environmental protection and the belief that the two must be coordinated. In pursuit of a clearer sky, greener land, and purer water, Shanghai strives to control atmospheric pollution and noise pollution, carrying out various measures to improve the environment for enterprises affected by pollution, and establishing wetlands conservation in the outlying regions of Pudong.

The economic goal is to maintain annual double-digit economic growth up to 2010, in spite of the global financial crisis. In February 2009 the online magazine *e-Pudong* reported that the impact of the global financial crisis on Shanghai's Pudong had been limited.

From a Disaster to a Business Case Model

What is true about Pudong is coming true in another field.

China's state-owned enterprises (SOEs) were special zones of a different kind from the successful special economic zones. The development of the SOEs started from a very low point, under circumstances that are hard to imagine, and turning the SOEs around was one of China's biggest challenges. In the early years the first Chinese entrepreneurs appeared, seemingly out of nowhere, and their achievements were no smaller than those of their widely known and highly praised American counterparts. Most architects agree that it is much harder to renovate an old house with an old structure than to build a new one. The SOEs were not only "old houses"; in many cases they were ruins.

In 1984, a thirty-five-year-old bureaucrat, Zhang Ruimin, was sent to run such a state-owned ruin, an electronics company in Qingdao. Nearly 600 employees produced not even 100 substandard refrigerators per month. The company was on the verge of collapse, and the workers' morale had hit rock bottom. Work started by eight A.M., but at nine A.M. people started to leave. By ten A.M., Zhang recalled later, "you could have thrown a hand grenade into the factory without hurting anybody." Zhang said that the work environment was at the same level as the employees' diligence. The ground was so dirty that after a rain you had to hold ropes under your feet or your boots would have been sucked off by the mud. The first thing Zhang did was to post notices on the walls: "Forbidden to urinate or defecate inside the factory."

But it took more to force a turnaround from the hostile workers.

Zhang's outburst of frustration made Qingdao's sledgehammers probably the most famous in the world. His fury boiled over when, once more, a customer complained about the lousy quality of a refrigerator. Zhang, an autodidact who had studied western management models, lined up seventy-six defective models he had sorted out on the factory floor and ordered those responsible to smash the refrigerators with sledgehammers: seventy-six refrigerators, each worth two years of salary, smashed to pieces. That woke them up.

The message got through. He would not tolerate ratings such as A, B, C, and D. There were only two: "acceptable" and "unacceptable."

Over time, in a step-by-step process, Zhang turned the lackluster state-owned refrigerator factory into what we know today as the Haier Group Company, China's largest appliance maker, with $2.1 billion in annual sales. Zhang, as its CEO, keeps embarking on new strategies; he is now expanding into computers, televisions, and DVDs. He has also opened a refrigerator plant in the United States and plans to expand into Europe. "We want to become a global company," he says. As a young man, Zhang turned to the West and Japan, to learn from them. Today Haier's business case studies are included in textbooks used at Harvard University, the University of Southern California, Lausanne Management College, European Business College, and Kobe University. Zhang is praised for his management ability and his diversification. Haier is just one of countless examples of how China's future is unfolding.

Chinese Miracles

Back in 1984, Zhang Ruimin was only one of the first generation of entrepreneurs who finally found an environment where they could flourish. We do not know which was smaller, Steve Jobs's garage ten years earlier or Liu Chuanzhi's tiny guardroom at the entryway of his former employer's compound, a prestigious computer research institute in the northern Beijing district of Zhongguancun, where he had worked as an engineer. Bored and frustrated because he had practically nothing to do, he founded a company and raised seed capital—about $35,000—from the Academy of Science in exchange for a state share of 61 percent in his company. The challenge was to find out how to translate English operating systems and make them work in Chinese. Under the company's name, Legend, in 1987 the "Chinese Character Card" was developed.

Legend's first bumpy years and its slow transformation from the Chinese Premium Computer Company to China's biggest technology company are well documented. The next step was to create a new name. The new CEO, Yang Yuanqing, changed the name to Lenovo. At the beginning of 2005, Lenovo burst on the world scene when, after several years of negotiation, it bought the PC division of IBM for $1.25 billion and became, virtually overnight, the world's third largest PC producer, after Dell and Hewlett-Packard. Twenty years after Li Chuanzhi boastfully announced that his company someday would make 2 million RMB, Lenovo reported a turnover of more than 20.5 billion RMB ($3 billion).

But not all companies founded in these first years of burgeoning entrepreneurship achieved success and fame. In the hot Pearl River delta in the south of China, the manager of a small county-level alcoholic beverages factory noticed that people in Guangzhou were drinking something called Coca-Cola. He picked up the idea of a special non-alcoholic drink and returned to his factory with the idea of combining it with a drink that would stimulate athletes' performance. In the early 1990s Jian-li-bao, the "oriental spring water," together with Coca-Cola and Pepsi, was the best-selling nonalcoholic beverage in China. It would hold the position of the most favored fortifying health drink for the next fifteen years. But over time poor management and increasing competition led to a total debt of more than 1 billion RMB ($121 million) in 2005. In February 2007, Zhang Hai, the former president and CEO of Jian-li-bao, was sentenced to fifteen years in jail for embezzling public funds.

A story with a much happier ending is that of Wang Shi, a young man who started his entrepreneurial life in Shenzhen, buying and selling corn. He took advantage of the special economic zone to import products with foreign exchange, and of a ferocious appetite for imported goods. The initial capital he made was the foundation for a company he called Vanke. Today Wang Shi is one of China's largest real estate developers and one of its most successful entrepreneurs.

As the environment for entrepreneurs became better and better inside China, the outside world slowly started to register China's economic potential and opportunities.

One year after Zhang Ruimin's workers got their wake-up call with sledgehammers, and ten years after China's first ambitious entrepreneurs entered the market economy, the Australian lawyer Geoff Baker visited China for the first time. Baker worked as a lawyer in Tokyo, where Japanese clients were seeking a way to break into China's emerging market. "True frontier work at the time," he said. His first on-site experience with China came in the winter of 1994. Baker has colorfully narrateded his first meetings with officials in Beijing, Shanghai, and Guangzhou. "The meetings were held in cold large boardrooms with the icy winds blowing into the rooms through open windows. The officials hurried into the rooms wearing modest clothes but they were so eager to do business and saw opportunities everywhere.

"Life then was still very tough for most people. Many buildings were run-down and a lot of foreign businesses were being operated out of hotel rooms, as there were not enough office buildings. People still dressed in drab clothes, giving me an idea of how the uniformity of the Cultural Revolution must have weighed on them.

"But nevertheless, when I landed in the old Tianjin Airport I was amazed and somewhat overwhelmed at what I saw. In this first trip, when I traveled from Tianjin to Beijing, Shanghai, and Guangzhou, I was not sure what affected me most as I struggled to come to terms with the vastness of the country, the speed of activity, and China's sheer dynamism. I felt China could change my life forever but I did not realize how much and how soon it was to be realized."

Today Geoff Baker has established himself in China as a qualified lawyer, a director of several private and public companies, a director of the Australian Chamber of Commerce in Beijing, and, together with his wife, Zhang Haihua, the coauthor of *Think Like Chinese*.

Signposts for Politics

Whereas the success of China's economic development is obvious, China's political progress is underestimated and underappreciated.

Motivated by the goal of blessing all nations with western democracy, the West quickly drafted an outline of how emerging China should cross the river to reach a western shore. China's refusal to follow these instructions astonished and exasperated westerners.

But China cannot put the cart before the horse, even if the western shore were the direction in which the Chinese wanted to go. And it is not. China's direction has been written in the Chinese constitution and was repeated in the charter in October 2007: "The strategic goals for the economic and social development by the year 2021 [the hundredth anniversary of the founding of the party], are to reinforce and develop the rudimentary achieved goal of modest wealth and to create a society on a higher level, and to bring further advantages to more than a billion people."

Although establishing a western democracy is the highest goal in the eyes of the West, China has its own highest goal and its own strategy for how to get there. Creating a society at a "higher lever" underscores that the Communist Party of China will not stop at economic goals but move on. During Prime Minister Gordon Brown's visit in 2008, Premier Wen Jiabao affirmed to him that "democracy on the mainland would be developed from the ground up."

There is no schedule for when China will reach the other shore, and no estimated time of arrival. We cannot determine exactly where China is in its journey to the other side. Our best estimate is that it is only about one-third of the way. But we are convinced that the speed will increase as the Chinese come closer to the other side. It takes some time until results appear, but the Chinese have much more patience than westerners. "The forefathers planted trees; the successors rest in their shade," they say.

The Communist Party of China is slowly appointing people outside the party to leading government positions. At the highest level, the science and technology minister is Wan Gang and the health minister is Chen Zhu; they are the first noncommunist cabinet ministers appointed since the opening up and the reforms began.

Wan is a member of the China Zhi Gong (Public Interest) Party and was appointed in April 2007. He was formerly an automobile engineer at the Audi Corporation in Germany and was president of Tongji University (based in Shanghai) before his appointment. Chen is a scientist who was trained in Paris and has no party affiliation. He was appointed health minister in June 2007. At the Seventeenth Congress in October 2007, President Hu Jintao said that the party would "select and recommend a greater number of outstanding non-CPC people for leading positions."

Hu also said, "Promoting harmony in relations between political parties, between ethnic groups, between religions, between social strata, and between our compatriots at home and overseas plays an irreplaceable role in enhancing unity and pooling strengths."

Signposts for Communication

One of the most delicate areas in China's reforms and opening up has been policy regarding the media. Relative freedom of the press has come a long way. In 1980, when a photographer took a picture of a group of small-time entrepreneurs on a street in Shanghai, the picture could not be published, because certain things could be in the media only to an "appropriate" degree.

But despite all progress, the 2008 Summer Olympics in Beijing focused international attention on the role of government and the media in China. Reports of news restrictions and statements that the government continued to detain and harass journalists kept appearing in the western press. It is true that no newspaper or television station, or any other medium, could run a "Free Tibet" or "Free Taiwan" campaign. Still, there is much greater diversity in China's media, and there is an increasingly sophisticated audience. China's problems are covered quite directly, and criticism is increasingly harsh. Here are some recent headlines we have seen in Chinese newspapers:

"Party Boss Sacked for Molesting a Child"

"Officials Jailed for Bridge Collapse"

"6,000 More Coal Mines to Close"

"Corrupt Official Gets Death Penalty"

"Porn Goes Mobile with Cell Phones"

"Unemployment Rates Climb"

China does not hide its response to what it deems inappropriate media activities, and statistics about this are widely available in Chinese publications. For example, more than thirty journalists and fifty cyberdissidents are currently jailed in China; and the government confiscated more than 45 million illegal publications in the first half of 2008, including 1.6 million pornographic publications.

Western commentators say the growing Chinese demand for information is testing a regime that is trying to control the media in an effort to maintain power. As we wrote in the chapter on Pillar 2, only state agencies can own media in China, but a privatization process is beginning as outlets subcontract administrative operations to the private sector. Ashley W. Esarey, an expert on the media in northeastern Asia, says it is also likely that the Internet will play a role in Chinese media reform, because its "absolute control has proven difficult, if not impossible."

Censorship Is Not a Chinese Invention

In the United States of America, said to be the freest country in the world, James Joyce's *Ulysses* was confiscated 1918 by the U.S. Post Office. It was published again in 1961, and again confiscated. Not until 1966 was the censorship ended by the Supreme Court. In 1938 Henry Miller's *Tropic of Cancer* was banned from being imported, and that embargo was not lifted until 1961. Over the years, many American states have banned titles from libraries and schools.

The most vigorous period of persecuting different thinking was the early 1950s, the era of Senator Joseph McCarthy, the Hollywood blacklist, and hearings conducted by the House Committee on Un-American Activities. Charlie Chaplin, Leonard Bernstein, Orson Welles, and Arthur Miller—to name just a few famous people—were called before the U.S. Congress to be questioned about their political views and activities. Many people were blacklisted, and a number of tenured university professors were fired because of their political views.

The name John Naisbitt also appeared, most publicly when Walter Winchell, in his popular Sunday night radio news commentary, warned the students of America against John Naisbitt, the student body president of the University of Utah, who was leading a student campaign to discredit Senator McCarthy, whom Winchell supported. John had started an organization called American University Students for Academic Freedom. This national organization was wholly devoted to fighting for the freedom of speech, and that meant freedom of speech for Senator McCarthy as well as those who opposed him.

All this took place almost 200 years after the American modern democracy was born.

Stumbling Stones

China has made its changes in fast motion. Freedom of speech has not yet matured to full freedom of speech, but speaking out is by no means as limited as it is often reported to be in the western press. There are three ways of looking at media in China: the western view, the view of the Chinese people, and the view of the Chinese leadership.

No matter how China-friendly a viewpoint one takes, the media in China cannot be said to be as free as those in the West. But it is also true that reports in the West often are more colored by personal opinions than based on facts. It is legitimate and important to fight for freedom of the press in any country of the world. As with so many things, however, China wants to set its own goals and approach them at its own speed. The harder the West pushes, the harder China resists. Reflecting on the reporting of the Olympic Games in 2008, Victor Paul Borg, a Maltese writer, remarks about fairness in *China Daily*:

"Fairness presupposes correct diagnosis of the subject, as well as knowledge of larger issues and background insight, and this is where foreign journalists begin to show their failings and limitations. I read journalists, who write with analytical lucidity and empathy about their country or similar countries or cultures, but then the same journalists travel to different countries or cultures, particularly in Asia, they churn out garbled stories that draw bizarre conclusions. As the effect of extended regulations for foreign journalists diffuses—the opportunity to mix in a more unfettered manner with a range of people will improve journalists' understanding of China—the likelihood is that foreign journalists will increasingly analyze China on its own terms and merits."

Who likes to be lectured? Would Angela Merkel follow Hu Jintao's instruction on handling eastern and western German affairs? Is Barack Obama going to copy China's model for an economic turnaround? China never instructs the West on how to handle western affairs and will not accept westerners' interference in its own matters.

China will let go slowly. Crossing a river on slippery stones, after all, is a balancing act. China still may stumble, but it will not fall. The strong will to maintain harmony and stability, combined with pride, still leads to overreactions, and certainly any tolerance stops when it undermines political authority and endangers the interests of the motherland and the "harmonious society."

Elizabeth C. Economy, director of Asian studies at the Council on Foreign Relations in New York, thinks the Chinese government is in a state of "schizophrenia" about media policy as it "goes back and forth, testing the line, knowing they need press freedom—and the information it provides—but worried about opening the door to the type of freedoms that could lead to the regime's downfall." Haven't most countries undergone the slow growth of freedom of speech? It is true that China goes back and forth, but China has been "crossing the river by feeling the stones" in most of its matters.

The media are seen as a tool to meet the needs and demands of the government in its strategy for dealing with public matters. But there is also an awareness that the media must meet the demands of the society. There has been much more open reporting about drawbacks and grievances and how local and central institutions and politicians deal with them. When Premier Wen Jiabao was attacked by a shoe-thrower in Cambridge, many people told us that until recently this would have never been reported in the Chinese media. But this time it was on television. There was open reporting, and there were even caricatures of the scene.

The Chinese media were quick to report the severe earthquake in May 2008, and for the first time the National Congress meetings were opened to the foreign press in 2007. Official guidelines and self-censorship might still color reporting by brightening it, but what of reporting about China that is colored by being darkened? Most people who talk to us about China have never been there. They think that China's people are suppressed, exploited, and kept under harsh governmental control. When we returned to Vienna from Beijing in early February 2009 a neighbor, young and intelligent, asked, "Is China interesting?" We looked at him, quite stunned. "You know," he continued, "I have a chance to go there in June. But I have read so much that worries me, and a friend who was there last year told me that the military is all over and people are totally restricted. I wonder if I should go there." We hear variations of this all the time.

How do the Chinese feel about freedom of the press? We noticed that the negative western reporting during the Olympics resulted in stronger patriotism. Even if the Chinese agree with criticism from the West, they do not like to be lectured. And whether the West likes to hear it or not, the three so-called "forbidden T's"—Tiananmen Square, Taiwan, and Tibet—are much less on Chinese minds than the West imagines.

The Foreign Correspondents Club of China reported that during 2007, 180 foreign correspondents were detained, harassed, or attacked in China, despite the nominally relaxed regulations. In addition, China continues to filter foreign and domestic content on the Internet. In its press freedom index the watchdog group Reporters Without Borders ranks China number 167 out of 173 countries. The United States is number 40; Germany is 20. However trustworthy or biased those rankings are, they reinforce the image most of the global media have of China.

What is really disturbing is that all this magnifies a very small part of China. This picture of China does not reflect the fact that the Chinese are concerned about their country, love their country, are proud to be a part of it, and make their own judgments about their government. Most people in the West believe the Chinese are unaware of their government's monitoring of the media and the Internet. But a survey funded by the Markle Foundation in New York reports that most Chinese approve of Internet control and management, especially when it comes from their government. At the beginning of 2008, when asked about online content, 87 percent of 210 million Chinese Internet users believed that pornography should be controlled, 86 percent believed the same for violent content, 83 percent for spam, 66 percent for advertisements, and 64 percent for slander of individuals.

The Human Factor

The issue is: who decides what's good and bad? If there is control, who controls the control? The Internet is still at a primitive stage, and over time the world will work out more sophisticated mechanisms to deal with its unwelcome aspects. And China, over time, will find the right balance for the Chinese between control and protection and personal freedom.

Two rather banal examples can give two different pictures. It was absurd when, in spring 2008, a good friend of ours applied for a visa to visit China that summer, close to the beginning of the Olympics, and was asked to sign a paper saying he would not write anything about China during his visit. This friend is a very well-known author who has sold millions of books, also in China. He had no plan whatsoever to write about China and even if he did, so what? He was just excited to go there and enjoy it. He didn't sign. At about the same time, we applied for a visa extension for China in Brazil. We did not know that if you don't live in Brazil, you can't get a Chinese visa in Brazil. But the general consul of the Chinese consulate in São Paulo was very unbureaucratic and made an exception, so we had our visas the next day, with no conditions added.

Both cases involved Chinese officials, one who probably was overly bureaucratic and one who felt free to interpret the rules as needed. Perhaps the people who are afraid to make mistakes, who are inflexible, and who self-righteously stick to the letter of the law give China a bad name; but "the government" does not stand behind everything, good or bad, that happens in China, or in any other country. The difference is that the China bashers grab negative reports, generalize them, and tell us how terrible "the government" of China is.

Just think about what opinion we would have of freedom in the United States if we based it on a story that was published in the *Economist* on May 8, 2008: "Christopher Ratte, a professor of archaeology, recently tried to buy his seven-year-old son a bottle of lemonade at a baseball game. He was handed a bottle of Mike's Hard Lemonade, an alcoholic drink, by mistake. Officials noticed the boy sipping the drink and immediately whisked him off to a hospital. He was fine. But the family was condemned to legal hell: the police at first put the seven-year-old into a foster home and a judge ruled that he could go home only if his father moved out. It took several days of legal wrangling to reunite the family."

As we wrote earlier, China's media are increasingly competitive and increasingly diverse. And there is also an increase in investigative reporting by Chinese news agencies. Chinese media broke the news of official suppression of information about the SARS outbreak in Beijing in 2003. But there was quite a difference between what happened on the ground and what was written in the western press. We were in Guangzhou, at the center of the outbreak, as it happened. We were at an IBM Forum attended by about 1,000 people. There was no secret about what was going on with regard to SARS; everyone talked about it. We were offered medication, which we turned down because there was no specific treatment against a possible infection. We did not get nervous; we did not wear masks. There was a simple consideration: yes, this might become a pandemic, but in all of China there were about a dozen deaths among a population of 1.3 billion. To put this in perspective, in the United States alone about 50,000 people die in car accidents each year out of a population of 300 million. Why in the world should we feel more endangered at the forum than in a car or on a plane?

But while we were having a wonderful time, friends and relatives in Europe and in the United States were very worried. On the basis of western reports, they pictured us in the middle of a medieval plague. To us the only scary scene was our transfer at the Hong Kong airport, where every second person wore a mask. The airport looked like a terrorist camp.

Nevertheless, Chinese reporting was slow, but China learned. After toxic chemicals leaked into a river and contaminated drinking water in the northeastern city of Harbin in 2005, newspapers and Web sites criticized the government's response, demanded greater transparency, and posted photos of local residents stockpiling bottled water. Bob Dietz, Asia Program Coordinator for the Committee to Protect Journalists, predicts that press freedom "will expand to meet the needs and demands not just of the government, but of the society."

How China will eventually deal with the communication tools of the twenty-first century will be worked out in a process of the trial and error, crossing the river stone by stone.

Coming under Net Scrutiny

The year 2008 was a milestone in awareness of the Internet. Chinese people are increasingly using the Internet as a bottom-up tool to voice their opinions and give feedback to the government: "In 2008, online public scrutiny became one of the key phrases in China's political scene," Min Dahong, one of the country's leading digital media and communication researchers, told *China Daily*.

The changes and growth in online activity have fueled a rise in public involvement in politics. When blogs became popular several years ago, most people in China wrote travel stories or diaries. Later, forums to discuss a wide range of political subjects were started, covering social and economic issues. But now users are no longer satisfied with just giving their suggestions online and sending e-mails to officials. They are actively pointing out possible instances of misdemeanors in official dealings and have become a perfect example of bottom-up participation in the vertical democracy.

"With the rapid development of the number of Chinese Internet users and the increasing awareness in participation in social issues, online public scrutiny will play an important part in the country's social development," says Sun Chunlong, an investigative reporter with the *Oriental Outlook*, a weekly magazine based in Beijing.

Sun ought to know. On a September evening in 2008, he made a bold move that he never thought would end up attracting attention at the highest level of government. On his blog, the thirty-two-year-old Sun posted an informant's letter addressed to Wang Jun, who had recently been appointed acting governor of Shanxi province. The letter asked Wang to make a thorough investigation into a fatal landslide that had happened in this region the previous month; apparently, the landslide had been caused by the collapse of an illegal mining dump in Loufan county, and it had reportedly killed eleven people. During his own investigation, however, Sun came to the conclusion that human error had led to the death of at least forty-one migrant workers. Two days later, Sun received a phone call from the State Administration of Work Safety and was invited to join an official team to reinvestigate the Loufan accident. Later he was told that Premier Wen Jiabao had come to know of the letter and had asked the relevant department to find out the truth immediately.

Internet collapses the information float; communication is instantaneous; and, as the case of Sun's blog showed, there is increasing significance in the bottom-up voices of the Internet. The number of Internet users in China reached 300 million at the beginning of 2009: the largest population of online users in the world. During his online chat with Chinese users in June 2008, President Hu Jintao himself said, "The Internet has become a distributor of all sorts of ideas and information, as well as a magnifier of public opinion, so we must fully understand the social impact of new media."

More and more local government officials have also begun to use the Internet to better communicate with the general public. Some have started blogs; others regularly chat with the online community through local official Web sites.

Since the mid-1990s, China's traditional media have joined hands with online media; and of the country's 10,000 news media, 2,000 have gone online. Popular Web sites have mushroomed and now play a unique role in news reports. Online magazines have developed rapidly, with a total circulation exceeding 360 million. After China Mobile launched cell phone television service in 2005, news images and text have been available on mobile phones, prompting a spate of new Web sites that also provide cell phone reports.

The newest trend in China's media industry is the formation of intermedia and transregional media operating on multiple patterns. The China Radio, Film, and TV Group, founded in late 2001, is now China's largest and most powerful multimedia group, covering television, the Internet, publishing, and advertising. The English channel of CCTV reaches U.S. audiences via News Group's Fox News network.

The Elixir of Life

During the first steps of the reforms, no one in China worried about the environment; people paid attention only to "economic stones." The only direction to go was: make money; better your life. But things have changed.

President Hu said, "Our economic growth is realized at an excessively high cost of resources and environment." With 20 percent of the world's population and only 7 percent of its water resources, China's starting position is not great. "For the Chinese, water is not just an economic resource but also an important cultural symbol. Even today, feng shui or wind water is what decides the aesthetics of everything, from homes to cities," wrote Alexis Hooi in February 2009 in his article "The Elixir of Life" in *China Daily*.

The Chinese are keenly aware of the need for a delicate balance between the environment and development, and they are working on it. For the country with the world's largest population in one of the most geographically extensive regions, the provision of water is on top of the agenda. "Start saving, or face a disastrous outcome," *China Daily* warned in this full-page article about China's numerous water problems, the pollution of its drinking water, and its lack of water in general.

The National Five-Year Plan for Environmental Protection declares that a rehabilitation of rivers and lakes is needed, and that a guarantee of safe drinking water for urban and rural residents is a main priority. The Water Pollution Control and Treatment Program has three major focuses: security of drinking water, environmental control of river basins, and urban water pollution treatment. Drinking-water security is a problem for 300 million rural people. Water shortages in Beijing will become a crisis when its population, as expected, reaches 20 million in 2010, 3 million more than its current resourses can support.

To forestall the water crisis, China has begun the South to North Water Diversion Project. As the name implies, it will divert water from the Yangtze River in southern China to provide 1 billion cubic meters of water to Beijing every year, starting in 2014. Northern China is a naturally dry region. It has less than 20 percent of China's water, but it has 40 percent of the population, more than half of the arable land, and, owing to its coal reserves, much of China's industry. All this, including an increasingly urbanized population, has made water consumption soar. "If climate change is included," says Lin Erda, one of China's experts in climate change, "the picture is even more dismal." Lin reckons that climate change will decrease China's crop production by 14 percent by the year 2050. Whether this prediction will be proved true or not remains to be seen. But "unless effective and timely measures are taken," Lin says, "China could see a food shortfall of 5 to 10 percent."

Shan Lun, China's seventy-six-year-old leading specialist on dry farming, who has done research in this subject for fifty years, says a lot can be achieved through prevention of canal leakage and installation of new irrigation technology. Agricultural irrigation accounts for 65 percent of China's annual water consumption of 560 billion cubic meters. An increase of 10 percent efficiency would conserve 56 billion cubic meters, enough to compensate for the annual water deficit in the north China plain. But it may never be implemented because of the prohibitive costs for farmers.

Further steps toward water conservation initiated top-down will not be enough if they are not supported and complemented bottom-up. Water affects every aspect in life, and sometimes an initiative comes from an unexpected source. In the small village of Zhenbeizhuang, in Dengfeng county in the province of Henan, two community leaders led an expedition deep into the Song Shan mountains. The reason was very personal. Men of this village had experienced huge troubles in finding wives who would be willing to move there. The reason was water, or rather the lack of it. But after nineteen attempts the two men finally struck water—offering a way to ease the thirst of not just a parched land, but also a generation of bachelors. In December 2008 an aqueduct built to channel water from the Song Shan spring passed the halfway mark, assuring the villagers that this time their hope for water would be realized. It was no big surprise when the two leaders of the water expedition won the local village elections, which took place around that time.

China between Eras

China is crossing the river as fast as it can. And sometimes the process is more like the spawning run of salmons—hopefully jumping up rapids rather than taking carefully chosen steps. Salmons can cover a distance of 300 miles in about three weeks; China is packing the changes of decades into a few years. And what is true for China on a huge scale is true within the small scale of families; within one generation, prospects in life have changed dramatically. Parents have to adjust to new values and desires of their children at high speed. And Chinese children have to walk a tightrope between respecting their parents and neglecting their parents' wishes. Such generational shifts sweeping China were spotlighted in a feature article in *China Daily* by Miao Xiaojuan in January 2009. The following is an edited version of the story.

For decades fifty-three-year-old Zhu Pijun of Sichuan province had been scrimping and saving, working as a migrant in coastal cities so his son could have a better life. Zhu sent his son to college to qualify for a secure job and be able to raise a family, only to hear that the son was rejecting his plans. Instead, the son wanted to start his own company.

The son, Zhu Bo, already had worked part-time in sales while studying at college, and he had learned to enjoy making his own money that way. Markets were booming, and young Zhu believed the prosperous construction market was creating good opportunities for decorators—he went ahead with his business plan.

"How can he be so naive?" the older Zhu thought about his son. "We were born farmers and we don't have the capital or connections. How can it be so easy to start a business?" These were concerns that the son was not willing to share. Instead, after graduating as an economics major in 2004, using the Internet he found new customers for his father, who was a carpenter.

Zhu Bo, the son, knew what he was doing and hoped to soon prove this to his father when he set up his own small interior decorating company in Guangdong one year later. At first his idea succeeded, and in 2006 his company showed an annual return of more than 170,000 RMB ($25,000). His staff of thirteen included plumbers, electricians, bricklayers, carpenters, and decorators; all of them came from rural areas, and half were from his home village.

For a long time Guangdong was considered the largest beneficiary of China's reforms, and it has more migrant workers than any other province. But a slower economy and a sluggish real estate market did not spare the city and brought tough times for housing and construction-related business. "Dry weather is suitable for decoration, and business should have been good in the second half of the year, but I have had just one contract in the past three months," said Zhu Bo.

"He should give up the company, and find another job," said his father. "From the beginning, I told him to take a safe job. I can always find carpentry work in the city or return home to farm the land—I don't worry about myself as long as I am strong enough to labor. But my son never did manual work."

Young Zhu is also rethinking his business future. But he is an adventurer and is determined to remain an entrepreneur and to go a different way. "I always wanted to be a successful businessman, I have found the right direction, and I will hold on to my dreams. My father is honest and industrious, but he is also very conservative. It is difficult to communicate if you think in different ways."

Zhu Pijun, the father, was born in Ziyan, thirty kilometers (about nineteen miles) north of Xichong county in Sichuan province, and migrated to Guangzhou. These, he and his wife live in a rented suburban house about thirty square meters (or yards) in size, because they could not afford to buy a house. His wife does odd jobs in the city to help make ends meet. His son's "ambitious" plans still bother him. "I still work hard, but I am happy with my life now."

"My father still feels like an 'outsider' in Guangzhou and will return to his hometown when he is too old to work," says the son. "I want to switch the company's focus to decorating offices and shopping malls, and start a lamp exporting business soon. I want a 100-square-meter apartment in the city, and I want to buy a car. I travel more than my father, and I want to broaden my horizons. I like to walk in parks and take a drink in a bar. My father's only entertainment is playing cards."

Zhu Pijun and Zhu Bo can see the huge gap between their generations: their different backgrounds and their different ideas about what they want to achieve. But they both admire the late Chinese leader Deng Xiaoping, though again for different reasons. The father is thankful for Deng's rural reforms; the son appreciates Deng's insight and strong spirit in hard times.

Implementing the Rule of Law

"We must implement the rule of law as a fundamental principal," Hu Jintao promised in his speech to the National Congress in 2007. Georg Blume says, in *China Is Not an Empire of Evil*, "One can blame Hu and Wen that their democratic confessions are nothing more than weasel words as long as there are no bolder moves in that direction. But one can concede to them that they guide China's discussion about political reforms in no other direction than democracy."

Westerners often rail about working conditions in China, but hardly anyone shows any interest when wages for more than 200 million migrant workers improve by almost 50 percent. Since January 2008 the legal rights of China's working class have been strengthened by a new labor law. Now more than 800,000 workers can demand a working contract, and their demand is backed by penalties that can be imposed. It will take a while until the workers really dare to do this, but it is a further advancement of individual rights.

China is enforcing the rule of law but also needs to improve its delivery. Fifteen years ago almost all judges were former officers of the people's army. Today almost all are fully qualified lawyers, and this trend gives more and more authority to the people. Since January 2007 it is the duty of the Supreme Court in Beijing to review each death penalty. In the past, each provincial party head was also the executioner of his territory; he could "correct" any verdict and thus decide about life and death. Now only President Hu Jintao can make such a decision, and it is not very likely he will ever do so. Since judges have become solely responsible for the death penalty, the number of executions has gone down by half.

Until the late 1980s all lawyers were state employees. Today China has 120,000 independent lawyers working in 12,000 approved law firms. In 2007, 143,000 lawyers were registered. This is still a very small number, compared with the population. But there is a gradual improvement in legal representation for those accused of a crime. Lawyers can now work closely with their clients on defense.

- In the province of Hunan experiments in solving minor crimes privately are under way. If the delinquent and the claimant agree, the prosecutor can abstain from prosecution.

  Many law edicts are marked "Put in force on trial." But the practical application still has to be improved. There is a lack of institutionalized checking of edicts in trial. That leads to their becoming obsolete, although formally still on the books.

- In Fuzhou (Fujian province) the city government is experimenting with the composition of law edicts. Not city officials but external panels, such as research institutes or universities of applied science, should draft local law edicts. This is done to ensure that decisions are not made in favor of certain interest groups supported by the local administration. As a first step, measures for control over parking areas will be drafted by independent specialists.

China is reforming its judicial system and—not surprisingly—is willing to learn from the West. At the end of 2008 the Chinese Education Ministry gave permission for a new China EU School of Law (CESL) initiated by the University of Hamburg. "China has already passed many good laws," says Uwe Blaurock, director of the Institute for Trade and Economic Law at Albert-Ludwigs-University. The bottleneck is education: "There are too few lawyers who have in fact studied law." Although Chinese law demands that a lawyer must have graduated from a law school, "many older collegues are working without a fundamental legal education."

To solve this problem the University of Hamburg has formed a consortium of sixteen European and Chinese universities, including Quinghua University in Beijing, as well as huge law firms such as Taylor Wessing and Clifford Chance. The new university will be led by the former EU lawyer Ninon Colneric and legal scientist Liufang Fang of Beijing. Clifford Chance will send two dozen instructors to teach subjects in which the Chinese are not yet well versed, but which are of increasing importance for China: "We will pay most attention to copyrights, data protection, banking and capital-market regulations."

Many Chinese laws and administrative norms leave considerable space for interpretation, which is naturally done by the Chinese. Such arrangements in the end protect Chinese interests and increase the dependency of foreign business partners. Harro von Senger, in his book *Supraplanning*, links laws that leave room for interpretation to a Chinese tactic: "Cloud the water to bereave the fish of clear sight." The Chinese legal system does give some advantage to Chinese entrepreneurs and companies, whereas western legal systems are often so overregulated that they turn against their own national economy.

The Rise of the Legal System

- The number of cases handled by the court system rose from 520,000 in 1979 to nearly 8 million in 2006, and almost 10 million in 2007.

- Courts across China handled an unprecedented number of cases in 2008: 10.7 million more cases, up 11 percent from 2007.

- Labor disputes rose 94 percent, almost doubling, to 286,221, as a result of the economic downturn and the new labor contract law.

- The number of cases handled by the Supreme People's Court was also up by about 30 percent, to 10,553. Following labor disputes were issues of real estate, company shareholding reforms, transfers of stock ownership, and foreign-related and maritime disputes. The president of the Supreme People's Court, Wang Shengjun, said that the courts will intensify efforts to maintain social harmony and stability through strict law enforcement, while fine-tuning mechanisms for handling people's problems.

- In 2006 about 152,000 unlicensed food businesses were shut down. Inspections at various levels of industry and commerce numbered 10.4 million in 2006 and uncovered problems in about 360.000 food businesses—comprising food processors, distributors, sellers, and eateries.

- The Standardization Administration of China will revise 600 national food safety inspection standards to bring them into line with international practice by 2010.

In the past thirty years the Communist Party of China (CPC) has worked to establish the first modern, economically developed, constitutional state in Chinese history. It has built new state institutions, new courts, schools, universities, and a central bank with much more authority. Everything is still under the control of the CPC, but all the institutions are developing a life of their own. Courts have become more independent, education has become more liberal and more universal, and the central bank has become more self-reliant.

Two Steps Forward, One Step Back

We wrote about the problems of the large number of backward, inelastic state-owned enterprises (SOEs). But once some SOEs started to make money, the next problem appeared. Bottom-up and top-down ideas about dividing the profits turned out not to be exactly the same. The forces collided in 1986, when Capital Steel, one of the first SOEs chosen to engage in an experiment of expanded autonomy, was asked by the Beijing municipal government to hand over a supplementary 108 million RMB of its profit. This demand violated the existing contract. The head of the Capital Steel factory refused to pay and instead wrote a letter to Chairman Deng. The main point of his letter was that you cannot ask for market performance without investing in technical improvements and human capital. In the end, Deng resolved the conflict by guaranteeing that Capital Steel's contractual terms would remain as agreed.

Despite Deng's intervention, solving the problem of the SOEs persisted for a long time; in fact, it was still China's biggest problem in 1996, when John had a private meeting with President Jiang Zemin: "President Jiang asked what I thought China's biggest problem was. I said I thought it was reforming the big state companies while not increasing unemployment too much by the necessity of reducing the bloated number of jobs to increase efficiency. We agreed it was a delicate problem. He said, 'We have a saying that we grasp the big ones and let the little ones go.' Meaning they attend to fixing the big ones and let the little ones be on their own, bottom-up."

China's SOEs have undergone dramatic changes since then. In July 2007, of the Chinese enterprises ranking in the world's top 500, the nineteen mainland enterprises were all state-owned. Of China's own top 500 enterprises, the majority were state-owned and state stock-holding enterprises. Non-state enterprises have become the driving force for industrial sectors, accounting for 50 percent in twenty-seven of the forty industrial sectors, and for more than 70 percent in some sectors.

China's Communist Party faces many challenges in addressing urgent issues such as water, pollution, social welfare, and sustainable economic growth. Hu Jintao has stated that China needs:

- Environmental conservation

- Implementation of the rule of law

- A basic medical and health care system

- Acceleration of the establishment of a social security system

- Higher priority for education in rural and urban areas

Megatrends, written more than twenty-five years ago, said about America: "As a society, we have been moving from the old to the new. And we are still in motion. We experience turbulence. Yet, amid the sometimes painful and uncertain present, the restructuring of America proceeds unrelentingly. The new American society is not yet fully evolved. Nevertheless the restructuring of America is already changing our inner and outer lives."

China's Megatrends describes the transformation of China. Each of the 8 Pillars examines one of the principles that work together to create the new whole. No one can predict the final shape of the new China—the new society that is evolving. China is "crossing the river by feeling the stones." This is good advice for any endeavor, but it has never before been applied on such an enormous scale, with more than 1 billion people feeling their way.

The vertical top-down, bottom-up dynamics allow China to focus on the goal while holding on to the flexibility needed to deal with any turbulence. There is no marked path, so opportunities can be grasped, hassles can be avoided, and shortcuts can be taken. And as with the restructuring of America, in the sometimes painful and uncertain present, the restructuring of China will proceed unrelentingly until it reaches the other shore.

Pillar 5

Artistic and Intellectual Ferment

No society ever changed for the better without artists and intellectuals in the front ranks of the parade.

While China's economy is the most pronounced manifestation of the great changes in China, it is only part of the historical shift that has occurred and perhaps not even the most important part. Early on, Deng Xiaoping said, "We have to build up two civilizations: the material civilization, and the spiritual civilization." The artistic and intellectual excitement in China today reflects the energizing of that spiritual civilization.

When we think of the Renaissance, names of artists and intellectuals—Michelangelo, Leonardo, Tintoretto, Shakespeare, Torquato Tasso, Gutenberg—come to mind. They were precursors of a huge shift in scientific, social, and political thought. Deng Xiaoping's visionary thinking inspired China's economic transition. The imagination and creativity of China's artists prepared the ground for creativity in other fields. Art reflects society and fortifies a country's identity.

In the old China, obedience was of high value, and a subordinate working class served very well in China's first stage as workshop of the world. But what will drive China into the next stage—the creation of distinctive Chinese products and design—will be the spirit of noncon-forming, talented, creative artists and intellectuals.

The Continuity of Chinese Art

In the western world, different eras shaped different styles; by contrast, Chinese art has been of astonishing continuity. Landscapes painted during the Qing dynasty (seventeenth to twentieth centuries) do not differ much from those of the Song dynasty (tenth to thirteenth centuries). Art has been strongly influenced by respect for China's history. It has not been a matter of creating something new, but a matter of staying in the traditions of the past.

After the communists took over in 1949, there was a profound shift in aesthetic values, a radical departure from all that had been before. Art had to be accessible and instructive and herald the ideal communist society for the masses. Paintings by older artists were often criticized for not contributing to the revolution.

Themeless Art

The first underground artists who became active were the No Name group. This group can be traced back to 1959, when Zhao Wenliang and Yang Yushu met at the Xihua Fine Arts Institute, one of the few private educational institutions that survived in the Mao era. In 1973, some talented students returned from their reeducation in the countryside and joined Zhao Wenliang and Yang Yushu's art circle. In 1975 the No Name group organized an underground exhibition in Zhang Wei's home called 203 Big Yard. Nonpolitical "themeless" art did not appear in public until 1979, three years after the end of the Cultural Revolution.

In late December 1978, the Central Committee confirmed the new leaders' policy of liberating minds, and two months later, in February 1979, an exhibition called "Twelve Artists from Shanghai" opened in Shanghai, showing works that were already moving away from revolu-

tionary realist art. This was the first show organized by individual artists since the Mao regime began in 1949.

In July 1979, with the support of Li Xun, a leader from the Beijing
Artists Association, the No Name group held its first official exhibition
in Beihai park in Beijing, and "No Name" came into common usage.
Two months later another avant-garde event, the Stars Group's first,
self-organized exhibition, took place. It caused a public sensation and
was shut down by the police.

Artists were at the front of Deng Xiaoping's spiritual parade.

A year earlier, in June 1978, a periodical devoted to modern art was
founded, with the rather grand title *World Art Magazine*. All this happened only a few years after the Cultural Revolution, during which
artistic freedom had been hit very hard. Noncommunist art of any kind
was banned, just as traditional Chinese opera disappeared from the
stage and was replaced by new operas with communist themes. Huge
libraries that had survived from old China were destroyed, and artists
who fell out of favor were arrested or even assassinated.

With the "opening up," the most visible early participants in the development of the "spiritual civilization" were artists. They got off to a
thunderous start with a "great leap" in a new direction, whetting the
people's hunger for artistic, spiritual, and intellectual experiences.

In the early 1980s the Central Academy of Fine Arts in Beijing oc-
cupied a modest plot of land near Tiananmen Square where the faculty,
not long before, had rigidly taught Soviet-style realist art to only about
200 students. If you visit the school today you will see a new thirty-
three-acre campus with more than 4,000 students, chosen from 60,000
applicants. Many of these students dream of following in the footsteps of
alumni, some of whom today make millions in international markets.

In the larger process of human self-liberation new art became common, the number of exhibits increased, and more new art magazines
were founded. Between 1985 and 1990, a group of more than 1,000
artists—who were living in an environment without galleries, museums,
or any systematic support for art, but who had matchless enthusiasm and
passion—led a profoundly influential movement. It marked the end of
the old communist regime's artistic model—"one art for all"—and

achieved a new freedom, opening a path for Chinese art to march toward international recognition.

85 New Wave Movement

In 1985 the celebrated "85 New Wave Movement" began, virtually institutionalizing the new art of China. This was neither western modern art nor historic Chinese art but a frame of reference that encompassed the whole world and China's place in it. The initiation of the New Wave, celebrated in 2007–2008 with a spectacular show and catalog at the impressive Ullens Center for Contemporary Art at the 798 district in Beijing, was clearly a direct cultural result of the reforms and opening-up policies implemented by the Chinese leaders. The early New Wave represented the most vibrant, most creative face of China's vast social transformation, and played the role of avant-garde pioneer and prophet.

Zhang Xiaogang, who was born in Kunming and now lives and works in Beijing and exhibits all over the world, describes his view of art: "Art should express the character of the individual. I have always felt that art should be, first and foremost, personal; only then can it become public."

Mao Yuhui—who was born in Chongqing, lives and works in Kunming, and exhibits worldwide—thinks that "art removes useless and dead concepts from people's minds, removing the dead while encouraging the living. Openness of art is to allow art to enter all aspects of life, dragging men from empty idealism back into living reality. Art gives people confidence. It does not deal out dreams but is a live force, perceptions of life itself. Art does not teach. It awakens."

Despite all the freedom artists have experienced in exploring and experimenting, China has showed as much prudery as western critics and audiences showed in the early days of their modern art. Also, in China there has been little appreciation of the aesthetic value of the nude human form. As early as December 1978, the Ministry of Culture issued a notice permitting the use of human models for teaching and artistic production, but it took more than ten years until the human body would achieve public acceptance.

The Nudes in the Airport Mural

The well-known story of the "hidden nudes" began in 1979, when the Ministry of Light Industry, during the first years of the reforms and the opening up, commissioned a group of artists to decorate the new Beijing airport. Forty artists participated in creating murals with themes ranging from ethnic folk festivals to literary references. It was an important project, and the opening ceremony was attended by Deng Xiaoping and other leaders.

Yuan Yunsheng's large mural *Water Splashing Festival* was a challenge to Chinese standards and became controversial. It showed three nude women from the Dai ethnic group bathing among clothed women, an image that once was thought capable of polluting minds, not emancipating them. People swarmed to the airport to gape at the unclothed figures, but only a year later the authorities decided that the mural was obscene, and the naked women were boarded over. The hidden nudes resurfaced in 1990, when cleaners removed the boards to clean the walls and revealed the full mural. It was then shown in its entirety but was later removed and, as far as we know, found a place in a restaurant at the airport.

We have been looking at art in China since our first visit there together. In 2000, when we started, some of the galleries were hard to find. A taxi driver would never turn down a fare just because he had no idea where an address was, but we did not know about this. Somewhere along the way the driver would ask a colleague, and in most cases we were lucky and ended up at the gallery we wanted. Sometimes, though, we were dropped off at the wrong corner; and, as we do not speak Chinese and few Chinese on the street speak English, that was just as bad as being dropped at the wrong end of town. One of the galleries we just had to see was especially hard to find. Holding on to the paper on which the Ritz-Carlton's concierge had written the address, we insisted that we would not get out of the cab until we found the gallery. Finally we found it, hidden in a backyard. We will never forget it, because one of the paintings there was by Zhang Xiaogang. The price was several thousand dollars. We thought it was too much and said we would look around, come back, negotiate, and see. But we did not have time to come back, and not much later we saw that the prices of Zhang's paintings were going through the ceiling.

The Globalization of Chinese Art

Chinese art has gone global. And very quickly, China has become a magnet for some of the world's biggest galleries, museums, collectors, and art speculators. By 2008 China had fifteen of the artists worldwide who sell their works for $1 million or more. A competition has begun over whether a westerner or a Chinese is the most expensive living artist. *Art Market Trends 2007* reported that five of the world's best-selling living artists at auctions in 2006 had been born in China. These artists were led by Zhang Xiaogang, then age fifty, whose works were sold for a total of $56.8 million at auctions in that year.

There is no better showcase than the world of contemporary art to demonstrate China's march toward a new era of individualism. Every artist is trying to express his or her individual experience and thought. Artists and intellectuals were the first to respond to the "emancipation of minds," followed closely by entrepreneurs.

The new individual freedoms have resulted in an explosion of artistic expression that is now spilling over into the world, along with China's economic assertiveness. China is moving in the direction of becoming the world leader in art, architecture, and design, just as the United States did in the twentieth century.

The Emergence of Chinese Design

Closely related to avant-garde art is the astonishing vitality of China's twenty-first-century design culture, which is also having a powerful effect outside China, showing the way for other countries to develop a cultural identity. China's impressive advances in design are a result of the emancipation of the mind and of the exploding market economy, in conjunction.

"Design China" emerged from a confluence of the consumer revolution and the new freedoms that gave rise to a new group of entrepreneurial designers. Until the early 1990s most designers worked for state-owned enterprises (SOEs); but as consumerism took hold, state-employed designers began to moonlight outside the official system. This led entrepreneurial graphic designers to set up their own private design practices. Today there are independent design practices all over China—in products, architecture, and fashion.

Leading the way in design development from the market side are Chinese companies such as the mobile phone manufacturer Ningo Bird, the appliance company Haier, and of course the big computer company Lenovo, which in 2006 had doubled its design team to eighty people.

It may seem surprising that Lenovo designed the 2008 Olympic torch. Yao Yingjia, executive director of Lenovo's Innovation Design Center in Beijing, said that the shape of the torch was inspired by a traditional Chinese scroll, and that the shape, texture, and technology evoked the Olympic spirit. "The imagery of the 'Cloud of Promise' represented the traditions of China," said Yao. "We approached the design of the torch with the same process we use in designing our personal computers. First we explore the connection between the users and the solution we create for them, looking at factors like size, weight, features, etc. Then we encourage the Lenovo design team to take a fresh approach to make the product uniquely and friendly to the customer, making it attractive to those who see it, and comfortable and light for those who carry it. In the case of the torch, our 'customer' is both the torchbearer and the spectator."

The emphasis on design is affecting China's new, big markets of tomorrow: cars, Internet services, information technology, and entertainment. Another measure of "design China" is that in 2008, more than 500 design colleges were operating all across the country.

In China's early automobile industry there was quite a bit of "borrowing arrows." Yin Tongyao, CEO of Chery, started in the best tradition with German quality at Chinese prices. Arrows made in Germany also came in handy when Volkswagen centralized its research and development in Germany and long-term Chinese developers switched to Chery. Then Yin bought a share of the Jia Jing Corporation, a young Chinese automotive design company that diverted some arrows from a joint venture between Citroën and Dongfeng Motor group. "I had the feeling of a fan meeting Michael Jordan," said Shen Haojie, one of the founders of the Jia Jing Corporation. Chery's two-thirds ownership added another twenty designers to the team. In addition, the CEO, Yin, engaged the Italian design company Bertone e Pininfarina, since he knew that the Chinese first pay attention to design, and only second consider hidden technical refinements. Yin also believes that an inexpensive car with great design will be very well positioned on the international market.

Chinese Architects and Architecture

For centuries there was no significant change in Chinese architecture. Most changes appeared only in decorative details. The architectural structures of a building, the number of levels, the measurements, and the colors had to follow certain rules, depending on the social status of the owner.

In the first decades of the reforms, almost any new building served the purpose of improving housing standards; but over time, demands became more exacting on the individual level and the public level. Soon architecture in Shanghai's Pudong, Shenzhen's city plan, and urban projects such as Songbei, which is almost as big as New York City, became well known and a symbol of China's progress.

After the year 2000 Chinese architects started to enter the global stage. In May 2006, thirty-four-year-old Ma Yansong of Beijing became China's first architect to win a competition overseas. An international jury chose Ma's twisting, fifty-six-story design for a residence to be built in Mississauga, Canada. One member of the jury called it the "Marilyn Monroe Building," and from then on that became its nickname. "I did not have Marilyn Monroe or a woman's body in mind,"

Ma says in an interview that can be watched on YouTube; "I wanted to make something irregular." The 500 units in the Absolute Tower (the actual name) sold in one day. And Ma immediately designed a smaller version, which also sold out right away.

After graduating from high school in Beijing, Ma studied in the United States, at the Yale School of Architecture, where he earned a master's degree. In 2002 he worked for such prestigious firms as Eisenman Architects in New York and Zaha Hadid in London before returning to China. He taught architecture at the Central Academy of Fine Arts in Beijing and in 2004 founded the company MAD (short for Ma Design). During the following two years Ma entered his designs in more than 100 competitions, winning several, although none of these designs were ever built. When the Absolute Tower project began, his own reputation rose with the building.

After the Canadian project, Ma soon gained fame in China, and he now has a score of designs being built in China and overseas. What happened to Ma was not different from what happened to the filmmaker Chen Kaige, who was not fully established in China until he received awards from the western film industry. Ma Yansong found no takers for his utopian designs in China, despite its building boom, until he was praised in the West.

Ma wants more Chinese architecture in China. In talking about the building craze there, Ma told the *Financial Times* in late 2007 that "there is no context for what is happening in China." People talk about the Olympics, but, says Ma, "that's not a real future. When society grows too fast and is too focused on the thing right in front of them, and not in the distance, that's a problem." He sees too many copycat versions of the western cost-efficient high-rises with conservative designs that show no evidence of fresh talent or creativity.

Ma wants to abandon the vertical, cubic skyscraper in favor of more fluid, less rigid structures that better reflect modern China's urban issues, such as population density and exhaustion of resources. He envisions a landscape of horizontal, organic, and—above all—human-friendly buildings. His company, MAD, now employs forty people and recently opened an office in Tokyo, thus becoming China's first internationally based architecture firm. Ma plans to open another office in Dubai, where the Tokyo Island "World" project has been commissioned.

"We have so many challenges and problems in everyday life, and the architecture has to be sensitive to that," says Ma. From the vantage point of his post-1989 generation, which grew up with social values more liberated than those of the past, it is only natural for Ma to want to revolutionize the way China gets constructed. (Almost all of the above was drawn from an article in the *Financial Times* by Michael Levitin.)

The Return of the Sea Turtles

Ma's story is like many other stories about China's so-called sea turtles. A growing number of Chinese who have studied or worked overseas are being lured back by the opportunities in China. These Chinese, often called "sea turtles," even have their own organization: the Western Returned Scholars Association. "Sea turtles" play an increasingly important role in China's economy.

Many of our Chinese friends are sea turtles. Some of the them belong to the first generation; these include Wang Wei, whose story we told in the chapter on Pillar 1; and Wu Ying, whose story we tell in the chapter on Pillar 7. Others, such as Zhang Haihua and Pu Xiaoyan, belong to the second generation who studied and lived abroad before returning to China.

The sea turtle community is male-dominated, but we are happy to know some women representatives of the group. One of them is Zhang Haihua (Helen), whose book *Think Like Chinese* we keep quoting because we have learned so much from it. When we first met her, we thought she must have grown up in England, because her English is flawless. But she was born in Tianjin, our Chinese hometown. There have been many interesting stages in her life, and very early on in the narrative of her life she tells us what seems so important for all Chinese: "From a very early age I knew that being a good student is a sure way to get the attention and favor from your teachers and your parents. I became such a good one that most of my learning was to pass exams."

At Peking University she "soaked up the unique atmosphere of the best university of China." In 1986, when she entered, students did not have to pay any tuition or board, and in fact they were given a small sum of money as a subsidy. Years later, when she had already left China and lived in Australia, the feeling that "only a respected degree will lead to a good job" pushed her to earn two master's degrees, both in finance and business.

Haihua had emigrated to Australia in early 1990, when the first large wave of foreign investments had come into China. She left China even though she had a great job at company that belongs to the Air Force Logistics Department—a job she had accepted after turning down an offer to become the personal assistant of the general manager of Bell Communication's newly established joint venture in China. After her graduation Haihua went back to her hometown, Tianjin, for some years and worked for the first American representative office ever established there. Her boss—a woman—had learned Chinese and was the first expatriate worker in Beijing in the 1980s, because she wanted to "become a big fish in a small pond."

Because of Haihua's superior Chinese education, her western postgraduate studies, her language skills (Haihua is truly bilingual in Mandarin Chinese and English), and her experience in the Chinese and western business world, the West offered her a great future. Also, Sydney is a great place to live.

Why did you come back? was a natural question for us to put to her. On the surface, the reason was simple. In 2002, her husband, an Australian lawyer, got a job offer to establish a law firm in Beijing. The legal industry was growing very fast, and many international law firms were entering or planning to enter the Chinese market. So Helen, as we call her, and Geoff Baker, her Australian husband, moved back to China, which Helen had left ten years before. "The reverse cultural shock was quite daunting to me," Helen said. "Roads I used to walk had either disappeared or been made three times wider, old traditional Hutong neighborhoods had become new business quarters, and the pace of life had become so much faster than I could recall. Everyone was interested in making deals and earning money. Now I understood why the comment of a former colleague at Peking University, when visiting Sydney, had been: 'Sydney is a great place to retire.'

"During the beginning of the new century China was going through further stellar growth. Foreign investment and domestic growth as well as government support took turns fueling the market, and the stock market, after low years, went through the roof. But in this 'get rich quick' phenomenon there was also suffering from shortsightedness and lack of awareness of personal and business branding. People invested in businesses and in the stock markets without a proper understanding of the risks.

"Many western companies and entrepreneurs that come to China to secure their share in this huge market have also lacked an understanding of the risks and demands doing business in China holds. A Chinese saying reflects the cultural gap very well: sharing the same bed but having different dreams."

Haihua and Geoff, who "come from two worlds sharing one bed," started their research on why businesses fail and where the risks and traps of doing business with China were. This research led to their book *Think Like Chinese*.

During the decade when she had lived in Australia, Haihua had became more "Helen" than she was aware of: "A few years ago, when people asked me whether I enjoyed living in Beijing my answer would have been quite reserved. In fact I would have packed up and returned to Sydney without hesitation. Now I see it in a totally different light. This is a country that is always learning, reflecting, and changing. This is the land that nurtured one of the most fascinating ancient wisdoms. This is the land that provides home for generations and millions of people. I feel I am on a journey of constant learning and change, and during this fascinating journey, my motherland, China, is going through all these changes, too."

Although the first-generation entrepreneurs, such as Helen's mother, are known for their experience and passion, they often lacked any business education. They sent their children overseas to study western technology and management theories—and to learn how to do business globally.

One of those is Pu Xiaoyan. While Wang Wei left China in early 1985, and Helen in 1990, Pu Xiaoyan left China as late as in 2004. Her background differs, and then again, seems very Chinese. Other than the first generation, which left China to study overseas, her generation relatively has less of the sense of mission of making history. They focus more on self-improvement and self-fulfillment. Studying abroad is more of an opportunity and a chance for them to rediscover the meaning of life, to reinvent themselves, and to live up to all of their potential. The western world is a totally new world, full of possibilities. In her memory, her classmates spent "tons of time on entrance exam preparation for overseas education." But Xiaoyan knew, on the very day she left, that she would certainly come back to China. Her career and life is here in China and there are more opportunities for her in this piece of land. The journey in the United States was just for recharging, for learning, for giving her different perspectives on life. She describes the several years right before she left China as China's most vital and also most restless period in her memory. "The entire country was undergoing dramatic changes, both socially and economically. Millionaires and billionaires were minted out every day. Everybody around me was talking about starting their own business, replicating the myth of wealth from the other side of the ocean. Beijing was the Wild West back then."

Like many other Chinese, she went to the United States, where she earned an MBA from the University of Texas at Austin and worked as global sales and marketing communications manager for Freescale Semiconductor, Inc. But although America offered a decent life, she could not hold on to her old dream and dream big, so she decided to come back to China to pursue it.

"When I breathed in the polluted air," she said to our surprise, "I felt home. The aspiration and energy excited me." She moved back to China in 2008 after accepting an offer to be general manager of Huaso Digital Film/TV production company, which is a joint venture of Sony Pictures in China with China Film Group, and is producing TV drama series, films, and content for new media in China. We asked Xiaoyan how the country changed in her eyes, and she listed the following:

- The entire society is calming down from high-speed growth. The rules of the game are set up and the playing field has been leveled. A new generation of entrepreneurs is rising. Compared with the old generation, they're more educated and connected to the western world and focused on nontraditional industries.

- People pay more attention to the balance of work and life now, and pursue things more than just money. Peace of mind plays a big role in the sense of well-being. It may explain why all kinds of religions are booming in China. The Chinese middle class is returning to the traditional value system, or actively seeking new value systems to live in after the wealth-creation carnival.

- The government is becoming more service-oriented. Now Chinese enjoy more equal opportunities and the society is making progress in this area.

- The society is more diversified, more tolerant, less cynical, and better connected with the outside world. The supervision of different voices is not easy anymore, thanks to the Internet.

- Local companies are rising up. Before I left China, Fortune 500 companies were the first career choice of the majority of university students. Now local companies are becoming more competitive in attracting talents.

- In this country, learning is the fundamental element of daily life since things change so fast and new things appear every day. Compared with China, U.S. society is relatively mature and stagnant.

- With the rising of China, Chinese people are becoming more confident and proud of their identity. Nationalism and populism are also gaining more attention among the younger generation.

Sea turtles are still the minority, but as China's economy develops, there will be more and more Chinese who return with a backpack filled with western know-how.

Rebirth of Performing Arts

Many of the sea turtles bring back a love of western music. However, "The crisis in music education is in the United States, not in China," the Chinese concert pianist Lang Lang said in an interview with the *Financial Times* in April 2009. "Perhaps mirroring Asia's ascendancy, while classic music in London and New York seems to be greying rapidly, in Taipei or Hong Kong, it sometimes seems as if the average age of the audience is about 10. In the U.S. the budget deficits mean that the first thing they cut is music and art and many of the schools don't have a music program anymore. There is no training [in] how to listen to Beethoven and Mozart. You can't expect someone who has never listened to classical music to start listening to it when he is 30 years old."

"It could be that one of the most important defenders of classical music will be China," said Lorin Maazel, music director of the New York Philharmonic, after the orchestra's hugely successful concert series in Beijing in September 2008. This is also the view of Curtis Price, the principal of the Royal Academy in London. "Chinese people," says Maazel, "who have shown their passion and high sense of aesthetics, are an ideal spawning ground for burgeoning interest in classical music." These and other very positive observations on the future of classical music in China were widely published in the United States. Most provincial capitals in China are building new concert halls. Someone, perhaps a new generation of musicians, will have to perform in them. More than 20 million young people in China are learning the piano, and 10 million the violin, so this new generation will surely include some of these.

China's performing arts are flourishing. A long list of stars and world-famous companies appeared on China's stages in 2009. The first was the Chicago Symphony Orchestra, which performed on February 13 and 14 at the National Center for Performing Arts with its principal conductor, Bernard Haitink. Now all of the "big five" American orchestras have performed in Beijing. In September 2007 we naively tried to get tickets for one of the concerts by the New York Philharmonic, only to discover that all tickets to all performances had been sold out for months. "Touch of Vienna" was the title of an article in *China Daily* about a concert by the Vienna Philharmonic Orchestra. With Viennese musicians; an Indian conductor, Zubin Mehta; and the Chinese soloist Lang Lang, this was international collaboration at its best.

In 2008 the National Center staged 661 shows, and box office earnings exceeded 300 million RMB ($44 million). The National Ballet of China, the Shanghai Ballet, and the Guangzhou Ballet presented their famous repertoires throughout the year.

The Center for Performing Arts presented four new shows in 2009: three operas—*La Bohème*, *Women Teachers in the Countryside*, and *Xi Shi*—and a drama, *Jane Eyre*. The center's first opera festival ran from mid-April to late June, featuring a dozen operas, including the western classics *Tosca*, *Turandot*, and *Carmen*, and the Chinese *Jiang Jie* and *The Prairie*. *Turandot*, directed by Zhang Yimou, was presented in the Bird's Nest, the great stadium that the world saw during the Beijing Olympic Games.

Dramas presented throughout the year included the avant-garde director Meng Jinghui's *Rhinoceros in Love*. *Secret Love in Peach Blossom Land*, first created in 1986 by Stan Lai's Taiwanese Performance Workshop, was acclaimed in China and across the world. *Secret Love in Peach Blossom Land* is an unusual experience. Two plays are enacted simultaneously in the same theater. One, *Secret Love*, is a modern tragedy in which an old man reminisces about a long-lost love; the second, *Peach Blossom Land*, is a broad comedy about a cuckolded man who finds his way into a fabled utopia—the Peach Blossom Land of the title. As the two productions jostle for control of the stage, the plays' themes interweave.

When Lin Zhaohua's *Hamlet*, an extreme interpretation even by western standards, in the Little Theatre of the Beijing Film Academy, was performed in 1990, it created queues hundreds of meters long for tickets. In March 2009 Lin Zhaohua's *Hamlet* was played in Beijing's Capital Theatre in a new production. It is honored as the most experimental theater work in China. Lin's concept, "Everybody is Hamlet," involves switching the characters' parts, to show that the characters share all the elements of good and evil, honesty and falsehood. Tickets for students were offered at only 60 RMB (nine dollars).

For those who were less enthusiastic about classical music or experimental theater, many other shows were presented. Sarah Brightman and Oasis performed, as did Gehua Live Nation and two well-loved Chinese singers: Xu Wei and Joanna Wang. It was the first time Brightman appeared in Beijing after her duet "You and Me" with the Chinese tenor Liu Huan at the opening ceremony of the Olympics.

Blockbusters in the Film Industry

China's moviemakers started late, but the number of movie screens nationwide has nearly tripled since 2002, from 1,400 to more than 4,000. In 2008 the top five moneymakers were domestic productions, including the young director Ning Hao's black comedy *Crazy Racer* (*Fengkuang de Saiche*) and the romantic *Look for a Star* with the popular actors Andy Lau and Shu Qi.

According to Tong Gang, president of the State Film Bureau, about 300 film producers made 406 features in 2008, including the action director John Woo's *Red Cliff* (*Chi Bi*) and the popular director Feng Xiaogang's *If You Are the One* (*Feicheng Wurao*), which grossed 100 million RMB ($14.7 million). "Eight years ago, 100 million RMB would have made a film the box office champion," according to Huang Qunfei, general manager of the Beijing-based theater chain New Film Association Company; but there has been continuous growth of 25 percent since 2002. "Now we have eight of these winners in one year." The film industry's box office is booming. Revenue for 2008 reached a record-breaking 4.34 billion RMB ($636 million), an increase of more than 30 percent over 2007. "As for ticket prices, leave those to the market," says Yin Hong, director of Tsinghua University's Center for Film and Television Studies. "Theaters are the most market-oriented part of the Chinese film industry."

"There is one movie screen for every 500,000 people in China, while 8,000 people share one screen in the United States," says the film bureau's president, Tong. "Many small and middle-size cities have no theater at all."

Huang is concerned: "There is a long way to go. The annual gross is still less than a single Hollywood blockbuster such as *Dark Knight*, let alone *Titanic*," he said. "And remember, we import only twenty foreign films a year. The quota has been very protective."

Culture in the Countryside

It seems that President Hu Jintao's announcement at the National Congress in 2007 was not just empty words: "We must stimulate cultural innovation and enhance the vitality of cultural development. We must uphold the principla of letting a hundred flowers blossom and a hundred schools of thoughts contend."

Whoever knows the Chinese would not be surprised if "Chinese country music" soon became a moneymaking machine. "Wang Qing Song," and "Song of Sanitation Workers," composed and sung by farmers, all members of the Wangqing County Federation of Literary and Art Circles, were reportedly very well received. Farmers in the federation create literature, music, calligraphy, paintings, photography, and Quyi folk art. In Wangqing county alone, 7 million people participated in fifty-eight events in 2007. A Chinese Dolly Parton may soon conquer the market, moderate a television show, record CDs, and compete in a Grand Prix of Chinese Folk Music. As reported in *Jilin Daily*, to accommodate farmers, art associations are being created at county, township, and neighborhood levels throughout the country, and farmers are joining the literary and artistic ranks in growing numbers.

The desire for entertainment grows bottom-up, complemented by a leadership that encourages and supports a wide range of efforts to bring a richer cultural life into cities and villages.

- In the year 219 BCE, Emperor Qin Shi Huang sent Xu Fu, a court sorcerer, to sail from the city of Zhucheng to Japan to find the elixir of youth. After he embarked on a second mission in 210 BCE, he did not return. Little hope of finding the elixir remains today; but in an attempt to cheer up the population, Zhucheng created "a two-kilometer cultural circle of rural communities" around the city in 2007, so that farmers within the circles could enjoy cultural facilities. The city began to implement ideas about the construction of such facilities in rural areas.

- *Dazhong Daily* reports that beginning in 2007, the city has built 170 cultural "courtyards" serving 800 surrounding villages. The facilities and services include a library, a press room, a cultural and information resource room, an administrator, a part-time cultural volunteer, and literary and artistic volunteers. More than 600 singing and dancing teams and artistic groups are giving 5,000 performances and exhibitions. *Dazhong Daily* says that these rural community cultural activities have changed farmers' monotonous life of "work when the sun rises and rest when the sun sets." Their lives have been transformed and enriched by the new cultural atmosphere.

- Jilin is a popular city for tourists. Each winter they come to view the magnificent rime ice on trees along the banks of the Songhua River. This rime ice is a natural phenomenon that occurs every year during January and February. But in the future Jilin might also become known for its cultural activities. *Jiangcheng Daily* has reported that a large-scale "culture rostrum" was opened in Jilin in early 2008. Fifty lectures, free to all citizens, were already scheduled. The subjects included current affairs, traditional culture, mental health of teenagers, science, and finance. These cultural lectures are becoming increasingly popular.

- In Yunnan province, the city of Kunming in southwestern China, often called "Spring City" because of its year-round temperate climate, is now reaching for the highest levels of entertainment. According to *Kunming Daily*, the municipal government established the focus of its cultural industry as "China's future Hollywood." It is reported that 30 billion Hong Kong dollars will be invested to build a new film and media center. The project is in four parts: film and television, new media, education, and service.

Hu's encouragement of "promoting Chinese culture to build up the common spiritual home for the Chinese nation" fell countrywide on fertile ground.

Competition to Be "Culture City"

- *Nanchang Daily*, in the capital of Jiangxi province in southeastern China, continues to report on cultural activities there. Nanchang is famous for its scenic lakes, mountains, rich history, and cultural sites. In 2008 it set a goal for itself: to become a "culture city." Its spring festival—the most important of the traditional Chinese holidays, which begins on the first day of the first month in the Chinese calendar and ends on the fifteenth—lasts seventeen days and features a series of seventeen activities, "rich in content, new in form, participatory, and interactive." These included a light-and-color art exhibition, calligraphy, and a painting exhibition, all meant to inspire the pursuit of traditional arts and culture, "promoting the heritage, innovation, and development of Nanchang."

- In the flat, low-lying Jiangsu province, along the east coast of China, Taizhou, the hometown of President Hu, borrowed from foreign experience and initiated a "1 percent culture plan," which began in the summer of 2008. Major construction projects must set aside 1 percent of construction costs to invest in public sculptures. The result has been sculptures that can be seen at public building sites, on major streets, and in residential areas.

- In the relatively poor and underdeveloped province of Guizhou—a mountainous, subtropical, humid region—a peasant poetry group is rising in Jinzi village of Suiyang town. Recently, a reporter for the *Guizhou Daily* found a journal called *Fenghua Poetry* in Fenghua county, where Suiyang is located. The journal was the work of a few peasants in Jinzi. All the authors were farmers, some of them middle school students. In 2006, under a proposal by the chairman of the cultural league, Jinzi village set up the Jinchen Poetry Institute as a platform for peasant poets. Every month, poetry lovers come to the new village office, where peasant poets gather for two days. There are more than twenty farmer writers in the village, and their sixty-four-page journal, *Fenghua Poetry,* printed in color, is now sent to all provinces, municipalities, and autonomous regions of the country.

- To promote the prosperity of rural culture and enrich farmers' spiritual and cultural life in Yining county, the county government is paying more attention to rural cultural talent, and grassroots amateur theatrical teams have become a major force in the local cultural life, as the *Yili Daily* reported. Facilities in the rural areas have gradually improved, and professional arts have been presented in the countryside, but when Yining county sends programs to its countryside, it always requires that the locals contribute their best programs to the performances.

- Zhangzhou city, in the past better known for its alcoholic beverage Baijiu than for its spiritual activities, has been taking urban culture to the countryside and rural culture to the city. This is an important effort to enrich the spiritual and cultural life of urban and rural citizens and build a harmonious culture. *Jiangxi Daily* reports that more than 1 million RMB ($147,000) has been spent to construct village and cultural facilities, providing a venue for performances in the countryside by city arts associations.

All these bottom-up local cultural initiatives find support in the Chinese leadership. Hu Jintao acknowledged those ambitions: "We must support the Chinese people in their increasingly ardent desire for a richer cultural life."

The Rock Scene

"You would not have seen such a flourishing music scene in Beijing two years ago," said Chen Nan in 2008 in a music review in the *China Daily*. The opening of the music market in China and cooperation between the music industries in China and western countries has brought increasing numbers of foreign bands into China, says Jiang Wei, publicity manager for Guitar China, which organized a recent Dark Tranquillity (a Swedish, melodic-death-metal-band) concert in Beijing. "But now the situation has changed. They are right in front of you." The construction of venues for live shows in Beijing contributes to the booming music scene. "Venues like Star Live, Mao Live House, 13 Club, and D-22 offer performers high-quality equipment, the same as in western countries," Jiang says. "There is a huge fan base for music in China. Watching live performances has become a way of life for music lovers. It is now common for big-name heavy metal bands to perform in the China rock scene. On a given night in Beijing you can catch Lacrimosa, Testament, or Napalm Death. Maybe in five or six years many people in New York or London will have their favorite Chinese bands."

The first three CDs released by a local label, Maybe Mars Records, came out at the end of 2007. These were albums by Carsick Cars, Snapline, and Joyside—three largely unknown Beijing rock bands. The label's founder says, "Today's Beijing is like San Francisco in the 1960s, when only insiders knew how good the scene was. In a few years the whole world will know."

The Return of Books

The fourth annual Bookworm International Literary Festival was held in Beijing in March 2009, and was reportedly 25 percent bigger than the previous year. Our first visit to Bookworm, a very lively bookstore, was in 2007, when our friends Haihua and Geoff in Beijing arranged a presentation of *Mind Set!* Among a wide variety Bookworm carries all western books otherwise not available in Chinese bookstores. This is not allowed, but it is not forbidden. Very Chinese.

The Bookworm festival continues to be more international, with new participants from the Middle East, India, Norway, and Australia. Justin Hill, the British author of *The Drink and Dream Teahouse*, who was a volunteer worker in China and Africa for seven years, says that China has renewed cultural clout, and that the festival reflects this. "China is here and now. There are more interesting conversations than in England," he said. "I write about China because it is important. There's more at stake here; it is more fundamental and raw than the West." The festival is organized by the Bookworm, our favorite bookstore in Beijing, and we hope to attend next year.

In early February 2008, when we were in Beijing, our Chinese agent, Stella Chou, introduced us to Mrs. Wu Wei, an official of the State Council Information Office, in charge of foreign affairs publishing. She had read *Megatrends* twenty-five years ago and was pleased that *China's Megatrends* would soon be published.

We have never doubted that the Chinese have spiritual needs. But we do sometimes fall into the trap of prejudice. We expected Mrs. Wu to be a bureaucrat, and were surprised when we learned that Wu Wei is an author herself, known for her *Epic of King Gesar*, about the most beloved legendary hero of the Tibetan people. This tale, we know now, is one of today's few living epics and represents the highest achievement of ancient Tibetan culture. It is an encyclopedic masterpiece. About 140 ballad singers are still performing today, presenting the 1,000-year-old songs about fearless King Gesar, who ruled the legendary kingdom of Ling. Back in Vienna, we listened to a monk singing the poems in the ancient Tibetan language on YouTube.

Wu Wei, commonly called Madam Wu caught our attention. Usually we don't ask for personal stories, although this is quite common in China, but in her case we did.

Wu Wei was the youngest child of an official in the government. Her childhood was happy; she felt spoiled and loved by her family. But as with almost everyone, the Cultural Revolution brought a big change in her life. The members of her family were not united in their political opinions; some took the side of the Cultural Revolution, but some took the other side—and those were soon to be persecuted. Everyone was busy: parents, siblings, and other relatives. The most painful consequence for Wu was the end of schooling. She loved to study and loved reading.

During the next three to four years all studies were possible only intermittently. Hunger for literature was not very popular during those "reeducation" years. Intellectuals and artists had to bend their heads over assembly lines and their backs in rice fields instead of reading or writing books. Wu showed little conformity, though, and somehow she and her friends managed to keep up with reading. They read famous Chinese literature and even foreign classics: The *Dream of the Red Chamber*, *The Romance of the Three Kingdoms*, *Journey to the West*. They even got hold of a handwritten copy of Gene Fowler's *The Second Handshake*.

Maybe all this would not have been so interesting for her and her friends had it not been politically incorrect. She did not even understand all the Chinese words—after all, the Chinese must deal with a minimum of 3,000 to 5,000 characters. But whatever Wu understood fed her love for the written word and, as a welcome side effect, improved her vocabulary and built a foundation for good literature.

At the beginning of the reforms, teaching became the most urgently needed profession, but very few students showed interest in becoming teachers. Working in a farming village or a factory, or being a soldier in the People's Liberation Army, was much more attractive at the time. Wu was the only one in her class who volunteered to become a teacher. But, as she told us, neither her school, which recommended teaching, nor she herself was totally unselfish in making this choice. The school hoped to get her back after graduation, and she saw teaching as the best chance to continue a life surrounded by books.

Nevertheless, Wu did not remain a teacher, but she soon continued her studies, and in 1985 she graduated from Capital Normal University, in art studies. After that she was admitted to the Academy of Social Science. At that time, as her research project, she had started work on a model to put the *Epic of King Gesar*, which has more than 1 million verses and about 10 million words, into a three-volume format that would retain the full essence of the epic. As we write these lines, a beautifully illustrated issue of *King Gesar* lies on our table. It won the National Book Award.

Not surprisingly, after her graduation Wu signed up to work in the China Tibetology Publishing House, where she was responsible for the research and publishing related to Tibetan culture. She stayed there for eight years. During those years, she was also writing her own books and doing translations.

From this job Wu Wei was transferred to the State Council Information Office, where she eventually became deputy director of a department. As we mentioned above, she is in charge of overseas publishing, and that was the reason we met with her. "For so many years," she said, "owing to various reasons, there were lot of difficulties in the communication between China and other countries." We agreed.

At that point she handed us a big package. Inside was a large golden-backed, ten-pound English-language *China Encyclopedia*. Madam Wu had worked on it for three years as editor in chief, and it was her present to us. *Megatrends*, which Madam Wu had read twenty-five years ago, described the transformation of America. She was happy to hear that now such an analysis of China was being written, and the *China Encyclopedia* would provide important data.

A few days after our dinner with Madam Wu, we again had dinner with her, and with former minister Zhao Qizheng, who had come from

Shanghai to meet us. We had not seen him for eight years, and we were very happy that Madam Wu had brought us together again. Just a few days earlier, Zhao had been appointed spokesperson for the Chinese People's Political Consultative Conference, China's top advisory body. In our conversation we addressed many problems China faces. As Zhao said, the question is not whether to take part in globalization, but how to take part, how to use advantages and avoid disadvantages, and how to realize advantages at the appropriate speed. We agreed that education has to be the number one economic priority. Zhao, who has a strong background as a scientist, said, "Whoever possesses the best of human talent occupies the height in science and technology."

Spring Awakening

At the meeting of the National People's Congress in the spring of 2009, Ouyang Jian, the vice minister for culture, said that the government would set up three major groups to develop China's wealth of culture and give a boost to the cultural industry.

He said, "We will establish first-class companies in animation, show business, and digital cultural content." He announced that his ministry was already in negotiations with partners to set up an animation group based in Beijing and Tianjin with 1 billion RMB ($147 million) in registered capital and a possible production value of more than 10 billion RMB ($1.47 billion). "It means," he said, "the company could go public in three to five years."

- Shanghai has completed 108 community cultural activities centers, providing cultural facilities, training in theatrical performance, book exhibitions, films, and other nonprofit cultural services.

- In western China the Sichuan Fine Arts Institute, which has a reputation for training great painters, received more than 64,000 applications in 2008 for 1,600 openings.

- On December 21, 2007, the media company Liaoning Publishing became the first domestic publishing enterprise to be listed on the Shanghai stock exchange.

- Jilin University has begun recruiting deans globally. In 2008 six people competed for two positions: dean of the life sciences college and dean of the physics college. Two of those competing for the physics position were Chinese living in America. One of those competing for the life sciences position was a graduate of Jilin University working in the United States. The *Jilin Daily* quotes the president of Jilin University, Zhou Qifeng: "Our goal is not to create a bigger school, or enroll more students, but to build a high level research university, and to do that the most important thing is to improve the quality of teaching and leadership in the university."

As its economy develops, China is also exporting culture to the world. By March 2009, there were 256 Confucius Institutes worldwide, and fifty-eight Confucius classrooms established in eighty-one countries. These are nonprofit language and cultural schools. The Chinese Language Council International expects that by 2010, Confucius Institutes will number more than 500 worldwide.

Putting Prizes Back in the Game

Opening up can be experienced in all fields: art, literature, architecture, entrepreneurism, commercial design, television, magazines, fashion, farming—and sports. During Mao's Cultural Revolution, competitive sports were denounced as "trophyism," and athletes, like intellectuals, donated their potential in rice fields and on assembly lines. The Beijing Olympics and China's 100 medals restored Chinese trophyism at a global level.

Talent in China is strongly supported, but there still is disparity between rural and urban areas. In March 2008 China's leadership started an education campaign to narrow the gap. It began to establish libraries in towns and villages, not by top-down orders but by handing over responsibility to the farmers, leaving it to them to manage the libraries. Each library has at least 1,000 books, thirty newspapers, and 100 videotapes. More than 200,000 such libraries were built by the end of 2009. By the year 2015, 640,000 villages are to have farmers' libraries. Buying newspapers is not as common in China as in the West—but reading newspapers is. In many Chinese cities and towns we see people, mostly men, lined up in front of newspaper bulletin boards reading the news.

When the opening up of publishing began in the late 1970s, it was an emotional time for China's intellectuals. Qin Xiaoying, a researcher with the China Foundation for International and Strategic Studies, said that the government's release of reprints of thirty-five previously banned popular and foreign books in 1978 was "like a warm spring breeze to thaw the frosty winter; the inspiring news set free the long-confined emotions of a large number of intellectuals."

All the reprinted books arrived at major bookstores nationwide. Starved readers, who flocked to these bookstores, couldn't believe their eyes, says Qin, when they saw Chinese and foreign masterpieces, such as *Anthology of Tang Poems*, *Anthology of Song Poetry*, *Midnight*, *The Camel Xiangzi*, *Informal History for Academia Home*, *The Arabian Nights*, *Quatre-vingt-treize*, *David Copperfield*, *Anna Karenina*, *Les Misérables*, and *The Divine Comedy*, on the shelves. Though book lovers in China had always felt respect and affection for these great cultural works, they were labeled "feudal" or "capitalistic" and were prohibited during the Cultural Revolution. Qin says not many people know that Deng Xiaoping was an active supporter and promoter of the campaign to lift the ban on "prohibited books," as part of emancipating people's minds.

In September 1979, the Zhejiang People's Publishing House announced a decision to republish *Gone with the Wind*, the popular American novel by Margaret Mitchell. Soon after the announcement, circulation departments from more than ten provinces, as well as a number of institutes of higher learning across the country, wanted copies. The provincial publishing house had to increase the number of copies from 100,000 to 600,000. Soon after the first volume was published, a violent academic storm blew into the faces of the book lovers. "Socialism, too, will be gone with the wind," was the tenor of a series of critical articles that ran in some newspapers. But Deng's positive attitude toward this novel calmed the tension. His remarks brought an immediate end to academic debates about the book.

Today, says Qin, "such debates may well be unimaginable." Anywhere in the world, education is the key to economic progress. Education is no longer only socially desirable; it has become the number one economic priority. What is the key to raising the level of education? Competition.

The United States has the best universities in the world because of the competition among them.

There is no difference, in this regard, in China's educational system. And competition in education usually begins with private schools. The first steps have been taken. The first law on promotion of private education went into effect on September 1, 2003. The development of private schools results in an increase in the overall "education supply" and a change in the traditional pattern of providing only government-funded schools to meet educational needs. By the end of 2007, there were 95,500 private schools of various types and levels, with a total enrollment of 25.83 million; these included 295 private institutions of higher education and adult colleges.

The government has made a commitment to provide and improve educational opportunities to raise the overall level in the next two decades. In parallel with raising the educational level, increasing attention is being paid to supporting "spiritual civilization." Libraries, museums, and the preservation of cultural treasures and the richness of cultural heritage, combined with new cultural directions, are all fertile ground where artistic and intellectual talent can flourish and grow. Artistic and intellectual ferment creates the color China needs if it is to find the balance in its "national and the spiritual civilization."

In the new China, there is an opening of boundaries as well as an increase in ambition, so that the skills and talents of the Chinese people are free to unfold. Not all the Chinese are intellectuals, and not all have artistic tendencies, but as our friend Wang Yukun has said, noodle makers can make the best noodles, waiters can provide the best service, and assembly-line workers can contribute their share to a great whole. For some the sky is the limit; others stay closer to the ground.

Artists and intellectuals are the first to detach themselves from rules and restrictions, opening their minds to imagination and fantasy. Creativity is unleashed. Artists and intellectuals will always be front-runners, but because of them the level of the whole nation will rise.

In the early 1990s, John experienced how early ambition, artistic talent, and an entrepreneurial spirit are sometimes displayed, when he visited an experimental school in Beijing that Madam Sun Yat-sen established after her husband died. It was a class of six-year-olds, graduating into the first grade: twenty-five lively children, more girls than boys, who sang songs and displayed some of their projects. When the time came to say good-bye, each of the children gave John a little card. Each card had an individual painting, made by the child—a flower, a bird, a tree—and in the middle the name of the child; on the back of the card, to his surprise, was the child's telephone number. Twenty-five little business-cards; twenty-five first impressions of tomorrow's artists, writers, doctors, politicians, and entrepreneurs.

The environment of children growing up in China today creates a great variety of prospects and choices through which future generations can nourish their talents and enhance their contribution to the new China.

Pillar 6

Joining the World

China's aggressive economic, political, and cultural engagement with the rest of the world is an assertion that China claims a role in the global community that matches its own progress.

In the year 1250 BC, thousands of kilometers westward and about 200 years before the Zhou dynasty began to rule in western China, the Greek city of Mycenae was building its city gate. The gate would be the first impression any visitor would have of the city; it had to represent its importance and wealth. Mycenae's Lion Gate was built with four monolithic blocks without mortar, each weighing several tons, and a load-relieving triangle. It was adorned with a relief of two lions, which gave the gate its name. It is still an outstanding monument, visited by people from all over the world.

China's Gate to the Modern World

More than 3,000 years after Mycenae built its gate to the ancient world, China built its gate to the modern world, as a symbol of what a city and a nation can now achieve. Beijing International Airport's "Terminal

Three" is a cultural emblem; it symbolizes China's open door to the world. It is bright, open, functional, and inviting. Daylight enters all parts of the building through the roof; no matter where you are, there is always natural light. At night a glow of yellow, orange, and red lights—colors associated with China and Beijing—can be seen through the roof.

And to the Chinese it is just as symbolic that Terminal Three, the largest building in the world—much bigger than all of London's terminals at Heathrow together—was built in record time. From the first groundbreaking in March 2004, it took the construction teams only four years to finish the project in February 2008. Also, the interior design has been shaped by human and cultural considerations. The feng shui of the airport is calming and inviting, and the arrival area reaches out into the surrounding landscape, welcoming visitors.

What a contrast to the airports at New York or Los Angeles! We find it very sad to experience the run-down airports in many of the main destinations in the United States. They make us feel as if a country that was once the glorious leader of a new world has missed the departure for the next station.

In May 2001, just before China joined the WTO, some Chinese asked us, "Does globalization mean Americanization?" "No," was our answer; "the world is changing America much more than America is changing the world." Today, that question is obsolete. Wherever we are, China, not America, seems to be the elephant in the room. "When will China overtake the United States? Will China take away our jobs? Should our children learn Mandarin?" are questions asked around the globe.

China is on everyone's mind. Few people have visited it, but not knowing much about China does not keep anyone from having an opinion about it. People's views range from loving China to bashing China. Most of the media focus on what is separating China from, rather than connecting China with, the rest of the world. Still, no matter from which angle one looks at China, there is no doubt that it has powerfully entered the stage of the world. And this new player will shape its own role.

China's Knowledge Imports

China's first step before entering the world stage was a change in mind-set. As we know, China embarked on a process of social, cultural, economic, and political emancipation. A new self-awareness allowed China to learn even from countries that for many years had been considered enemies or had been ideologically condemned. China reached out and moved from its isolation to become part of the economic, political, and cultural fabric of the world. After "100 years of humiliation," followed by thirty years of reinventing and reforming itself, China should be accepted and respected by the rest of the world.

Since 1978 China has been busy catching up with the world. What Zhao Qizheng wrote in *Mapping Out Pudong Development* is true for all of China: "Planning functions as well as infrastructure with the wisdom of the entire humankind and according to the world standard and vision—that is an important secret underlying Pudong's successful development."

China has built a nationwide modern infrastructure as a crucial element in economic progress. Its logistics market grew to $500 billion in 2006. China's airlines are the safest in the world; 185 million people flew in China in 2007; 3 million tons of cargo were transported. China's domestic air cargo market grew to $3.1 billion, according to *China Economic Review*.

In joining the world, China knew it had to do something about its terrible commercial air safety record. During the 1990s China's airlines were the world's most dangerous. Today China is a global leader in air safety, with a better record than the United States or Europe. This spectacular turnaround was engineered by the deputy director of the China's Civil Aviation Administration, Yang Yuanyuan. His brilliant approach to fixing the problem was to join the world: to get advice and help from others in the global airline industry. The Chinese were feeling the effects of complacency and runaway growth; and early on, Yuan negotiated a cooperative agreement with the U.S. aviation authorities to coordinate assistance from the industry. Thirty U.S. companies from all areas of the aviation industry organized themselves to provide technical help.

For its part, China recognized that it could have no secrets about matters of aviation safety, and according to American aviation officials, its participation was completely open.

No Chinese jetliner has crashed since 2004, although this has been a period of rapid growth when China's planes have flown more than 8.5 million hours. That is the best safety performance in the world.

Setting Foot on the World Stage

"One World, One Dream," the theme of the 2008 Olympic Games, is a simple expression of a profound idea. It is a theme of China, and also of the world. It conveys a lofty ideal of the people in Beijing and throughout China: to share in the global community and civilization and to create a bright future hand in hand with the people of the rest of the world. It expresses a firm belief of a great nation with a 5,000-year history on its way toward modernization, a nation that, according to the organizers, "is committed to peaceful development, harmonious society, and people's happiness. It voices the aspiration of 1.3 billion Chinese people to contribute to the establishment of a peaceful and bright world."

The year 2008 was significant for diplomacy in China. More than 180 heads of state or government visited China. Foreign Minister Yang Jiechi pronounced, "Now China's fate is increasingly closely linked to that of the world." Surely those heads of state imagined that the fate of their own countries was increasingly tied to China.

When China joined the WTO in 2001, it expanded the frame in which the world would do business in China and in which China would do business with the world. After it joined the WTO its export trade increased in volume by 20 to 30 percent annually. By 2008 China's foreign trade volume reached $2.5 trillion. China's role as a major player in the global markets was obvious.

Not all voices had been optimistic. Japan issued a white paper warning that China's rise could get out of hand, and the China-bashing began. In his 2001 book, "The Coming Collapse of China," the overseas Chinese lawyer Gordon G. Chang, a freelance journalist writing for the *New York Times* and the *Asian Wall Street Journal*, said that China's prosperity was a chimera and its setback inevitable. Smith Barney, now a division of Citigroup, predicted that "five years after joining the WTO [that would have been 2006] China would see 40 million unemployed and sooner or later the fall of the government."

But not only did China successfully join the WTO; its efforts at developing foreign relations are the most vigorous in the world. Its entire economy is now tied to the international marketplace. As President Hu Jintao has said, the door to China "has been resolutely opened to the outside world."

The traffic goes in both directions. China has become the biggest manufacturer in the world; and the bigger China's share of global production becomes, the larger is its hunger for natural resources. Oil, gas, copper, zinc, wood, cotton—and the list goes on. To purchase these commodities in the world's markets, China has developed its own strategies.

China is creating a nourishing environment for its own entrepreneurs and for direct foreign investment. Since the 1980s the government has promulgated more than 500 economic laws and regulations to provide legal and other guarantees for foreign investors in China. The mainstays of these policies have been the Law on Chinese-Foreign Joint Ventures, the Law on Chinese-Foreign Cooperative Joint Ventures, the Law on Wholly Foreign-Owned Enterprises, and the related rules for their implementation. By the end of 2007, foreign investors had established 591,000 foreign-funded enterprises, and 450 of the world's top multinationals have invested in China. China has begun to institutionalize a system of intellectual property rights, to a large extent driven by its own increasing numbers of patents and other intellectual properties. China's Olympic slogan—"One World, One Dream"—signaled a desire to become an integral part of the world.

China–United States Relations

How times change! In 1978, when Deng Xiaoping was just taking charge, President Jimmy Carter was secretly negotiating to establish full diplomatic relations between the United States and a poor, even destitute China.

Thirty years later, President Barack Obama has to deal with a China whose wealth and influence are essential to salvaging the world economy.

In 1978 the United States still recognized Taiwan as "China," and its annual bilateral trade with the mainland was less than $1 billion. With concessions on both sides, Jimmy Carter and Deng Xiaoping worked out an agreement to establish full diplomatic relations. The result was announced on December 15, 1978, and America switched its recognition from Taiwan to the People's Republic of China. Secret negotiations had gone on for two years before the breakthrough came in late 1978, with the emergence of Deng as China's new leader. Today, bilateral trade is reaching almost $400 billion. And China and the United States constitute the most important bilateral relationship in the world.

"After thirty years of cooperation and friction," says Shen Dingli, director of the Center for American Studies at Fudan University, which is based in Shanghai, "Beijing and Washington have both realized that dialogue and cooperation are the only way to peace and a win-win result. Strategic dialogue mechanisms promoted by the leaders of the two countries will be further strengthened." Shen also said, "It is expected that mutual trust between China and the United States will be enhanced as the two sides deepen cooperation in dealing with the current financial crisis, and other thorny global issues. There are good reasons to believe that a steady Sino-U.S. relationship will bolster peace and prosperity in the world."

Extraordinarily, it has been many years since either China or the United States was concerned about the ideological differences of socialism and capitalism. China's leadership likes to call its market economy "socialism with Chinese characteristics." That's OK. The United States is evolving toward "socialism with American characteristics."

Strategic Economic Dialogue

On the morning of November 5, 2008, the day after the American election, President Hu Jintao congratulated Barack Obama on his victory. Hu was one of the first heads of state to do so. "China and the United

States share broad common interests and important responsibilities on a wide range of major issues concerning the well-being of humanity," Hu said in his message. "In the new historic era, I look forward to working with you to continuously strengthen dialogue and exchanges between our two countries and enhance mutual trust and cooperation with a view to taking our relationship to a new high and bringing greater bene-fits to people of our two countries and the rest of the world."

In making the announcement that he was appointing Jon Huntsman Jr. as ambassador to China, President Obama said, "I can't think of any more-important assignment than creating the kinds of bridges between our two countries that will determine the well-being not just of Ameri-cans and Chinese, but also the future of the world."

The best legacy of the Bush administration was the establishment of the Strategic Economic Dialogue (SED) which began in 2006, as a re-sult of a joint agreement by the two heads of state. It was a cabinet-level endeavor, cochaired by United States' secretary of the treasury, Henry Paulson, and his Chinese counterpart, Vice Premier Wang Qishan, meeting twice a year alternately in China and the United States.

Top officials on both sides of the SED have expressed hope that the Obama administration will continue this high-level economic dialogue between the two countries. At its last meeting in December 2008, Pre-mier Wen Jiabao told its members, "Over the past two years, the five rounds of SED talks reached 189 agreements, with forty alone during this fifth dialogue. The decision to establish the SED mechanism was indeed visionary and productive."

Though this is generally little known in the United States, there have been debates in political and economic circles about whether the SED should continue during the Obama administration. Opponents say the mechanism has failed to persuade China to appreciate its currency. But probably, China will never allow the exchange rate of its currency to be driven by any force other than its own strategies. President Hu has ex-plained the three principles of the reform of the RMB's exchange rate: "One, maintain its own initiative, based on China's development needs; two, keep things under control avoiding financial turbulence or an economic turndown; and three, carry out the reform through a gradual process considering short-term needs and long-term development interests." The SED should also induce China to open its financial sector more widely and take effective measures to ease trade imbalances.

Supporters of SED argue that it is necessary for the two economic powers to continue an open, regular dialogue. Some have even suggested the United States and China set up a Group of Two, the G2. Although there have been debates in the United States about the desirability of continuing the SED, it has never been an issue in China. From the Chinese point of view, this mechanism was established to provide both sides with a format for consultation on issues of strategic significance.

As for the increasing talk of a G2, China should "resist the tendency to believe that, with their size and wealth, only a partnership between China and the United States was needed to decide important world matters," says Huang Ping of the Chinese Academy of Social Sciences. "Once you start to go that way, how would the Japanese, Koreans, Russians, Indians, and all our neighboring nations think of you?"

China-Japan Relations

The year 2008 was the thirtieth anniversary of China's reforms and opening, and the thirtieth anniversary of America's diplomatic recognition of the People's Republic of China. It was also the thirtieth anniversary of the signing of the Sino-Japanese Peace and Friendship Treaty.

On October 22, 1978, China's new leader, Deng Xiaoping, traveled to Japan to sign the Sino-Japanese pact and to visit the country. It was also the first time since his studies and work in France that Deng had set foot inside a "capitalist" factory. An endearing incident of that visit is recorded in Wu Xiaobo's book *China Emerging*: "Deng had made a special trip to see Matsushita Electronic and also met with the owner, the 83-year-old Konosuke Matsushita. Matsushita asked Deng what he might find of interest in Japan. Deng Xiaoping replied that winters were extremely cold in China, and people had to burn briquettes to stay warm, with the result that they often fell prey to carbon monoxide poisoning. He wondered whether Japan had briquettes which did not produce carbon monoxide."

Deng was the first Chinese official to visit Japan since the founding of the People's Republic in 1949. It was symbolic that he made this one of his first foreign visits after assuming his new responsibilities. It was of course not lost on Deng that Japan was having a very successful experience in rebuilding a war-ravaged country. A closer relationship with a booming neighbor would help China in its own rebuilding through shared experience, trade, and economic development.

The last thirty years of an increasingly better relationship with Japan has vindicated Deng's early judgment and first steps not only to open China up but to bury an old hatred, and build new relationships to enable China to "join the world."

During President Hu's visit to Japan in May 2008, there were two surprises. First, he used unusually blunt language in speaking of the past: "The invasions and wars led by Japan's militarism gravely damaged the friendship between the two countries; they were a grave disaster for Chinese people and the people of Japan." At the end of his speech at the elite Waseda University in Tokyo, he said to his audience, "We lay emphasis on the idea that history should be kept firmly in mind, not because we want to carry on hatred. Instead, we should learn from history, move forward, treasure and safeguard peace, so that friendship between peoples of both countries can last for generations."

The second surprise came when Hu showed a side of his ambitions and mastery that was usually not revealed in public. In the sports hall at Waseda University, he took off his glasses and his coat and showed off his table tennis skills against two world-class players: the Japanese champion Ai Fukuhara and the Chinese woman champion Wang Nan. The spectators cheered as he slammed winning points against both; and the *South China Morning Post* tactfully suggested that the matches were a draw, and said that they memorably showed the sixty-five-year-old Hu's stamina and tough, competitive streak.

These games brought back memories of the "Ping-Pong diplomacy" of the 1970s, when an exchange of table tennis players helped thaw the icy relationship between Beijing and Washington.

The China–Japan–South Korea Summit

An overall shift in the early twenty-first century is the transfer of economic importance from West to East. As a consequence the East, just like the West, will make its own decisions and build its own partnerships. The East will understand itself to be an equal of the West. This shift will change the global political and economic balance, and result in a new understanding of the roles of the West and the East. The East is claiming its position in the world with increasing self-confidence.

This shift was underlined on December 13, 2008, in Fukuoka, Japan, when South Korea, China, and Japan, which together account for 75 percent of the East Asian economy, held the first-ever tripartite summit. It is surely of great significance that the three countries put aside their historical disputes to form this partnership.

The representatives of the three countries had met often on the sidelines of meetings held by the Association of Southeast Asian Nations (ASEAN) but had never before held a separate summit away from ASEAN. The leaders representing the three countries were the Chinese premier, Wen Jiabao; the Japanese prime minister, Tara Aso; and the South Korean president, Lee Myungbak, who had called for the meeting of the leaders in October to discuss the global financial and economic crisis.

In a meeting with Wen before the summit, Lee said that the $26.3 billion currency swap between the central banks of China and South Korea was an important step toward addressing the financial crisis. This was the first such deal China had signed with a foreign central bank. The three countries vowed to encourage domestic demand, infrastructure projects, and a regional web of trilateral currency swaps, while trying to avoid imposing new barriers on investment or trade for a year.

In a joint statement, the three leaders said they expected Asia to "play a role at the center of world economic growth to reverse the downward trend of the world economy." The trilateral summit will become an annual event to strengthen cooperation.

The China–African Connection

As we have written in other chapters, China thinks in huge dimensions with regard to time and accomplishments. There is a lot of speculating about the Chinese-African connection, almost all of it from a western perspective.

The only way to understand China is to find out what China has in mind and not what the West imagines China has in mind.

In many cases, China does not hold back with its plans. According to Premier Wen Jiabao, Africa will be China's biggest trading partner by 2010. By the end of 2008 the China Africa Fund had invested about $400 million in twenty projects, and it will expand its investment from a total of $2 billion to $5 billion. By 2007 trade between China and Africa totaled $62 billion. To alleviate Africa's food shortage, China will establish fourteen agricultural technology demonstration centers, beginning the construction at the end of 2009.

President Hu Jintao's affinity for Africa began when he went there in 1999 as vice president. In the last few years no other foreign politicians have visited Africa as often as Hu Jintao and Wen Jiabao. In 2006, at the Beijing Summit of the China-African Cooperation Forum, President Hu announced China's eight-measure African policy. It includes assistance to Africa; preferential loans and credit; the building of a conference center for the African Union; the canceling of debts; further opening of China's markets to Africa; the establishment of trade and economic zones; and the training of African professionals.

The West has its own interpretation of what China has in mind and is accusing China of being greedy for natural resources and of exploiting Africa. But what happened after the last western colonial power left the African continent? For most of the countries there, the most urgent tasks were fighting poverty, installing basic services, and establishing security for the people. How much has the West contributed to helping Africa realize even these basic goals?

China's trade policy has not involved judging African governments and lecturing them about their ethical standards, their observance of human rights, and environmental considerations. And, yes, that forbearance may well be influenced by China's own dislike of being lectured.

As part of its trade negotiations, China offers to help African countries build infrastructure, in return for lucrative exclusive contracts for natural resources, which stretch many years into the future. Although in many cases the moral judgments of the West are justified, the question remains whether the western approach, which has included large amounts of aid, rather than trade, has made a more important impact on Africa than the Chinese strategy of building streets, canals, power plants, and railroads.

China can offer most products and services much more cheaply than western suppliers while offering the same standards of quality. Despite the prevalent corruption in many African countries, many Africans claim that what matters most is the improvement of social conditions. Without infrastructure, there will be little economic progress; and without economic improvements, there will be little social progress. A different case is of course Darfur, where the issue is not corruption but systematic pillaging, rape, and murder inflicted on a portion of Sudan's population. In this area, China has proved to be a frustrating ally for the West, because China steadfastly holds to its policy of not interfering in other countries' internal affairs. Instead, its policy is to provide a role model for what Africa can do.

Three decades ago, China's economy was as low as Malawi's; but it catapulted itself out of the mud and into the twenty-first century. Deng Xiaoping, when the president of Ghana visited China in 1985, said modestly, "Please don't copy our model. If there is any experience on our part, it is to formulate policies in the light of one's own national conditions." That continues to be China's position on interference in the affairs of other countries.

The Chinese Method

In 2008 the World Bank issued a report titled *Building Bridges: China's Growing Role as Infrastructure Financier for Sub-Saharan Africa.* In the report Obiageli Katryn Ezekwesili, the bank's vice president for the Africa region and formerly Nigeria's education minister, said, "Today, China's growing infrastructure commitments in Africa are helping to address the huge infrastructure deficit of the continent. The growing South-South cooperation, driven by strong economic complementarities between China and Africa, is a win-win model."

Take Angola. Its illiteracy rate is 60 percent; 70 percent of its people live in absolute poverty; it has experienced thirty years of civil conflict during the same period that China has spent building up a modern country. Angolans have "unlearned" how to work, whereas the Chinese are eager to add their share in creating modest wealth. In January 2009 China's minister of trade, Chen Deming, announced that Angola had become China's largest trading partner in Africa, with bilateral trade volume hitting an all-time high of $25.3 billion in 2008. To help Angola's economy the Chinese government has exempted more than 67 million RMB ($9.8 million) in debts Angola owed to China and has given Angola favorable duty-free treatment for more than 450 categories of products.

It is only natural for China to join the West in playing an increasingly large role in global relations. The declining influence of westerners in the Middle East, central Africa, and South America is in stark contrast to China's increasing influence and its willingness to jump in wherever the IMF or the World Bank refuses to go. The World Bank reported that in 2001 China's investment in Africa was less than $475 million, but that it rose to $4.5 billion in 2006 and to $7 billion in 2007. On the other hand, at the Group of Eight Summit held in Britain in 2005, Africa was promised economic aid of $25 billion before 2010, but as the World Bank's report of 2008 noted, only 14 percent of the commitment had been fulfilled.

Despite the increase in China's imports, only 14 percent of Africa's oil goes to China; 40 percent goes to the United States and 17 percent to Europe. China has invested only $10 billion in the oil fields of Africa, whereas western companies have invested $168 billion. Westerners who claim that China is taking advantage of Africa's natural resources might want to think again about who is currently gaining the most from Africa.

The 2006 Sino-African summit in Beijing emphasized that any partnership should be of mutual benefit. Hu promised to reduce or write off debt owed by African countries. His remarks were immediately met by suspicion and disbelief. Will China, like the West, default on or reduce its promised aid to Africa? Only time will tell, but so far China has delivered.

Africa is not the only region of the world to move closer to China than the West might like. Russia proclaimed 2007 the "Year of China." Sino-Russian military cooperation has advanced steadily. Trade structure has improved remarkably, investment on both sides is expanding steadily, and the range of cooperation has widened. There is hardly a place on earth where China does not leave its footprints.

Not to Overlook Latin America

Trade between China and Latin America has increased from $8.3 billion in 1999 to more than $102 billion in 2007. In November 2008, when President Hu Jintao visited Peru, he called for a new era of cooperation in Latin America. He said that the world's largest developing country and the major developing region should unite more closely.

During Hu's visit the Chinese Ministry of Education announced that it would provide more scholarships to students from Latin America. In 2007, a total of 2,930 students from Latin America studied in China, including 652 on Chinese government scholarships.

To spread Chinese culture, seventeen Confucius Institutes have been established in eight Latin American countries: five in Mexico (the first of these institutes was established in Mexico City in 2006); three in Peru; two each in Colombia, Chile, and Brazil; and one each in Argentina, Cuba, and Costa Rica.

China's trade with Latin America has grown dramatically since the year 2000, reaching a record of more than $140 billion in 2008, 40 percent higher than in 2007. It is now the region's second largest trading partner, after the United States. China replaced the United States as Brazil's top trade partner as of April 2009. As in Africa, China is expanding its lending to Latin America as it pursues long-term access to commodities and natural recourses.

In November 2008, Beijing published its first policy paper on Latin America, outlining its intention to strengthen "comprehensive cooperation" in the region in politics, economics, and culture, as well as peace, security, and judicial affairs. China's goals, the paper said, were to promote mutual respect and trust, achieve win–win results, and boost common progress.

Expansion through Education

China has been rapidly developing active cooperation and exchanges in education with the rest of the world. No other country has more people studying abroad than China. Since 1979, more than 1 million Chinese have studied in more than 100 countries, and nearly 300,000 have returned home after finishing their studies. The number of foreign students in China has also increased rapidly. Since 1979, more than 1 million students from 188 countries have studied at 544 Chinese universities.

Learning the Chinese language has become a popular pursuit around the world. Since 2004, China has opened 226 not-for-profit Confucius Institutes in sixty-four countries around the world, with the aim of spreading the Chinese language and culture. More than 40 million people abroad are studying Chinese at some level. And more than 8,000 schools in nearly 100 countries have included the Chinese language in their curricula.

Greater efforts will be going into attracting outstanding overseas talent to work in China. The Ministry of Education has a talent development office; its director, Lu Yugang, says, "High-level talents with overseas education and work experience will greatly strengthen China's all-round development, especially as the country is implementing its strategy of invigorating the nation through science, technology, and education."

One of the ministry's programs is targeting scholars with doctoral degrees and outstanding records. Begun in 1996, the program has funded more than 12,000 individuals and 200 groups of scholars and researchers to serve the country on short-term visits. One of the participants is now China's minister of science and technology, Wan Gang. Wan was part of a German automobile research team that got financial support from the program in the late 1990s. Wan returned to China in 2000 and became president of Tongji University in Shanghai in 2004. He was named a minister in 2008, one of two members of China's ministerial cabinet who are not members of the Communist Party.

Someone we know, Rao Zihe, was a participant in another of the Ministry of Education's programs—the Changjang Scholars Program. Rao returned to work in China in 1996, after ten years overseas. "I gave up my research work at Oxford University and came back to China, attracted by the promising outlook of my motherland and good offers from universities." He is now president of the Nankai University in Tianjin, one of the universities that host the Naisbitt China Institute.

China is now the fifth most popular country for American students. In 2008 there were 11,064 Americans studying in China, up from 8,830 the year before. American students who study in China are increasingly picking subjects related to economics rather than culture, language, or traditional Chinese medicine, favorites of the past. More than 81,000 students from the mainland are currently studying in the United States, up 20 percent from 2007 according to the Ministry of Education.

China Is Decentralizing Faster Than Any Other Country in the World

One of the chapters in John's earlier book *Mind Set!* describes a shift from nation-states to economic domains and the twin paths of globalization and decentralization. What we have been witnessing is a globalization not of countries but of economic activities. In consequence, the economics of the future will be built in a new way.

Decentralization is an effective tool of the market economy. The more centralized and regulated an economy is, the less flexible it will be, and the less adaptable to changing market conditions. In the past decades China has proved that economic considerations overwhelm political considerations. "Economic development is the central task," Hu confirmed in his speech at the Party Congress. Only if China continues its decentralization process will it stay united as a whole.

In this regard China is well on course. As part of its decentralization, power is shifting to local provinces and companies. They are now encouraged to deal directly with companies in other countries, bypassing the central government.

In March 2009, China officially authorized its provinces—effective immediately—to approve proposals for foreign direct investment (FDI) up to $100 million. The result is that today the vast majority of new international deals are handled at the provincial level. Until this new authorization, all FDI proposals, irrespective of size, had to be ratified by the Ministry of Commerce, although many provinces had been dealing directly with international clients for some time. Such a decentralization of investment authority had been expected, but the Chinese government acted out of concern that the global economic downturn was slowing direct investment, which has been one of the main engines of China's economic growth.

The *China Daily* quoted a spokesperson for the European Union Chamber of Commerce in China as saying, "We welcome the policy as it relaxes and decentralizes the regulation of foreign investment activity in China and provides a level playing field for all businesses. It is a strong encouragement to potential foreign investors." And they keep coming.

Investments go in both directions. By the end of 2007, Chinese businesses had invested in more than 10,000 enterprises overseas, with an overall value of $118 billion. In 2008, overseas direct investment, not counting financial institutions, was more than $40 billion, an increase of 63 percent over 2007. In March 2009, the Chinese Ministry of

Commerce simplified its approval procedures to encourage Chinese businesses to invest overseas.

During 2008, the president of the China-Britain Trade Association and a former mayor of London, Granville White, led a delegation to Dalian to promote cooperation between it and the United Kingdom in finance and other areas. As the *Dalian Daily* reported, the British prime minister Gordon Brown and White traveled to Dalian to encourage British financial firms to set up offices in Dalian; Brown and White also wanted to encourage British companies to help Dalian build a regional financial center.

Financial markets have been opened gradually. Under the Qualified Foreign Institution Investors (QFII) program foreign companies are authorized to invest in mainland stock markets, from a minimum of $50 million up to a maximum of $800 million. The system allows such institutions to invest in local currency and use the specific accounts to invest in local securities markets. The return on the investment, the dividend, and the capital gain can be legally exchanged into foreign currency and repatriated. The total investment grew from $7.145 billion in 2006 to $9.545 billion in 2007.

In late January 2008, the government of the city of Wuxi and Japan's Mizuho Corporate Bank signed an agreement in Tokyo that created the first outsourcing project for financial services. As the *Wuxi Daily* reported, part of the outsourcing arrangement is the first data center of a foreign bank located in Jiangsu province. The project is the beginning of financial international outsourcing in Wuxi.

Connected or Disconnected?

For individuals, the most effective tool for joining the world is the Internet, and this is true of the Chinese as much as of anyone else. There is much talk about the Chinese government's control of the Internet. And here again the West measures the Chinese model against its own beliefs and perceptions, which—although not necessarily either good or bad—lead to different results regarding how the Chinese feel about such control.

The Pew Research Center, a well-respected nonprofit, nonpartisan institution located in Washington, D.C., published a study on the social impact of the Internet. The results regarding China were headed "Few in China Complain about Internet Control."

"Most Americans and Europeans assume that China's Internet users are both aware of and unhappy about their government's oversight and control of the Internet. But in the new survey, most Chinese say they approve of Internet control and management, especially when it comes from their government," according to the Pew study.

As reported in the West, the Chinese Internet community sometimes appears to be an ocean of bloggers with only one thing in mind: to bring down the Chinese government. But like most American bloggers, most Chinese bloggers write about less earthshaking matters: their families, their hobbies, their jobs, gossip, and personal thoughts.

Maybe the Chinese government would have a heavier hand in Internet content, if it could. And if such intervention reduced the large presence of pornography, including child pornography, it would not in every regard be a loss for mankind. The Chinese government feels it has to protect its citizens from anything "that damages China's unity and sovereignty; harms ethnic solidarity; promotes superstition; portrays violence, pornography, gambling, and terrorism; violates privacy; damages China's culture or traditions."

A serious worry in China is another effect the Internet can have on children. Many stories in China's media warn about how time-consuming the Internet is. Given that most Chinese regard education as the indispensable key to a better life, addiction to any medium is seen as disastrous. China's "six-pocket little emperors" (two parents and four grandparents) are the pride and hope of their families. Time spent at the computer surfing the Net would not be seen as time spent valuably.

With the closer balance between top-down and bottom-up forces, we believe that censorship of Web sites and blogs will continue to decrease, as will the blocking of articles critical of the government. As with liberation and opening up in other fields, China will decide on its own timetable.

Actually, most of the concerns about the Internet are in westerners' heads. "Alongside outside criticism and internal pressure for liberalization, other evidence suggests that many Chinese citizens do not share Western views of the Internet. When asked who should be responsible for controlling or managing the Internet, more Chinese identified the government, 85 percent, than any other entity."

The survey findings discussed here, drawn from a broad-based sample of urban Chinese Internet users and nonusers alike, indicate a degree of comfort and even approval of the notion that the government authorities should control and manage the content available on the Internet.

The survey concludes that "despite negative press and despite anxieties and fears about dangers lurking online, Chinese users appreciate the Internet for unprecedented opportunities to play and be entertained with cheap games and movies, and to be in touch via blogs and discussion boards with friends about movie stars and bands. Nonusers, especially young people, pick up cues that they will be left behind if they don't get online."

China in the World and the World in China

Whatever one's view of Internet access, what is clear is that the Chinese have more access to information than ever before.

The balance now is between having the Chinese join the world and keeping the world out of China.

The first technology to monitor Internet usage of course came not from China but from the United States, and many blamed Cisco for having supported the repression and crudeness of the Chinese government by selling mirroring routers to China. Cisco said it also sold to any other organization that needed to monitor. Many U.S. organizations, such as libraries and schools, use similar blocking methods to prevent users from visiting gambling, pornography, or hate speech sites. But whatever favor Cisco did for the Chinese government several years ago by selling it the technology that the "Great Firewall" is based on, the Chinese now can buy routers from many sources, including the homegrown Huawei.

The digital divide between urban and rural areas also has narrowed. There are now 74 million rural Internet users, up 70 percent from the previous year. At least 94 percent of them have broadband, according to government figures.

But although China has its own approach to the Internet, it is well aware that "the Internet is new engine powering China's economic and social development," and that "international cooperation is essential for promoting the health and orderly development of the Internet industry because of its global nature." These remarks were made by Cai Ming-zhao, the vice president of the State Council Information Office, in a keynote speech at the Second U.S.-China Internet Industry Forum in Beijing in November 2008. In another speech, Microsoft's chief research and strategy officer, Craig Mundie, said that a communication mechanism based on mutual trust and close cooperation is critical to innovative applications, and to ensure the security of electronic transactions and combat online crime.

Reporting on this forum in *China Daily*, Zhou Yan said that China's online population is growing at an average of 240,000 a day and might reach 500 million in three to four years, according to official figures. And Hu Qiheng, chairman of the Internet Society of China, said that the biggest concerns regarding China's Internet development include the security of users' information, the transmission of illegal and obscene information, piracy, spam, and encroachment on privacy.

Whenever we use the Internet we become part of a network. This network cannot be limited ideologically or geographically. The moment you enter, you become part of the global Internet community. To be connected very much matches Chinese thinking. Village life in China is still a very collective way of life. Perhaps some of the government's worries about blogs and critical sites are rooted in this connectedness of the Chinese, which could turn a snowball into an avalanche.

When China entered the global stage as a serious player, the established actors assigned it a supporting role. But the new actor was too good a performer to remain on the sidelines. It made its way into the limelight and not only joined the act, but changed the allocation of roles and the setting of the stage.

The world's stage in the second half of the twentieth century was dominated by two superpowers: the United States and the Soviet Union. And the roles they played were as opponents. When the Soviet Union broke up into its separate parts, America became the only superpower, economically and militarily. The United States sets the standard against which other nations compare themselves: the European Union, which neither is one economy nor speaks in one language or one voice; and China, the only challenger on the horizon. In the years ahead, the most fascinating bilateral relationship by far will be that of China and the United States.

The United States is a $14 trillion economy. The GDPs of Japan, China, and Germany are all within the $4 trillion to $5 trillion range. China had just passed Germany to become the number three GDP in the world and is likely to pass Japan soon to become number two. Germany and Japan will stay at the $4 trillion to $5 trillion level without noticeable growth, and even with some shrinkage, for the foreseeable future. Both the United States and China will continue growing, but China will grow at a much faster rate. China and the United States will be the world's two largest economies, leaving all others a considerable distance behind.

For the first time in history, the two most powerful nations will be not opponents but partners in an economically interdependent world. The European Union, ASEAN, NAFTA, the G8, the G20, and the great gains in world trade are all building blocks of a single, integrated economy for the whole world. At the end of the twentieth century, China was joining the world. In the twenty-first century, China can become its most important player.

Pillar 7

Freedom and Fairness

This pillar is about the struggle to balance what is economically possible with what is socially desirable, the freedom for the few to become financially successful with the need of the many for social services.

The debate between socialists and capitalists has always been about freedom and fairness. Do we choose a system where all are equally treated so that no one gets too far ahead of others? Or do we choose freedom for individuals who through their talents and hard work gain levels of achievements far above others? The whole world wrestles with these considerations.

Very early on, in the cold days of January 1978, Beijing's people had a first glimpse of a new dawn. *Xinhua News* wrote, "A hint of sun is finally breaking through the coldness, bringing a small measure of warmth to people's lives. In this huge city, with its crowded apartments, its narrow checkerboard streets, the masses of people can begin to feel some relief." Gradually, as we wrote in the preceding chapters, emancipating minds, seeking the truth from facts, and widening the frames in which people could operate improved life in China.

There was no such a blatant announcement as "To get rich is glorious," which the western media keep citing as Deng Xiaoping's approval of further steps toward the creation of wealth. In fact, Deng never said this at all, let alone with the implied intention. What he really said, in an interview on western television in 1986, was, "To get rich is no sin." And then he continued, "What we mean by getting rich is different from what you mean. Wealth in a socialist society belongs to the people. To get rich in a socialist society means prosperity for the entire people. The principles of socialism are: first, development of production; and second, common prosperity. We permit some people and some regions to become prosperous first, for the purpose of achieving common prosperity faster. That is why our policy will not lead to polarization, to a situation where the rich get richer while the poor get poorer."

What is socially desirable is not always practically realizable.

Closing the gap between rich and poor while allowing individual talent to be rewarded has always been as much socially desirable as practically unrealizable. During the twentieth century there was a lot of discussion of policies between capitalist countries emphasizing freedom and socialist countries emphasizing fairness. China is now developing its own system of dealing with the limits of freedom and the limits of fairness. The government's stated overarching goal is to eliminate abject poverty and develop a society in which middle-income households are the majority by 2020. President Hu Jintao at the Congress of 2007: "We need to deepen the reform of the income distribution system and increase the income of both urban and rural residents."

China started from a very low base and has come very far, but it still ranks quite low internationally. When its GDP is divided by its 1.3 billion population, the per capita GDP is only $3,315. This can be compared with other figures for per capita ADP, according to the IMF in 2008: United States, $46,859; Germany, $44,660; Japan, $38,559; India, $1,016.

Of course when GDP is averaged out, it loses all meaning. China is at different stages of economic development simultaneously. Provinces in the south and eastern coastal areas with prosperous cities are well developed; but provinces and cities in the west, northeast, and central regions are way behind. China of course is not alone in having such geographical economic disparities, and they contribute to making per capita GDP difficult to interpret.

Social Security—The Basics

It is not easy for China to catch up with advanced countries at its current level of social security, which can guarantee only basic living standards for its citizens. China has to establish pension insurance that maintains a moderate living standard for workers after retirement, unemployment insurance that maintains subsistence for workers without jobs, and medical insurance that covers ordinary demands.

President Hu: "We must do our best to ensure that all our people enjoy their rights to education, employment, medical and old-age care, and housing, so as to build a harmonious society." Social harmony for the Chinese is not only morally desirable, but essential to the sustainability of the system. Top-down and bottom-up adjustments and the alignment of central and local governments allow long-term extensive planning and support efforts to create a functioning, effective system.

- The Qingdao Development Zone has fifteen indicators of comprehensive protection involving social assistance, social welfare, and social security. There has been a substantial increase in social assistance to meet the minimal needs of the urban and rural areas and an increase in housing maintenance subsidies; this zone also has a new rural cooperative medical care system, new medical aid standards for the seriously ill, and new minimal-needs and minimal-assurance student grants. The *Qingdao Daily* has identified the city as the first "to achieve really seamless coverage of the social security system."

  By the end of 2007, 201 million people had participated in basic old-age insurance, 220 million in medical insurance, and 116 million in unemployment insurance; and almost all provinces and regions have set up a basic rural social security system. In rural areas without such a system, 5.6 million poor people receive regular subsidies from local governments. The national programs are supplemented by bottom-up programs.

  In an effort to at least narrow the gap between the winners and losers, a system to provide a basic minimum standard of living has been established in all China's cities and counties, for residents with family per capita income below the local standard. In 2007, 22.71 million urban residents were receiving such support, and all low-income people meeting the requirements are covered by insurance. The system is now being extending to many rural areas. As so often in China, local governments supplement national programs. Many start on a very small scale.

- The government of Wuxi city, whose administration spreads over 4,787 square kilometers, has established a "living security standard in its Binhu District." This means that the lowest living security standard of rural areas is to be the same as that of urban areas, with any shortfall made up by the local government. *Wuxi Daily* said that this was the first district to establish such a standard in the whole city.

- Huairou district is a municipality of the administration in Beijing. It has an area of more than 2,000 square kilometers, twelve cities, two rural communities, and 287 villages, and includes more than 90 percent of Beijing's mountain area, where more than 100 households grow chestnuts. Because workers and farmers often fall from the trees when harvesting the chestnuts, all are now covered by personal injury insurance.

- In Tiekuangyu, another village of Beijing Huairou district, more than 170 villagers receive "personal accident insurance" before starting a job. The insurance costs only 130 RMB ($19) per year; 90 percent of any personal accident loss can be written off.

Since the 1990s, China has actively pursued reforms in its old age, unemployment, and medical insurance systems. Now, quite separate from enterprises and institutions, a social security system managed by the government is taking shape; this system integrates old age, unemployment, and medical policies, as well as minimum living standards. It includes increased pensions for retired personnel, a new medical insurance system for urban residents, an advancement of the rural basic social pension insurance system, and the establishment of a subsidy for people seventy years old and older, as part of a "centenarians' living subsidy system."

The one-child policy leaves an increasing number of old people without the once solid social network of an extended family. An "empty nest" initiative for elderly people who do not live with their children or have no children has been established in the Huaibei community, in Xuanwu district; these elders are offered free dining paid for by the local government, at designated restaurants. A "Service Circle" issues cards that can be used for three free meals a day in certain restaurants.

As *China Daily* reported in February 2009, China has now built a network of nearly 700 million social insurance personal accounts. And "people have their say" about the new social security system; these comments add up to "more extensive, less costly, and fewer restrictions," as bottom-up demands for China's newly drafted social welfare system.

Some efforts have gone the wrong way. Several social insurance scandals have been detected and revealed to the public. Shanghai's former party chief Chen Liangyu was removed from his post and sentenced to eighteen years in prison after being linked to a scandal regarding a social insurance fund involving 3.7 billion RMB ($542 million). President Hu said, "We must hold up integrity and combat corruption." Despite all its efforts, China has its own Madoffs.

The Chinese government has proposed that by 2020 it will have built a basic social security system for urban and rural residents. With the new and comprehensive law, China aims to regulate its social security system and safeguard the funds. Since China has about one-fifth of the world's population, this will also constitute the world's largest social security system.

Health and Medical Care—The Basics

In 1978 China spent 11.5 billion RMB, about ten RMB ($1.60) per capita or 3.04 percent of the GDP, on health care. When reforms began, health care started to improve slowly; but it took until 1992 before China changed its health care system to suit the needs of the people and the market economy. Since 1984, China has established several policies concerning social welfare, but various regulations sometimes overlap and affect social insurance on the whole, leaving the government unable to cover all citizens.

The dramatic case of a little boy whose life was in danger because of a lack of money and insurance was reported in *China Daily* on February 19, 2009. The story was most probably reported because China's premier, Wen Jiabao, got involved, and especially because he solved the problem. Nevertheless, a single case can raise awareness of a problem much more effectively than even the most accurate statistics.

It happened at the Tianjin train station, one end of the new rapid Beijing-Tianjin service (which achieves a speed of 350 kilometers, or more than 200 miles, per hour, shortening the travel time to only thirty minutes). The parents of the boy were waiting for a train to take them home to Hebei province. There had been no way to finance further treatment for their son's aggressive leukemia at the Blood Research Center in Tianjing.

The boy had the good fortune to be in the train station at the same time as Premier Wen Jiabao, who was returning to Beijing. Wen, a very popular leader, was applauded by the crowd and started to walk around shaking hands. When he saw the mother with her son sleeping in her arms, Wen asked her where they were going, and so he learned of their story.

He took the mother's hand and said, "Come to Beijing and I will make arrangements for your boy's treatment." On Wen's instruction the boy was sent to Beijing's Pediatric Hospital, where the doctors promised to do everything to save his life.

Networks for medical treatment, disease prevention, and health care have taken shape at county, township, and village levels. The health of urban and rural residents has been greatly improved; the average life expectancy is now seventy-three years, close to that of intermediate developed countries. "Prevention first" is one of the important principles in all health care in China.

- Changchun, one of the most important industrial cities in northern China, is moving to provide access to private doctors and develop a health file for each of its millions of residents by 2010. In order to realize this goal, the municipal government has provided funds for hygiene service centers in forty-six communities in the city. The *Urban Evening* reported that 70 percent of the residents in Changchun already had their own health files and a private doctor at the beginning of 2009, so the program is well under way.

A new rural cooperative medical system began in 2003. It focuses on health insurance for major illnesses and is based on three kinds of support: payment from the individual, support from the collective, and subsidies from the government. By 2007, about 700 million people were covered through this new system, and the goal is to have everybody covered by 2010.

- The *Henan Daily* reported that since February 1, 2008, farmers in Henan province, part of the autonomous prefecture of Huanguen, who participate in a new-type rural cooperative medical plan have used one card to see a doctor at any hospital in the province. This is the first such program in China.

- Shanxi province has established a direct report system called "Unexpected Public Health Affairs," a network for covering all counties in the province. Already, 131 disease-control agencies and 594 other medical institutions in Shanxi province are reporting at the provincial, city, and county levels. Information, monitoring, and systematic precautions for unexpected public health situations have improved greatly. More than 700 "Network Direct Report" institutions have begun operating. The largest concern, of course, is infectious diseases.

- *Beijing Daily* reported that, to lead communities and families in comprehensive prevention and treatment of chronic diseases,

Beijing started the "family health scheme" in 2007. More people are developing high blood pressure, diabetes, coronary heart disease, and other chronic disorders. Initially 1,000 family members who had been through professional training became active in the 126 communities of Dongcheng district to popularize this new health scheme.

Although by 2007 the number of general hospitals had grown to 29,852 and spending had reached $8.6 billion, the Chinese kept criticizing their health care system. Public complaints about medical fees, inaccessibility of medical services, poor doctor-patient relations, and low medical insurance coverage have risen dramatically, even though large cities like Beijing, Shanghai, Tianjin, and Chongqing have built hospitals specializing in cancer, cardiovascular disorders, ophthalmology, dentistry, and infectious diseases. Medium-size cities throughout China have also added general and specialized hospitals with modern facilities.

At the beginning of 2009 the government announced its long-awaited health care reform plan, pledging to spend $124 billion in the following three years to provide accessible and affordable health care to the country's 1.3 billion people. The government said that it will build hospitals and improve medical services at the county level and in remote areas, and expedite the reform of state-run hospitals, strengthening their administration, operation, and supervision. It will also regulate the drug system, which is considered a major source of corruption in the medical sector. The new plan provides for an expansion of the medical insurance network to cover 90 percent of the population. The aim of the reform is to make the government bear most of the medical expenses of its people by 2011.

Traditional Chinese Medicine

Some ten years ago, when John was meeting with China's minister of health, Chen Minzhang, he asked how much traditional Chinese medicine and how much western medicine was practiced in China. The minister answered, "About half and half. We tend to use western medicine for diagnosis and Chinese medicine for treatment."

Compared with western medicine, traditional Chinese medicine (abbreviated TCM in headlines in the Chinese press) has independent theories and diagnostic methods, including frequent pulse taking, applying acupuncture, and using herbal medicine as its main treatment. Today China has more than 3,000 hospitals using TCM; these have more than 300,000 hospital beds and are staffed with more than 500,000 practicing doctors and their assistants; 167 hospitals offer combined treatment.

In China's cities, 90 percent of community medical centers offer traditional medicines, about 70 percent of counties have TCM hospitals, 75 percent of township hospitals have TCM departments, and 40 percent of village doctors treat patients with traditional medicine or integrate it with western medicine. Western medicine is practiced throughout China and available through relatively high-level clinical treatment.

In China today medical professionals use both TCM and western medicine, particularly to diagnose and cure difficult and complicated cases. In order to find more optimal ways for such integration, the government has provided impressive support in building twenty-seven specialized departments and eleven hospitals, all providing combined treatment.

It should be noted that, according to statistics published in *People's Daily* in April 2009, China has about 5.5 million doctors trained in western medicine, while it has only 400,000 doctors trained in TCM, 20 percent fewer than half a century ago. Currently, most TCM doctors are above age fifty, and the number of young people studying TCM is getting smaller and smaller.

The Future of Migrant Workers

When China's reforms and opening up started in the rural areas in 1978, collectively owned farms were reduced to individual families, freeing up some 100 million peasants from farmwork. Initially about 60 million of these farmers were given jobs in village-run enterprises, which were being created at a great rate. The flight to cities started slowly. But when more and more investments came into China for construction, factories, and mining, creating jobs that most urbanites consider too demanding and dirty, migrants began flooding into urban areas. In the first decade of the twenty-first century 250 million Chinese migrant workers left their villages for jobs in the cities: more than the whole adult population of the United States, and the largest migration in history. There is hardly any sector where migrant workers are not found.

Migrant workers in the United States are typically thought of as people coming up from Mexico to harvest crops, workers who come and go with the seasons. Similarly, though on a much smaller scale, in Europe migrant workers from Poland, Romania, and Hungary come to Austria, Germany, and Italy to harvest asparagus, potatoes, sugarcane, and grapes.

As in the West, Chinese migrant workers receive low pay, are not treated very well, and are often taken advantage of. Most of them must work overtime; some work seven days a week. But conditions are improving. Between 2005 and 2007 wages increased by about 30 percent. The prediction of an increasing shortage of uneducated workers and demographics that suggest China's workforce will begin to shrink by 2015 also drive up wages.

Much stricter laws are slowly developing workers' awareness of their rights. They have begun to dare to stand up against their bosses and against unfair and illegal practices.

- In late January 2008, *Shenzhen Zone Daily* reported on reforms by the the Shenzhen Municipal Labor Department. This department was the first to announce that arbitration fees paid for by petitioning workers had been abolished. Its policy became a national law in May. If, for example, a company is found guilty of withholding wage payments, it will be blacklisted, and so will be unable to apply for bank loans or business licenses.

A big step was taken earlier, in 2005, when the first trade union for migrants was established in the northeastern Liaoning province.

- "Trade Unions Help Migrant Workers to Survive the Crisis" was the headline of a story in *China Daily* in March 2009. The global financial crisis had led to unemployment for more than 20 million migrant workers. Action was taken. The All-China Federation of Trade Unions (ACFTU) announced an extension of aid to more than 10 million migrant workers in February 2009, strengthening vocational training, covering about 5 million workers with job training, and letting another 5 million pursue their legal rights. The ACFTU will also urge state-owned enterprises (SOEs) to shoulder more social responsibilities. Companies that close down will have to provide full, timely payment for their workers. "It is necessary to introduce migrant workers into trade unions," said Professor Wang Wei of the National School. "We should study how to organize them, increase their 'rights awareness,' and help them protect their interests actively and effectively."

- *Inner Mongolia Daily* reports efforts in the Dalate district in Inner Mongolia, where trade unions are responsible for the supervision of workers who are paid at the work site, to better prevent misappropriation of and deductions from migrant workers' wages—abuses that had been common the past. A payment system for preventing postponements of and deductions from the wages of rural migrant farmworkers has been established, and a migrant workers' payment card system has been put in place at construction sites and in factories.

  In addition, President Hu demands an "increase in transparency in factory affairs to support workers' participation in management."

The Constant Churning of Jobs

There is no way to keep an economy healthy and at the same time hold on to outdated jobs. Ice-cutters were replaced by refrigerators, coach makers by automobile manufacturers, typists by PC keyboarders, factory workers by automation technologists. As out-of-date jobs disappear, inventions and innovations create new ones. The workforce in the obsolete occupations will either make the change or be left behind. During its first three decades of reforms, China had to deal with two changes of enormous scope: the laying off a huge part of the workforce in SOEs and the migration of millions of farmers into China's cities.

Migration in China is in general seen as a path to a better way of life. Younger and better-educated people are not so much driven by poverty as they are attracted by the opportunities of the cities.

Georg Blume, who has visited migrant workers at their factories, traveled with them to their villages, and experienced their difficult legal situation, writes in his book *China Is Not an Empire of Evil*, "I have very seldom met unhappy migrant workers in China. Most of them come from practically feudal village conditions and were happy to have escaped them. They were proud of the little money they earned, because their parents made much less as farmers." Blume says western moralists do not want to admit that "most of the Chinese are living a much freer life with more dignity than they did several years ago."

Nevertheless, there are winners and losers. A story of a migrant worker who saw himself stuck in the dark side of life was published in *China Daily* in February 2009, headed "When Life Passes You By."

Luo Lian was a migrant worker who had left his work at a furniture factory in Foshan—in Guangdong province in the south of China—to visit his parents for the traditional mid-autumn festival. He did not arrive and has not been seen since. All that is left of him is a note his brother found in his dormitory: "I will work and work for my entire life. But I see no hope of success. I feel so exhausted and I've lost my direction in life. I don't have a career. I have nothing to support my parents. Can I be more miserable?"

Luo's supervisor at the factory portrayed him as neither diligent nor intelligent; his colleagues described him as tight-lipped and withdrawn.

Luo's story has refueled discussions of the plight of migrant groups. Many people expressed sympathy for him; others dismissed him as irresponsible and unrealistic. The columnist Xu Zhiyuan thinks that Luo's anguish is typical of thousands of young migrants working in the Pearl River delta. Migrant workers such as Luo feel they contribute as much to progress as urbanites but are treated as second-class citizens.

Problems are undeniable, but China has become more and more attentive to migrants' needs and problems, and many towns, cities, and provinces have been responding to the plight of migrants, offering training and supporting self-employment.

Henan's provincial government has taken action in several directions. It offers subsidies for vocational training in skills that range from welding to computers, and it encourages migrant workers to start their own businesses. The government has earmarked 800 million RMB, about $90 million, to support the development of small and middle-size enterprises in Henan.

- *Jiujiang Daily* reports a wave of migrant workers returning to Lushan district to set up businesses. The district government has established a service center for all aspiring entrepreneurs, to provide policy, advice, training in business skills, and microcredit.

- In Jiangsu province, Donghai county has granted a three-year tax break to returning migrant workers, and their tax payments for the following five years will be cut in half. During the first half of 2008, more than 20,000 migrant workers returned to Donghai county and established 13,000 businesses in silicon processing, agriculture, building materials, and machinery.

Entrepreneurial initiatives are a good way to start absorbing a surplus of rural labor and to contribute to the general economy. The first step often is to start small primary processing factories for agricultural products. But Hui Guojun, a town village head, said, "Planting vegetables alone won't bring much wealth to us. We need to promote the processing industry and big farms so that more people will be willing to stay." This development is gaining momentum.

To close the gap between China's east and west, the government launched a campaign called "Develop the West" in 2000. Western China, bordered by more than ten countries, is rich in land resources and mineral reserves, and many believe that it will become the next golden area, following the development of eastern China's coastal areas. By the end of 2007, more than 3,000 enterprises with foreign investments were founded in western areas in logistics, IT, commerce, finance, security, and trade.

For decades, migrant workers moved to where the factories were, but now some big Chinese companies are moving to where the migrant workers live. The owner of the sportswear giant Li Ning, who became famous as a gymnast and later carried—better, floated—the Olympic torch into the Bird's Nest, lighting the Olympic flame 150 feet above the ground, made an investment of 3.2 billion RMB ($470 million) in a manufacturing and distribution center in the city of Jingmen, in central China, in 2009, creating 20,000 to 30,000 new jobs for migrants. Baron Davis of the Los Angeles Clippers is the latest of NBA elite players to be signed to help in the marketing of Li Ning shoes.

The workforce that Li Ning's facilities will need almost equals the 30,000 migrant workers who returned to Jingmen during the economic slowdown. "Migrant workers who return home to work for Li Ning's manufacturing center will be able to purchase apartments from the government at a discount," Deputy Mayor Zhou Songqing told *China Daily*. "What's more, they will be entitled to the same medical benefits as the residents of the city. Their children will also be able to go to normal school like all other children." Such initiatives for fairness are being created bottom-up all over China.

- Guangdong's skilled migrant workers have been offered low-cost housing and free education for their children as part of a series of measures to help them counter the effects of the global financial crisis.

- Hangzhou city built a total of 100,000 square meters (nearly 120,000 square yards) of apartments for migrant workers during

2008, with a monthly rent as low as 300 RMB ($44) for an apartment of forty to fifty square meters. The apartment complexes will have libraries, community rooms, and other facilities to meet the workers' leisure and cultural needs.

Still a Class Society?

Fairness begins with equal opportunities in education. The national college entrance examination, reinstated in 1977, is one of the fairest ways to give many Chinese a chance to change their fate. The exam is held nationwide every summer and it is open to everyone, and if you fail you can always try again. Age restrictions were removed in 2001, and in 2008 Chinese newspapers ran a story about a seventy-nine-year-old man who was taking the exam for the eighth time.

Although anyone can take the national exam, Chinese from rural areas are still tied to the countryside by a residence-based population-opportioning system that issues identity cards called *hukou* to residents. "The existing *hukou* 'permanent resident permit' system, which impedes free human movement and discriminates against people as either rural and urban, is not based on a fair and just model, " *China Daily* wrote in an editorial on February 25, 2009. "The *hukou* system restricts free flow of the population within their country and has caused countless heartbreak since its adoption more than 50 years ago. People without *hukou* often are treated like second class citizens in cities where they have worked and paid taxes for years."

Hukou—identity cards—are issued in the town or city where a person is born. The *hukou* system prevents people from rural areas from enjoying benefits such as insurance, housing, and education that are provided to the local urban population. Making a living in another city and paying for all the services that locals enjoy free is one reason most migrant workers leave their children back in their hometowns with the grandparents. But the education system is of a much lower quality in rural areas than in the coastal areas, so it is harder for migrant children to move up the social ladder.

President Hu addressed the problem in his speech in 2007: "We must ensure that children from poor families and rural migrant workers in cities enjoy [the same] access to compulsory education as other children."

The government of Shanghai made a first step toward equal availability of education, although many think this was too small a step. It announced five requirements for getting a *hukou*: holding a local residency permit for seven years, participating in the city's social security system, paying taxes, having a mid-level professional title, and violating neither the family planning law (the one-child policy) nor other laws. Although this was only a minimal step, it has sent a signal that the long-standing problem should be addressed at all levels. Other measurers followed.

- In January 2008 the Pudong district of Shanghai announced the first private schools for children of migrant workers, starting with four schools and 3,900 students. The migrant children are provided with the same subsidies as Shanghai students, and with teachers of the same quality.

- More than 93,000 children of migrant workers now attend public primary and secondary schools under a program of free compulsory education in Dalian. In recent years, Dalian city has consistently required children of migrant workers to go to school; this policy is meant to promote education and to be a fair and constructive measure for a harmonious Dalian. The *Dalian Daily* reports that children of migrant workers attending public school account for 17.3 percent of all students in 2008, compared with 3.2 percent the previous year.

- All unemployed men in Fengtai district in the Beijing area can take unlimited, free training in vocational skills; and all the costs are paid by the government. The yearly cost is about 3.3 million RMB ($484,000), according to the *Beijing Daily*.

Learning Networks

An unquestionably positive use of the Internet is to connect China's rural population to an education network equal in quality to that for urban students. President Hu in 2007: "Distant learning and continuing education will be promoted to make ours a new society in which every citizen is committed to learning and pursues lifelong learning."

During 2003–2007, central and local governments allocated 10 billion RMB ($1 billion) to implement modern distance-learning projects in rural elementary and middle schools in central and western China. Junior high schools have been equipped with computer rooms; facilities to receive satellite-transmitted teaching programs have been installed in rural elementary schools; and DVD players with complete teaching sets have been supplied to elementary teaching centers.

With 3,000 branch schools and a staff of 50,000 people, the Central Agricultural Broadcasting and TV School has grown into the world's largest distance education institute for rural areas. With the help of radio, television, satellite networks, the Internet, audiovisual materials, and other teaching methods, this school also provides farmers with training in practical technology, according to *China 2008*.

- *Yili Daily* reports that Nilek county has fully established a distance education network in sixty-three new sites. Farmers can watch television programs by satellite broadband transmission and ask questions to get help to solve their problems and exchange information.

- According to the *Guangxi Daily*, "peasant classrooms, field classrooms, and network classrooms" in the county of Xingye, Shigui village, have expanded the tea cultivation area from thirty-three acres to 885 acres, and families involved in cultivation increased from several to more than 160 households. The value of the annual output reached 5 million RMB ($730,000), and per capita income increased dramatically.

The Freest Economy in the World

The concept of "fairness" is often associated with redistribution of wealth, social programs, and charity. But such measures only ease the symptom; they do not deal with the cause. Access to education and an entrepreneurially-friendly environment are the most effective and efficient tools to fight poverty and social inequity.

It is significant that China has a model of economic freedom—the basic condition for using skills and talent for business opportunities—right in its midst: Hong Kong. Hong Kong has been named the freest economy in the world for fifteen consecutive years by the U.S. think tank Heritage Foundation. Among the ten criteria used, Hong Kong ranked first in trade freedom, financial freedom, investment freedom, and property rights.

As we wrote in the chapter on Pillar 2, Hong Kong cannot be called democratic in the western sense, and it has never had a democratic movement of any significance. Hong Kong shows how well capitalism, under the general administration of Beijing, can work for the benefit of the people. China is looking more and more like Hong Kong.

The Chinese Dream

Freedom means having an environment that allows you to achieve your goals. China keeps working on providing a nourishing environment for entrepreneurs. President Hu: "We will improve policies to encourage people to start businesses."

Under the banner of freedom to make the most of your talents and energy, many exceptional private entrepreneurs have emerged. Chen Xiaojun left his "iron rice bowl" in the financial industry in Zhejiang province to found the commercial bank Taizhou, one of the few privately held banks in China. His decision to leave a government job to start an entirely private bank broke new ground. *China Daily* wrote about him: "An emancipated mind transformed a loan clerk at a rural credit cooperative into one of the most prestigious bankers in the nation's financial community."

Another entrepreneur, Song Zhenghuan, forty-seven, created the Goodbaby Group. This seventeen-year-old company has held an 80 percent share of China's baby carriage market for ten years. About 80 percent of the company's sales are in overseas markets, and half of these are in the United States, where Goodbaby accounts for one out of every three strollers sold. Innovation is the secret of success, says Song. In 2008 the company opened a 20,000-square-meter research and development center in Jiangsu province, the largest of its kind in the industry anywhere in the world.

Zhang Yin is said to be the richest person in China—wealthier than any other woman in the world, including Oprah Winfrey. Zhang founded her company, Nine Dragons Paper, China's largest packaging manufactory, ten years ago. She turns trash into wealth by shipping several million tons of wastepaper from the United States and Europe to China, where she recycles it into corrugated cardboard that is used for boxes for electronics and toys. These products are stamped "Made in China" and shipped back to western countries. After the boxes are disposed of, the cycle starts all over again. Her approach to business is quite capitalistic and more black-and-white than we would see it. "In the world of business, there is no difference between men and women, only winners and losers," she says. What would the Chinese have said about such a statement twenty years ago? Today, President Hu says, "We must accelerate the growth of Chinese multinational corporations and Chinese brand names in the world markets."

How many American success stories have begun more or less like this?—"He arrived with only a few dollars in his pocket."

Wu Ying arrived with thirty dollars but gave five of them to charity in his first half hour on U.S. ground. He was one of many smart Chinese students who went to United States during the early years of the reforms. When he arrived in the United States in 1985, he had already served as an assistant professor at Beijing University of Technology. His talents and his English-language skills won him a coveted spot at

Stanford University, but the New Jersey Institute of Technology offered him a teaching assistantship, so he went there instead.

In 1987, after Wu Ying had graduated and was working at Bell Laboratories (Bell Labs), China was really starting to open up, and he wanted to be part of the action. As it turned out, he was at the center of the action, beating big SOEs and the powerful Ministry of Telecoms at their own game in the new freewheeling China and became an entrepreneurial hero there. He told us his story when we met him in 2008.

Wu based his system on what he found in something called the personal cell phone system, or PHS, that had been tested but rejected by Japan and Thailand. The equipment cost only a small fraction of what was required by the mobile systems being deployed across China. Wu Ying and his company, UTStarcom, positioned the PHS service, renamed "Little Smart," as an inexpensive mobile phone service for China's masses. He saw it as a market of 650 million phones. He figured that the top 20 percent of Chinese people could afford regular mobile phones, whereas the bottom 30 percent were simply focusing on getting basic necessities. It was the middle 50 percent that UTStarcom wanted. He made a compelling argument to local officials: you can make back your investment on my system in three months, instead of the eighteen months or more it would take for real mobile phone equipment.

The 50 percent came by the millions to buy the "Little Smart" at 80 percent less than the state company's competing product. Today Wu Ying is one of China's billionaires and is now investing in other entrepreneurial companies. Wu is a hero in China, especially among young people, for bringing technology to the people, and he is an icon in the IT community.

Wu's wealth did not come as a gift. He worked his way up and certainly was luckier but also more diligent than Luo Lian, the missing migrant worker who became a loser. Like Wang Wei, our partner and friend, and others who are called winners, Wu is very much engaged in any improvement for the new China. But the price he pays, as in other societies, is that he has very little time left for his family, almost no leisure time, and very long working hours.

The number of wealthy people in China is rising rapidly. If we go by the numbers published in the *China Economic Review 2009,* the best environment for becoming rich must be found in Guangdong. Of the ten richest men and ten richest women in China, three women and six men come from Guangdong. Only two came from Hong Kong.

According to a McKinsey 2009 report, China is expected to be the world's fourth largest country in terms of the number of wealthy households by 2015, following the United States, Japan, and the United Kingdom. China is expected to have more than 4 million wealthy households by then, the report said. By the end of 2008, there were 1.6 million wealthy heads of households in the country, accounting for little more than one-tenth of 1 percent of the population. The number is increasing by 16 percent annually.

Of those 1.6 million wealthy households, about 50 percent were not rich four years ago, and more than half of those that will be wealthy by 2015 are not rich today. McKinsey says the most striking finding is that the Chinese wealthy are much younger than those in the United States and Japan; about 80 percent of rich people in China are under forty-five, compared with 30 percent in the United States and 19 percent in Japan.

"To get rich is no sin," as Deng said. And to be poor has not much merit. Freedom and fairness mean different things to different people. In business, freedom is the possibility of working hard, earning, and enjoying the fruits of your own accomplishments. Fairness involves providing equal access to education for all levels of the population and sharing wealth with those who, for whatever reason, are not able to completely care for themselves.

In the endeavor to find a balance between freedom and fairness, China's model of vertical democracy has advantages. The constancy of the ruling political party allows long-term planning without the disruption and changing politics of thinking and acting that are focused on elections.

The Chinese model can establish local and countrywide mechanisms to reduce the number of social parasites, leaving more funds for those in real need.

The big frame of social welfare can be provided by the central government, leaving space for local governments and authorities closer to the core problems to find solutions with bottom-up participation.

But education, the key to enabling people to care for themselves, is at the top of the list. Education must be China's number one economic priority. Not only will education be the driver of China's future, but well-educated and well-trained people are much more likely to find solutions in times of turbulence and much less likely to seek public support. The key to opening the doors of freedom and fairness is education.

Pillar 8

From Olympic Gold Medals to Nobel Prizes

Look for China in the next decades to duplicate its Olympic success in economic performance and competitiveness. China's economic sustainability is now firmly linked to moving from imitation to innovation, from manufacturing for brands to creating brands. China is now taking the steps to become the world's "innovation country."

The name of this pillar is a prediction as well as a primary strategy for China. The competitive leadership China achieved in the 2008 Beijing Summer Olympics is a preview of what will happen in its global economic competitiveness. The organizers of the Olympics spent $1.9 billion on constructing venues and another $42 billion on urban infrastructure. To prepare for setting new standards for the Olympic Games, 1.5 million Chinese had to move out of their homes and make way for Olympics venues and beautification projects. China shut down 200 polluting factories and treated 90 percent of Beijing's wastewater. The goal was to outperform all previous hosts of the Olympic Games in the artistic standard of the official ceremonies, the architecture of venues, and the gold medals won. China succeeded in all its goals. What the world can expect from China in the next decades is a duplication of this success in economic performance and competitiveness.

Michael Porter wrote in the U.S. Council on Competitiveness Index that the ultimate goal of competitiveness is the prosperity of a nation's people. To become the most competitive nation in the world suits China in three ways: (1) It matches China's goal of achieving modest wealth for its entire population. (2) The country is run as an enterprise, led by a powerful leadership which sets long-term goals in a top-down bottom-up interplay of a vertical, increasingly democratic decision-making process. (3) The well-being of the whole is in the common interest of both the leadership and the workforce. The Chinese are united by a pride for what has been achieved and by ambition to rise to the next level of development.

In the first phase of reinventing itself, China changed from a country on the verge of collapse to the third largest economy in the world. In 1978 its 0.8 percent share of world exports was only as big as the share of Libya. In 2009 China beat Germany as the world champion of exports.

The economy of the twenty-first century will favor nations that reach for global markets. What nation could have a better starting position than the "workshop of the world"? In the Competitive Report of 2006, Michael Porter—who is famous for his book *Competitive Advantage*—wrote that the commanding economy "will favor nations that will embrace different cultures and absorb their diversity of ideas into the innovation process. It will be fueled by the fusion of different technical and creative fields and thrive on scholarship, creativity, artistry and leading edge thinking. These concepts are America's strength and our competitive advantage. These concepts are uniquely American." Were uniquely American.

China's goal to quadruple the per capita GDP of the year 2000 by 2020 and achieve modest wealth for all its people matches what Porter calls "the ultimate goal of competitiveness." In his speech to the National Congress in 2007, President Hu focused on China's new goal "to ensure sound and rapid economic growth and make China an innovative country." He said that China will:

- Enhance the educational attainment of the whole nation by providing much higher training of innovative personnel.

- Enhance China's capacity for independent innovation.

- Increase spending on independent innovation.

- Establish a market-oriented system for technological innovation.

- Continue to create conditions conducive to innovation, and work to train world-class scientists and leaders in scientific and technological research.

- Upgrade new- and high-technology industries and develop information, biotechnology, new materials, aerospace, marine, and other industries.

- Balance urban and rural development and build a new socialist countryside.

- Expand the areas of opening up and industrial upgrading; balance development among regions.

Whether China actually achieves all this will depend to a great extend on transforming the authoritarian, exam-driven structures of the educational system so as to liberate students to think for themselves. The goal of becoming an innovative society cannot be achieved while hierarchical, authoritarian patterns persist in education and in the workplace.

That goal must be seen in the greater context of a general reform of China's educational system. And the only way that China can quickly reform this system is through competition. As we mentioned earlier, the reason U.S. colleges and universities are the best in the world is that they are in competition with one another to get students, and they keep enhancing their offerings. To get results in general education, you have to shift to such a system, putting the schools in competition for students. The Chinese have to transfer their knowledge and experience in the commercial area—where companies compete by offering increasingly superior products and services—to education, where schools would compete by offering increasingly superior performance. This involves using a market mind-set to reform education. And the customers decide. Parents chose among the schools that are competing to educate their children. A competitive system can improve the schools in any country. For instance, when private schools, including slum schools organized by parents, became prevalent in India, they quickly attracted 50 percent of the school-age population. They became such a threat to the establishment that when we last checked, there were proposals in the parliament to close all the private schools, that is, to outlaw the competition.

The authors of a book we often mention, *Think Like Chinese*, say, "Due to the vast number of students the education system has been distorted to become learn-by-rote and exam focused. A good student may get very good marks in exams and know the material intimately, but may not necessarily understand the essence of what is learned to acquire knowledge. A good schoolteacher is one who has the highest number of students admitted into higher education. A bonus for a high school teacher is usually linked to how many students were accepted to universities," where again the same principle—learning by rote—applies. This is not the wood out of which Nobel laureates are carved.

A top-down call to "inspire the creative wisdom of the society" has been issued. But how will it be executed?

If America's problem is that children and employees are too undisciplined, China's problem is that they are too disciplined.

From Little Emperors to Big Thinkers

We had a demonstration of the value and level of discipline in education when we were in Tianjin in September 2008. Our institute has its office at Tianjin University of Finance and Economics (TUFE), a complex so modern and stylish that any university in the world might take it as a model. But each year in September something takes place that could never be seen on a western campus: the freshmen receive paramilitary training. You can see these new students, marching in formation on the university grounds, dressed in uniforms, each step synchronized with the group.

"This certainly gets the students attuned to discipline, but what does it say about encouraging creativity?" we asked. Once we heard the reason, it seemed evident to us: "The military training for students is supposed to give them a sense of responsibility, discipline, and teamwork. Most of the students are the only child in the family and are taken care of by four grandparents and two parents—in many cases, even by several uncles and aunts. They are too ego-centered and are often called 'little emperors.'"

Westerners might suppose it would be easy to do away with the military drill, and in the case of a two-week training session at a university, that seems reasonable; but the idea becomes questionable when students are already too eager to please their teachers. Pressure for conformity does not come only from the top down. Much of the pressure comes from inside the people themselves. More than anything else, the Chinese have to save face—*mianzi*, their reputation, their social status, their the image in the eyes of others. Mistakes and failure do not fit into this concept. The book *Think Like Chinese* describes it "as often more important than health or well-being." The real challenge for any "innovation initiative" is how to shift the mind-set that making a mistake means losing face.

The Chinese saying "The more you do, the more likely you will make a mistake" dates back almost 2,000 years and has been passed on through generations. To become a sage, or an ideal human being, is still a very desirable goal. To achieve this, however, you cannot do anything wrong. The less you do, the less you can do wrong! This is not a formula for developing an "innovative society."

Education remains one of the most conservative areas in Chinese society. Especially in rural areas, education carries the burden of a generation of teachers with yesterday's thinking, who are hidebound and obsessed with test scores. We asked President Zhang Jia Xing of TUFE for his opinion about adapting China's educational system for the needs of the twenty-first century.

"In an era of overwhelming information, the winners in the severe competition are those who are good at understanding new perceptions. It is crucial to be able to learn, put it in practice, and innovate. We encourage our students to first obtain a solid foundation of basic knowledge, to selectively add to it and use this base to generate new knowledge. Our mission is to open the minds of the students [to receive] new insights and theories, be prepared to apply them, and be bold in venturing out with new ideas, theories, and conclusions. Our goal is cultivate talents with the capability of riding the wave of the time, the wish to reach out into the future.

"TUFE is dedicated to build a state-of-the-art university with a global view and a global vision. We think that the globalization of economics will certainly push the process of globalizing education. As an educational institution for business and economics, we are at the forefront to prepare the generation which will determine the China of tomorrow. Therefore, we are engaged to keep our educational concepts updated, attend to philosophy and practice, and [develop] the Chinese characteristic into a more suitable, more scientific way of education. Ideally, a university should be a nutrient for the business world—as we call it, the material civilization—and a refuge for spiritual demands of the civilization."

Loosing *Mianzi* but Gaining Ground

"Now, don't take it personally," says the boss in an American company after he has dumped a load of disapproval and anger on his employee, Joe. "Lousy job. Make it again and make it better."

"Idiot," Joe mutters to himself as he walks out of his boss's office with fury in his stomach: "I'll show you."

Such a scene could happen in China as well. But the Chinese Joe would not walk out with his head held high in anger; he would wish to be swallowed by the ground. He has lost face. There is no way he cannot take it personally. The American Joe can push the criticism out of his mind or use it as fuel to motivate himself and deliver a better job. The Chinese Joe needs to keep his self-esteem, his *mianzi*.

In China, reliability within a social network determines a person's trustworthiness. A well-respected person earns trust, and a trustworthy person earns prestige. It would be unthinkable to gain a leadership position without such characteristics. And that's China's problem when it comes to criticism. We do not know which would be harder: to turn an American Joe into a respectful subordinate, or to turn his Chinese counterpart into an aggressive, inventive student or employee. The problem is that representatives of the two "Joes" will be competing in worldwide markets, and to date it has been clear that boldness is most likely to win.

America leads in Nobel Prizes, has the majority of companies listed in the Fortune 500, and is an innovative country, not because Americans are the smartest people in the world but because American society allows mistakes, encourages creativity, sees faults as something to learn from, and welcomes a failed entrepreneur back in the arena.

Respect and obedience may be of high value on an assembly line, and respecting ancestors, seniors, chiefs, and colleagues may be a socially desirable quality, but modern scientific breakthroughs need people who are willing to question their forefathers' points of view and their bosses' orders. As we have said, hierarchical, authoritarian thinking is China's highest hurdle in changing from the workshop of the world to a leading innovative country. It is one thing to say as President Hu did, that "the creative wisdom of the whole society should bring forth large numbers of innovative personnel in all areas," but another thing to create the social and cultural environment needed for such a development. China needs to change a mind-set that has been built up over thousands of years, and this change has to come within one or two generations. On the other hand, the good news is that it doesn't have to happen with all

1.3 billion Chinese people; it just needs to happen with enough people to create a critical mass.

For public figures in the West, nothing seems worse than being ignored, but in China being ignored is better than being questioned or criticized publicly. Our Chinese friends have repeatedly reminded us that in China you cannot praise a person in one regard and heavily criticize him or her in another. Yet this is common practice in performance reviews throughout the western world.

The situation in science is not as dramatic, but still serious. A challenge that is not often discussed is the lack of candid, honest communication among Chinese scientists. Vice President Song Chunping of Henan University spoke out about this recently, saying that the problem was universal in China and "stood against the campaign to exploit the nation's potentials."

An editorial in *China Daily* applauded Song's concern, saying that "academic criticism, if it does exist, has in many cases degenerated into a shameless exchange of peer acclaims." Critical intellectual reviews are rare. "We share Song's anxiety," the editorial said, "with an additional fear—a profound fear of moral corruption that goes along with it." The editorial ended on a surprising note: "Our society needs an injection of the sense of shame. We need to feel ashamed of receiving praise we do not deserve." That would certainly be a U-turn for the Chinese—to worry about fake praise instead of worrying about being criticized!

"One of the biggest problems we have in recruiting management personnel is that because the Chinese fear doing something wrong, they would rather do nothing," a manager of one of Beijing's five-star hotels told us. "We are educating our staff on all levels. Each employee is empowered to solve a guest problem on his own, right away, as long as the solution does not exceed 2,000 RMB" ($300).

The number of mainland Chinese in management positions is increasing as education and experience get better and better. Since mainland Chinese have the advantage of speaking fluent Mandarin, they also have a great cultural advantage over many foreign managers.

"Our number one priority is education," said Zhao Qizheng over a dinner in Beijing on the last evening of the Lantern Festival in 2009. He can be taken seriously. In his book the *Shanghai Pudong Miracle*, Zhao writes, "In our world today, human resources are more important than any other resources. Whoever possesses the best human talents will occupy the commanding heights in science and technology. Whoever possesses an abundance of intelligent human resources will enjoy an advantageous position in the ever-fiercer international competition."

The Pudong government has also maintained the importance of attracting Chinese scholars who are abroad and assisting them to return to China to start or develop their careers. Early on, the local government set up a leading group to work on this. In 2006 it expanded this group to include both government leaders and heads of the various related enterprises. They know that talent goes where it is best treated.

As part of its push for innovation, the government has put in place an ambitious plan to attract outstanding talent to the Chinese mainland. It was launched at the beginning of 2009, and by midyear the first group of ninety-six scientists and twenty-six entrepreneurs had been formed, elite personnel willing to do their work in China. The plan targets people with full professorships or the equivalent in developed countries. The government's relocation allowance is $146,000 in addition to salaries and research funding from universities and institutes that hire them.

The government says that China has about 38 million researchers and other scientific personnel, but only 10,000 are considered top-level experts. The people targeted in the innovation plan are those who are among the top five or top ten in their fields. In switching to an innovation-based economy, while reducing its reliance on export industries, China must compete with the world's most advanced nations by attracting more of the world's most advanced minds, says Miao Hong, of the Chinese Academy of Science. The academy, one of the agencies involved in the program, had itself received applications from more than eighty of these leading minds during the spring of 2009 for the second round of recruitment.

Zhangjiang Hi-Tech Park in Pudong— An Innovation Model

Zhangjiang Hi-Tech Park (ZHTP) is located in the middle of the Pudong new district and has a planned area of twenty-five square kilometers. It was designed to include several zones: technical innovation, biomedical, integrated circuits industry, scientific research and education, and residential. The ZHTP is the Silicon Valley of China and has the country's most advanced technology and most complete industry supply chain. Its Web site notes that by the end of 2007 it had attracted 5,359 companies, 108 of them registered as research and development centers and 306 as high-tech companies. By 2007, organizations within ZHTP had submitted a total of 9,142 inventions for worldwide patent application or registration and had been granted 2,205 patents.

This is also the site of the "Pharmaceutical Hub," with major research and development institutes in biotech and pharmaceuticals, including the National Human Genome Center, the National Center for Drug Screening, the National Center for New Drug Safety Evaluation and Research, the National Center for Traditional Chinese Medicine Innovation, and the National BioChip Engineering Research Center.

By 2010, the park expects to add a number of research and development companies, ten large domestic enterprises, and fifty small or medium-size medical device companies. Annual production value in the Modern Medical Device Park is projected to surpass 10 billion RMB ($ 1.47 billion) annually. The ZHTP has also become the Incubation and Entrepreneurship Center in China. It has now 382 start-ups and 182 high-tech enterprises. One successfully "incubated" company is Shanda Networking, which now has more than half of the total online entertainment market share in China

The Model of a "Living Circle"

Semiconductor Manufacturing International Corporation (SMIC) is one of the leading semiconductor companies in the world and the largest and most advanced in mainland China. The company has implemented many innovations at ZHIP and has had an important impact on other companies and cities in China. To attract the best talent globally while it was constructing its manufacturing plants in 2001, SMIC spent $100 million to build a "Living Circle." This corporate village has villa-type units as well as high-rise apartments; generous parking space; sports facilities; a village center with banks, restaurants, grocery stores, and other small shops; a bilingual school; and even a church. The company claims to sell these housing units at cost, and its own employees receive a discount of 15 percent when they shop at company-owned stores within the village.

Not surprisingly, education is a key element in innovation in the Pudong new district and at ZHIP. The availability of education is a key to the successful recruiting by SMIC, which offers private schooling in both English and Chinese. The English track has been granted a Level II code by the Educational Testing Service in the United States; this allows its students to register for the SAT or ACT assessment tests needed to apply at U.S. colleges. The Chinese track follows the official Shanghai elementary, middle, and high school curriculum to prepare its students to take the Chinese national college entrance examinations.

To reach Christian and other religious high-tech industry employees from the global talent pool, there is the Pudong Thanksgiving Church near the company site. Since we read Zhao Qizheng and Luis Palau's *Riverside Talk: A Friendly Dialog between an Atheist and a Christian*, this no longer surprises us.

In our field studies at ZHTP and the SMIC village, we have observed firsthand the vibrant social activities and intellectual exchanges among relatively young high-tech suburbanites who may or may not work for SMIC. The suburbanite lifestyle in the SMIC village and a dynamic social center like the Thanksgiving Church provide models of innovation within an extended metropolitan region that are being closely observed and studied by other regions in China, and they may have an impact well beyond the local city.

There Is More Than Beer in Tsingtao

Pudong is not the only district with high-flying plans. A new generation of cities may become role models for further steps toward China's next stage as an innovative country. President Hu said in 2007, "China is advancing towards an industrialized, information-based, urbanized, market-oriented, and international country."

One city with ambitious plans is Qingdao—or Tsingtao, as the name appears on beer bottles, which are where most people become familiar with it. Tsingtao brewery is the tenth largest in the world, and the first one, at least in our experience, where you are asked to type in your age before entering the Web site.

Fewer people are aware that Qingdao is a booming metropolis in the peninsula of Shandong, and one of the few bathing resorts in China. The Germans speak of it as "Naples on the Yellow Sea." Its harbor is the third largest in China and the ninth largest in the world. It exports fish, seafood, textiles, and household goods and is a site for globally successful companies such as Jean Pierre, Hong Ling, Shuangxin, and Haier. Seafood, by the way, is China's leading export to the United States. In Qingdao ten patents, on average, are approved each day. About 90 percent of these are used in production. China is now the leader in the world in improvements in production processes, making products cheaper and easier to sell anywhere in the world.

China Daily reported that Xia Geng, the mayor of Qingdao, has more than beer and bathing in mind: "Independent technological innovation is the core competitiveness of the city's sustainable economic development." If we measure the city's plans against the history of the company that is probably its most famous, Haier, we can conclude that there must have been some enduring spirit of German accuracy, which inspired Zhang Ruimin in his famous refrigerator massacre.

When we visited Qingdao in 2003, we were guests of the Laoshan Industry Park administration and took part in a roundtable discussion with Fred Li, the CEO of a Taiwanese software company; and General Guo, known as the father of Taiwan's software industry. The discussion was attended by city officials, academics, and industry representatives.

Laoshan is a scenic part of Qingdao and is designated as a site for high-tech industries. It was beginning an innovation drive, and the park had already completed an impressive administration building with meticulously planned grounds.

From the windows in our room in the new five-star hotel we overlooked a Disney-like amusement park. Across the four-lane road along the Yellow Sea, new western-style villas were waiting for buyers and renters. The city had a growth rate of 32 percent, and we felt its spirit of renewal. Business was booming, though there was still a gap in salaries. An experienced chemist or engineer leading a group of four to five people can make 6,000 to 8,000 RMB (about $1,200) per month in Qingdao, but in Beijing or Shanghai he or she could easily double that amount.

"To have more independently developed intellectual property in high-end technological fields is crucial for industrial improvement and development," said Wang Anmin, director of the Qingdao Science and Technology Bureau. To expand Qingdao's capacity for independent innovation, and to foster a talented workforce in high-tech innovation, the city is creating ten science and technology research laboratories. Six innovation centers, including Haier's national laboratory for digital household appliances, are being built.

Qingdao local government is also encouraging universities, research institutes, and companies to work together in technology research and the training of professionals. The city's science and technology plan calls for Qingdao to be an "innovation-powered city" by 2012. More than ten companies in Qingdao, including Haier and Hisense, have now established partnerships with about 100 universities and research institutes, including the Chinese Academy of Sciences, Shandong University, and the Ocean University of China. Already in production in Qingdao is a high-speed train (300 kilometers, or about 185 miles, per hour) that makes China the fourth country capable of independently designing and building such a train, following Germany, France, and Japan.

Ten industrial centers—including centers for software, digital high-definition television sets, new materials, and seafood—have been established, and are expected to generate revenues of 120 billion RMB ($ 17.6 billion) by 2010. The Qingdao city government plans to support thirty selected small and medium-size enterprises working in new materials, electronics, and bioengineering every year, to help them cultivate their own innovation ability.

A 600-Year-Old Dream Comes True

A hundred years ago, China had almost no science and technology at all; and according to one story, only ten people in the country understood calculus. But by the early twenty-first century, the gap in high-tech research and development between China and the world's advanced countries had obviously shrunk. Sixty percent of China's technologies, including atomic energy, space, high-energy physics, biosciences, computer and information technology, and robotics, has reached or is close to the levels of the advanced world.

In joining the world, in becoming a leading player in the global economy, and in gaining the respect of the global community, few things excite the Chinese people more than their adventures in space.

The breakthrough in China's space program was the successful launch of a manned spacecraft in 2003, when Yang Liwei spent twenty-one hours in space. The year 2005 marked another leap in Chinese astronautics when the Chinese could watch the televised launch of two men on Shenzhou 6. Following its successful Moon Probe Project in 2007, and the space walk in 2008, China planned to launch unmanned probes to the moon before 2010.

We were in Beijing on Saturday afternoon, September 27, 2008, when the astronaut Zhai Zhigang floated out of the Shenzhou 7 spacecraft to become the first Chinese to walk in space. On his space suit he wore the Chinese characters for *feitian* ("fly the sky") in President Hu's handwriting. Millions of Chinese were checking their watches that afternoon and finding television sets where they could see the live broadcast of this historic achievement. At 4:41 P.M. Zhai emerged from the orbital module holding a Chinese flag. We watched the scene on a huge outdoor screen while we were stuck in a traffic jam, sitting in a taxi decorated with doily-like seat covers and plastic flowers. The excited

Chinese voice on the radio sounded like the sportscasters reporting the Super Bowl when Pittsburgh beat Arizona in the last minute of the game. The taxi driver kept turning to us with a wide grin on his face, pointing at the screen and probably thanking his ancestors that he was stuck in traffic at the right time and in the right place.

China's space ambitions are at least six centuries old. A story is told that Wan Hu, an official in the early sixteenth century, during the Ming dynasty, was the earliest documented pioneer of rocket flight in both China and the world. One day, in an ambitious attempt to fly to outer space, he bundled himself into a chair attached to forty-seven rockets while holding a large kite in each hand. The result was fatal: the rockets exploded, and Wan died. It would take 600 years until manned spaceflight became a reality in China.

A crater on the moon has been named after Wan; and Zhai's walk in space began a new era and reinforced China's ambition to achieve a successful moon landing by 2012.

China Takes Off

Closer to the ground, China is spreading its wings to join the global aircraft industry. And there are signs that China will play a successful and significant role in this high-tech field, becoming a world-class aircraft manufacturer.

China has already entered the market of regional jets with the launch of its ARJ21, a locally developed plane with a ninety-seat capacity. The designation ARJ21 stands for Advanced Regional Jet for the Twenty-First Century. The first of these jets rolled off the production line in 2008, and has been undergoing testing. Its name, *Xiang Feng*, consists of two Chinese characters, meaning "flying phoenix" and symbolizes luck and harmony. The name was chosen through online voting.

The ARJ21 is a milestone in China's ambitious plan for its civil aircraft manufacturing industry. The Commercial Aircraft Corporation of China (CACC), the company making the new jets, did not start from scratch. Its history goes back to the years of Deng Xiaoping, who started to send aircraft construction engineers and students to western countries to learn new technologies and come back with their heads full of ideas. The strategy was not much different from the one used in the automobile industry. Importing was soon followed by what the Chinese in the automobile industry called "mutually shouldering risk," joint ventures with established aircraft manufacturers, moving from local assembling of imported parts to producing the parts locally and, as the final stage, moving to local development and production.

General Electric's aircraft leasing unit placed the West's first order for the Chinese-built jet: five planes, with an option to buy another twenty. First delivery is scheduled for 2012. Within China, domestic airlines have ordered more than 200 ARJ21s.

China has made parts for both Airbus and Boeing since the early 1980s, and has years of experience making military aircraft. China will follow with larger planes and advanced helicopters and is moving toward challenging the jumbo jets of Boeing and Airbus by 2020. At a meeting of CACC in 2008, Premier Wen Jiabao exhorted the Chinese people to "use their own two hands and their wisdom to manufacture internationally competitive large aircraft." Wen said, "It is the will of the nation and all its people to have a Chinese large aircraft soar into the blue sky."

China Plans to Be the World Leader in Electric Cars

A soldier, a tractor driver, a factory worker: these would have been the answers of Chinese boys had we asked them twenty years ago what they would like to become. A few years after the first Formula One race in Shanghai, the astronaut has replaced the soldier; the Formula One driver, the tractor driver; and the manager, the factory worker. The Olympic motto "Faster, Higher, and Stronger" is also energizing the manufacture of cars and education.

China will take time to be ready to enter the more mature markets of Europe and North America with middle-class cars, but it is already leading the world in the development of electric cars. At the end of 2008, BYD, a private Chinese automobile company, began selling an electric hybrid car in China, more than a year ahead of similar offerings in the United States and Japan. It is the first of a line of electric cars the company plans to introduce around the world, starting in China and then in the United States and Europe in 2010. One of the investors in this innovative Chinese company is none other than Warren Buffett.

The company was started in 1995 by Wang Chuanfu, a forty-three-year-old entrepreneur from Anhui province, with $300,000 he had borrowed from a cousin to make batteries for cell phones. Within five years the company was selling batteries to Motorola, Nokia, and Samsung, among others. The move to electric cars began early and became a passion of Wang's. "It's almost hopeless for a latecomer like us to compete with GM and other established automakers with a century of experience in gasoline engines," he said. "With electric vehicles, we are all on the same starting line."

On that starting line, BYD has more than 5,000 auto engineers and 5,000 battery engineers, most of them living in a complex of fifteen apartment buildings, each eighteen stories high, at the company's headquarters in Shenzhen. The Ministry of Science and Technology is run by Wan Gang, a minister who is not a member of the Communist Party, as mentioned earlier in this book. Wan was an auto engineer with Audi in Germany and then became the chief scientist for the government's research panel on electric vehicles before he was appointed minister. China plans to turn itself into one of the leading producers of hybrid and all-electric vehicles within three years, with the goal of being the world leader in electric cars and buses.

High-Flying Machinery Maker

"Be strict, progressive, and creative" is the spirit promoted by China's biggest maker of construction machinery, Xuzhou Construction Machinery Group (XCMG). It is becoming a serious competitor in construction machinery and ranks fifteenth in the world. Importing advanced technologies, XCMG develops new high-premium and high-tech products, which are distributed to more than forty countries overseas. Most of its products are market leaders both domestically and internationally. This group is also seeking to buy assets in Europe and the United States—not manufacturing facilities, but distribution companies.

In China, more than eighteen Sino–foreign equity joint ventures have been formed. Caterpillar Xuzhou is a joint venture between XCMG and Caterpillar, producing world-class hydraulic excavators. Several selling centers have been set up in the United States, Germany, Japan, the Middle East, and Southeast Asia. Also, XCMG is developing plants in Poland and Iran, moving toward overseas sales of 40 percent of its total revenue. With its newly developed crane, XCMG is counting on its overseas sales to increase 25 percent in 2009.

> *XCMG's vision:* "To be a world-class construction ma-
> chinery conglomerate with great competitive power,
> making the Chinese proud of it." What a difference
> from the mind-set of the state-owned enterprises!

> *XCMG's growth strategy:* "To become number ten in the
> construction machinery industry in 2010 with revenues
> of 50 billion RMB ($7.3billion). By 2015, to become
> number five with revenues of 100 billion RMB ($14.6
> billion)."

Moreover, XCMG plans to establish new segments for growth: in-struments, air conditioners, textile machinery, plastic machinery, and information development. It wants to "further widen the vision of glo-balization, [and] participate in the international economic and techno-logical cooperation and competition on a broader scale in more spheres and on a higher level."

Waiting for the Robots

Aren't we all waiting for a time when we can get rid of our less attractive routine daily work and delegate it to robots, the household helpers of the twenty-first century? This idea was dramatized in Karel Čapek's science fiction play *R.U.R.* The title is an abbreviation for Rossom's Universal Robots, and the play depicts humanlike robots that relieve people of tiresome work. It dates from 1920, and ever since then we have all been waiting for the robots to come.

Now help is on the way. China has taken up the cause. *China Daily* begins the story about times to come. Robots will teach kids English and clean houses when the owner is not at home. They will help fix cars and set up the wind power equipment in dangerous situations where no one would send a worker. They can carry heavy goods and fix tiny chips in a vacuum. All this can be done by robots made in China. If you want to see an example of how China is changing itself from a world factory to a high-tech producer, you can pay a visit to the workshop of Qu Daokui's company, SIASUN Robot and Automation, in Shenyang, capital of Liaoning province. This company is where the magic happens.

Qu Daokui was born in a coastal city in east China's Shandong province. Before establishing his company, Qu studied robots for almost twenty years. After finishing his undergraduate studies at Jilin University in Changchun in 1982, he continued studying at the Shenyang Institute of Automation with Jiang Xinsong, who is regarded as the father of robotics in China. In the early 1990s Qu went to Germany, to the lab of the Universität des Saarlandes, where he studied automation and robot science.

After he returned to China in 1993, he worked in commercial robotics and automation technology. When he became CEO, at the age of thirty-nine in the year 2000, he was an outstanding scientist in robotics and automation. Up to that time the Chinese domestic market had been dominated by multinational robot and automation companies such as ABB Robotics from Switzerland, FANUC and Yaskawa from Japan, and other firms from Germany and the United States; and China's leaders were eager to reduce its dependence on imported robots.

How can an eight-year-old company compete with multinational firms from Switzerland, Germany, and Japan? Qu says, "We can provide the same standard of product at half the price and ensure clients' problems are resolved in twenty-four hours." SIASUN's strategic goal is to take advanced manufacturing technology as the core and develop into an internationally advanced, strongly competitive equipment supplier and high-tech industry group. Last year, the company's independently developed system for automobile assembly lines won the GM global procurement bid and was exported to Mexico, India, Russia, and Canada. The system can lift an engine and install it in a car in less than two minutes.

Apart from robots for industrial use, home robots are a growing trend worldwide, Qu says. Although mass production remains a long way off, he expects advanced domestic robotics to play a major role in his company's future. He says, "The intelligent service robot will be the third generation of consumer electronics products, after the first generation of radio and television, and the second IT generation." Qu, who is now forty-eight and president of the company, continues to be the deputy director of the National Engineering Research Center on Robotics, and a professor.

Nothing Protects Intellectual Property in a Country More Than That Country's Developing Its Own Intellectual Property Rights

"How many books did *Megatrends* sell in China?" That's one of the standard questions John gets when he speaks in China about China; and when he answers, "As far as I know, millions and millions," you can almost hear the mental rumbling as his listeners calculate how much money he must have made. Must have, but did not.

In the 1980s there was a generous innocence about the idea of intellectual property. Didn't China share its inventions with the world? After all, gunpowder, porcelain, silk, and noodles had never brought the Chinese any dividends. When John was signing copies of *Megatrends* in China, he enjoyed noticing the creativity of, at last count, twenty-two pirated editions, each with a different cover.

But at the time of his latest book tour, the scene had changed; we did not see a single pirated edition. The reason is simple. With the increasing number of Chinese authors and publications the question of property rights has moved quickly from being a foreign issue to being a domestic demand. It was OK to pick the cherries hanging over the wall from a neighbor's garden, but the fruits in our own garden needed to be protected. And that also eased the problem for the neighbor.

China's leading politicians are aware of the importance of a sound legal framework for intellectual property rights (IPR). On a local level, the enforcement of laws needs to be improved substantially. China's institutionalized system of IPR was initiated in the 1980s. China has promulgated and implemented a series of laws and statutes dealing with IPR as well as related specifications for implementation and legal interpretation, including laws to protect patents, trademarks, and copyright; statutes to protect computer software, integrated circuit layout design, audio and video products, and new varieties of plants and intellectual property at customs; Olympic logos; rights to promulgate information online; and regulations to manage special markings. All this has contributed to improvements in China's IPR-related legal system.

Considering the 828,328 patent applications and 698,000 entries for trademarks the office of the IPR had to deal with in 2008, all efforts to improve the legal copyright situation in China seem absolutely necessary.

In accordance with "Action Outline for Protecting Intellectual Property (2006–2007)," issued by the State Council in April 2006, service centers for the reporting of, and for complaints about, IPR violations have been set up in fifty cities. The general office of the State Working Group for IPR Protection also established a Web site—http://www.ipr.gov.cn—in both Chinese and English, to offer specialized services to the public in China and overseas.

At the beginning of China's reforms and opening up, the strategy of sending out boats with straw to collect the arrows was a smart move; but as Chinese enterprises become more and more innovative, they themselves are adversely affected by a lack of IPR protection. Infringements of IPR will harm the national and international reputation of Chinese companies; by contrast, proper IPR policies will support the transfer of research-and-development results from public organizations to the Chinese economy.

The number of new Chinese patent applications has risen rapidly. With its new focus on innovation, "China is set to dominate as the world's leading innovator," by 2012, according to Bob Steinbridge of Thomson Scientific, a research division of Thomson Reuters. Inventions from China have been growing at a faster rate than those from any other region in the world.

China's Business Schools

Only a little more than thirty years ago, higher education in China was limited to a small minority handpicked by the Communist Party. About twenty years ago, in the 1980s, the illiteracy rate was still one-third of the population. Who would have thought that by the year 2009 education in China would reach the average level of middle-income countries?

China has implemented a nine-year compulsory education system; educational horizons are expanding; and the number of applicants for higher education has been soaring. The first law on promoting private education was passed in September 2003, and by the end of 2007 there were 95,000 private schools of different types and levels, including 295 schools of higher education and adult colleges. These brought competition into the educational system. Now China is about to become a high-end global competitor in MBAs. The favorite slogan of Chery's boss, Yin Tongyao, was, "Learn cost control from the Japanese, boldness from the Koreans, technological accuracy from the Germans, and marketing skills from the Americans." This might soon be complemented by "Get your MBA at a Chinese business school." It has been only a few years since China began to allow the private sector to be active in this area, but now private business schools are one of the fastest-growing phenomena in China. "Made-in-China business education, with China-relevant case studies and China-focused courses as drivers," the *Financial Times* reports, "will change both the content of business education worldwide and the competitive environment for business schools in China."

The China Europe International Business School, widely known as Ceibs in Shanghai, was ranked by the *Financial Times* among the top ten business schools in the world in 2009, alongside Wharton, London Business School, and Harvard Business School. Other outstanding Chinese business schools include the famous Tsinghua University's School of Economics and Management, Shanghai Jiaotong University Antai College of Economics and Management, and Zhejiang University School of Management.

Rolf D. Cremer, dean and vice president of Ceibs, says that three factors drive high-quality business education in China. First, there is a need to catch up. From its early days of reforms and opening up, China faced a wide gap between the capacity to develop competent and responsible managerial talent and the human requirements of the reforms. Second, China's educational environment is open to a wide range of approaches for developing the management resources required to support economic and social reforms. Third, the success and dynamism of economic development in China are very impressive.

"Chinese business schools appear to mirror, in their realm of management education and research, the development of China itself," Cremer told the *Financial Times*, "from a developing nation that followed and copied others into a leading international force."

The newly established Asian Business School at Tianjin University of Finance and Economics is taking a "made-in-China business education" approach. China is often called an economic miracle, and China's recent history can in fact offer many business stories, which unfolded in the context of the Chinese economy and culture. To summarize them and tell them to the world will also enhance the understanding of China's business rules for global entrepreneurs.

Wang Wei, the founder of the Asian Business School, says: "Students want to learn about reality, how business works. Many academics know nothing about business but are being bold enough to teach; that is a joke. The new business school will open the teaching positions only to business executives and regulators in government—and in certain cases, to someone who came out of jails, if it was only for business failure, but can pass on a valuable lesson to learn. We want to offer a business school which also serves the increasing number of foreigners living in China.

"In addition, many business schools are too expensive to attend and take too long to finish for market needs. Asia Business School will focus on training courses typically three days long. Our focus will be to make engineers rather than scientists."

A Framework for Innovation

Education:

It all starts with education. As long as China's education system continues to rely heavily on passive learning and exam-based performance, it will not be able to support innovative thinking, creativity, or entrepreneurship. Universities are a key factor in knowledge infrastructure. China needs a fair number of world-class universities that are less involved in research for practical use—which should be the task of the business sector—and more involved in basic research.

Competition:

America is still the most inventive country in the world. One of its secrets is competition. Competition has made American universities the best in the world; competition has driven America's enterprises to top performance. Competition is an important stimulus for China's economy, but it can be distorted by administrative interventions, which interfere with the normal functions of the markets and generate protectionism. The goal of becoming an innovative economy is also based on stronger intellectual property rights and a modern, properly enforced system of antitrust law.

Corporate Governance:

Many Chinese firms are not familiar with innovation strategy, although some Chinese companies have become role models. Haier's business case studies are included in textbooks used at Harvard and other universities, and Haier's CEO, Zhang, is praised for his management ability and his commitment to diversification. Companies like Haier must become the rule and not the exception: Haier is an example of how China's future can unfold. A top-down approach in which the government instructs the SOEs how to invest in research and development is not likely to support the goal of creating innovative enterprises. Instead, more market-based funding of research and development should be put in place, including incentives for investment in the business sector.

Finance:

China's banking system is more or less a monopoly. State-owned banks give loans to large SOEs that are operating at a loss; thus large amounts of nonperforming loans have accumulated. China must reduce such loans and instead meet the funding needs of small and middle-size private enterprises. This capital market is underdeveloped. Capital for financing new ventures as an important source of innovation is needed. Venture capital firms set up by the government and run by government officials do not always have the necessary entrepreneurial, scientific, and management skills.

China's efforts toward becoming an innovative society are characterized by different levels and dynamics of development. Beijing holds the biggest share of research in public institutions but does not have the industrial base to commercialize the results; Shanghai has an active business sector but no strong application-oriented basic research infrastructure. The creation of science parks like Zhangjiang Hi-Tech Park in Pudong, and technology incubators, which provide companies with low-cost office space and strategic advice on considerations such as management and financing, will have a role in correcting these mismatches.

China has made successful efforts to mobilize its human resources for upgrading the technological standards of the economy. But if we consider the number of science and engineering articles published per

1,000 researchers, and the number of patent applications, China still lags behind significantly.

President Hu affirmed China's scientific development in his 2007 Congress speech: "To make China an innovative nation we must have free compulsory education in a modern system of national education, we must enhance the rule of law, reduce government intervention in microeconomic operations, build capacity for independent innovation, keep up with times, and be oriented toward the world and the future." A good summary of the task ahead.

It may well be that China will not win a Nobel Prize tomorrow. But the achievement of launching a whole new socioeconomic system guiding more than 1 billion people from poverty to modest prosperity, and challenging the United States as the most innovative nation, should certainly gain the acknowledgment of the world.

Matters in Dispute

In the preceding chapters we have been describing the 8 Pillars on which the new Chinese society rests. But although the foundation is solid and strong, the facade still has some cracks that need to be fixed. Some people see those cracks endangering the whole structure; some say they can be repaired.

In some cases there is only one truth. Either the sun orbits the earth or the earth orbits the sun. But in countless cases truth has many faces; the more emotions are involved, the more vehemently one truth or another is defended. Such a highly emotional discussion arises about the true face of China. In the center of controversy are the "three forbidden T's": Tibet, Taiwan, and Tiananmen Square.

John has been lecturing in China for many years. But never has there been any word about what to say or not say, neither at John's many lectures and discussions with students at many universities nor in interviews in various parts of the country. In the media, there is a kind of self-censorship, about which Chinese journalists talk openly, but that has more to do with the approach to the reporting than with the content itself. The Chinese do not like to lose face, and if they feel accused, especially when they feel an accusation is unjustified, their reaction can be harsh. But in saying this we are already entering the territory of opinion, personal views, and emotions. In judging China's face, few people start from a neutral point of view; and once an opinion about China's face is made, it takes on a life of its own.

Western journalists are practically united in their criticism of China—so much so that sometimes there seems to be a need for an explanation or an apology when one is being positive about China.

"All love the Dalai Lama, all abhor the Chinese Communist Party which fights against unarmed monks with armed military police. Hardly any journalist or politician dares to openly show respect for what China has achieved in general," writes Georg Blume, the foreign correspondent for the German newspaper *Die Zeit*.

"There is no way Beijing can win the PR war on Tibet, when Tibet has in its corner the charismatic and amiable Dalai Lama, dressed for photo ops in his pristine saffron robe, while all China has are those poker-faced communist officials whose tough talk doesn't exactly endear them to the world's press. Given this disparity, how can China hope to win in the court of public opinion?" wrote Taiwanese businessman and former Stanford professor and essayist Fred Li.

It is good to make any violation of human rights public, to direct attention to those who cannot speak for themselves. Freedom of speech is of the highest value, and any restriction of it should be condemned. But freedom of speech should be accompanied by responsibility and fairness—exactly what we see missing in the reporting about China.

We admire China; we love the Chinese people; and we have come to know many politicians and officials who are anything but demons running an evil empire. Yes, there is corruption; yes, there are assaults; yes, there is questionable government at the local level. But if stealing, bribery, intrigues, and irregularities cannot be prevented within companies of a few hundred people, how can an enterprise of 1.3 billion people work without flaws? China's leaders are very well educated and well aware of the problems their country has to deal with; they have no desire to lecture the world but are eager to learn from it. And they are not so naive to think that in today's world a country of China's size can be run like a medieval realm. China's leadership, with the vast approval of the Chinese people, insists on modernizing China in its own way. And in doing so it claims nothing more than Europe and America claimed when they started their journey into modernity a few hundred years ago.

Our intention is to base our views on facts. Our view might be colored by our positive emotions, but if so, it may serve to balance the heavily weighted negative commentary.

From Heaven to Hell?

When we judge one thing, we almost always judge it against something else. We judge good against bad, rain against sunshine, sadness against happiness, heaven against hell. We judge other people's values and standards against our own. When we arrive at an opinion, it is usually built on information we have collected—unless we choose to adopt someone else's opinion. The picture we have about Tibet and China is different from the picture that is presented almost universally in the western media. If the accessible information is inconsistent, the best way to find out what comes closest to the truth is to look for facts and avoid emotions. This is what we did in the matter of Tibet.

The magnitude of a problem is often a question of attitude. How big a problem Tibet is can easily be checked. The common idea is that Tibet is tiny but very important. Although the latter might be right, the former is wrong. The autonomous region of Tibet is about one-eighth of China. The area claimed by the Tibetan independence movement is about one-quarter of China. When we are dealing with Tibet, we are talking about a huge part of China.

In 1959 only a little more than 1 million Tibetans lived in Tibet, under a feudalistic regime. The number has now risen to more than 2.8 million. Before 1950 the largest part of the population (more than 90 percent) were serfs, ruled by aristocratic landlords and monks. All the monasteries had huge estates. Serfs had no personal freedom, from birth to death. Life expectancy in Tibet was thirty-six years; since 1950 it has increased to sixty-five years. Tibet's economic growth is also high—14 percent in 2007—but it is mostly the Chinese who drive this growth, because many Tibetans lack skills, including the ability to speak basic Mandarin. Native Tibetans have an illiteracy rate of almost 50 percent.

The Tibetan language is beautiful, but more suited for expressing spiritual enlightenment than for making a living in the material world. Nevertheless, the Dalai Lama warns that if Tibetans concentrate on learning Mandarin, they risk losing their cultural identity, and thus falling prey to cultural genocide.

From 1966 to 1976, the Cultural Revolution turned Tibet's farms into communes and closed or destroyed monasteries and temples; but the same happened in all of China—Tibet was not singled out. After the Cultural Revolution ended, communes were disbanded and many temples repaired.

In traditional Tibetan religious practice, worshippers prostrate themselves on the ground for hundreds of miles, but they now have to do so at the feet of tourists snapping photos, while breathing in the exhaust fumes of automobiles. Many of the more "assimilated" native Tibetans have moved out of their harsh homeland, and many Han and Hui people have moved into the Tibetan people's homeland.

Tibetans enjoy a number of privileges. The key to wealth in China is education. Education used to be a privilege of the monks and the nobles; it is now available to all, and Tibetans need to score only half as high in the entrance examination to get into the best of the highly competitive schools. Tibetans are allowed to have three children and will still have all the state-provided benefits; before, they had none. Han Chinese are still under the one-child policy. Tibetans have guaranteed seats in the Chinese People's Congress, and since the 1980s the Communist Party picks its officials in Tibet from among Tibetans.

Apart from what China has done wrong, the Chinese did abolish slavery and unpaid labor. They established secular schools, breaking the educational monopoly of the monasteries. They provided running water and electrical systems in Lhasa, the capital.

On January 1, 2008, the Tibet autonomous region raised the minimum wage standard, which had been established three years before. Minimum wages in Tibet are in the forefront of the national average and only slightly lower than those in Beijing, Shanghai, and Tianjin. Employers cannot circumvent the minimum wage standards by using a piecework system. In addition, men and women and farmers and workers from towns and cities must be paid equally for equal work for the same employer.

In recent years, the Huangnan Tibetan Autonomous Prefecture has undertaken the improvement of the health of peasants and herdsmen as the key task of medical and health work, focusing on building the county, township, and village medical networks. As of 2008, thirty-seven township hospitals and 252 village clinics were completed, covering virtually 100 percent of the prefecture. At last count, the number of peasants and herdsmen who had participated in the program was more than 293,000. So far, 285,000 farmers and herdsmen have received compensation claims of more than 2,382 million RMB ($350 million).

Fred Li on Lamaism and Tibet

The Dalai Lama's description of pre-communist Tibet: "The pervasive influences of Buddhism amid the wide open space of an unspoiled environment resulted in a society dedicated to peace and harmony. We enjoyed freedom and contentment." Tibetans love the Dalai Lama and miss life as it once was. But how was life when the Lamas ruled Tibet?

Accounts of Tibet's history are controversial. There is a continuous political and academic debate about serfdom in Tibet. According to the Chinese, 95 percent of the Tibetans lived in "feudal serfdom" before 1950. Chinese narratives portray Tibet prior to the arrival of the PLA as "hell on earth" for the lower classes and especially for the untouchables. And from the Chinese point of view, freeing such a large percentage of Tibet's population from serfdom gives China the moral authority to govern.

According to research by Michael Parenti, a scholar, writer, and educator who studied at Yale, those narratives reveal a feudal, corrupt, and unbelievably brutal picture of the Tibet of the past: "Crushing taxation, unspeakable sexual slavery of women and young boys, shocking mutilation of escaped slaves, and frequent and ongoing infighting between various sects of Lamaism. In Lamaism large portions of the population did nothing economically productive but read scriptures and contemplate the great mysteries." Melvin Goldstein, a Tibetologist, wrote in 1971, "Tibet was characterized by a form of institutionalized inequality that can be called pervasive serfdom." Others say that "serfdom" is a misleading term and instead describe pre-1950 Tibet as a caste-like society.

Tibetologist have offered a range of opinions as to the accuracy of this characterization. There is no consensus on the topic.

A Tyrant Called Modernity

To the lamas there is a bigger threat than China. A tyrant called "modernity" threatens their privileged way of life. The tyrant moves on irresistibly, mauling everyone who gets in its way, regardless of how enchanting and mystifying he may be. The Han Chinese in Beijing have lost their traditional alleys, their *hu-tongs*, and people in Taiwan lost their bucolic paddies to skyscrapers. Globalization has caused less functional languages to slowly disappear. Nobody in Cornwall speaks Cornish anymore, and only a few specialists in Wales speak Welsh.

A market economy simply cannot support a system where large groups of young men do nothing but pray, contemplate, and turn prayer wheels. Drepung Monastery, where the protest in May 2008 began, used to own 185 manors, 25,000 serfs, 300 great pastures, and 16,000 herdsmen. In the twenty-first century, such feudalism could not continue.

As we noted above, many Han and Hui Chinese are moving in, and—although this is seldom reported by the media—large numbers of better-off Tibetans are moving out: to other provinces of China, to India, to Switzerland, to Berkeley, to Colorado, and to Oregon. Given a choice, most people would move out of the harsh land and settle elsewhere. Beijing poured billions into Tibet to make it attractive for people to stay. Now commercialism will take over, and in the long run people will become less religious and will be unlikely to continue supporting the lamas in the way to which they have grown accustomed.

The Beijing government pays the monks a monthly salary. They are provided not only with food and clothing, but with cell phones and, probably, Internet service through which they can obtain information and coordinate actions. They don't have to earn a living; they can read scriptures and long for the return of the Dalai Lama because he symbolizes their old way of life. Many of the poker-faced communist officials of Tibet who speak to the press are ethnic Tibetans!

We said that there is not only one truth. Ultimately, everyone has to form his or her own opinion on Tibet. *Asian Arts News* wrote in June 2008: "Over the past two decades, as Tibet has slowly opened up to tourism and scholarly research, much of the mystery of the place in the minds of foreigners has been replaced by reality. Walking the streets of Lhasa today it is difficult to imagine the cacophony of the culture of the once dominant Tibetans. A world in which religion, culture and art were uniquely blended. The meeting of traditional Tibetan and Chinese art has brought together a new way of looking at the world, as well as a fresh way of looking at local cultural experience."

Mainland and Island

In the traditional Beijing opera, faces play an important role. Facial expressions, from grimaces to smiles, are highly stylized, and are often understood only by insiders. Some operas last many days and run through more than 100 acts. In the long-lasting Taiwanese Chinese performance, the players are also acting with mime and gesture; but while onstage the faces often signal high drama, behind the curtains a different play is taking place.

"Taiwan and China End Political Ice Age," the Beijing correspondent for a German television station reported in April 2009. The report said that both sides were counting on "one China" politics, although each side understands it in its own way. Taiwan sees a democratic, not a communist, China. The mainland does not share this view, but as the unity of the country is not questioned, it is acceptable as the starting point. The report adds that the new policy of détente will be a new impetus for economic relations. China is Taiwan's main trading partner. About 50,000 Taiwanese companies manufacture in China. Now there are more than 100,000 joint ventures on the mainland with Taiwanese partners. Taiwanese entrepreneurs have invested more than $50 billion in these joint ventures. Taiwan in recent years has emerged as one of China's biggest investors.

"Ever Cuddlier" was the title of a report in the December 18, 2008, issue of the *Economist*. This should not have come as such a surprise. While the world has paid most attention to political posturing and fury grimaces, behind the masks much friendlier features were hiding. Taiwan and the mainland have been moving toward economic integration for quite a long time.

Taiwanese companies have been allowed to invest in the mainland since 1979. And now the reverse has become possible as well. On April 26, 2009, representatives of the mainland and Taiwan signed an agreement that, for the first time in sixty years, allows mainland companies to invest in Taiwan. The new agreement is a huge advance in the development of relations across the Taiwan Straits. Details of the agreement are to be worked out during the balance of 2009. Already in 2009, on April 30, *China Daily* reported the first direct investment of a mainland SOE, China Mobile—$528 million—which acquired a 12 percent share in Taiwan's Telecommunication Company FarEasTone. The companies also agreed to work together on procurement, roaming, data- and value-added services, and network and technology advancement.

However, whereas the flow of investment was increasing with little trouble, traveling between mainland and island was not a smooth ride. You could not fly directly from Taiwan to the mainland in either direction. Fred Li, parts of whose essay on Tibet are used in this chapter, is one of Taiwan's investors in China. He often has complained about the time-consuming detour via Hong Kong on flights from Taipei to Shanghai or Tianjin. Hundreds of thousands of Taiwanese business-people and their relatives live and work in China. Changing planes in Hong Kong, as many weekday travelers previously had to do, often took the better part of a working day. But finally, with the new Taiwanese government, in 2008, direct travel of mail and people between Taiwan and various destinations in China again became possible.

The main opposition party, the Democratic Progressive Party (DPP), remains skeptical, saying that the links threaten the island's security. But a jubilant Chinese official declared it "the final part of our economic circle with Taiwan."

In the year before Ma Ying-jeou was elected Taiwan's new leader, we got to know him during a televised discussion. After that visit in Taipei we flew to Beijing (at the time, still via Hong Kong), and we were very much surprised when our Chinese friends told us that they had watched John on television with Dr. Ma. We had no idea that the Chinese could watch Taiwanese television stations. But footage of the interview had been broadcast on China's big national network, CCTV. In the interview, John was asked to predict who the next leader of Taiwan would be. "He is sitting right next to me," John answered.

Half a year later we had the pleasure of being invited to Dr. Ma's inauguration, and it was good to hear him say that he would work to ease relations with the mainland. Ma belongs to the younger generation of the Kuomintang Party (KTM)—a generation of people who have no connections to the party in China before 1949. He was born in Hong Kong in 1950 and later moved to Taiwan and studied law in the United States. Taiwan's relationship to China was Ma's central subject during the election. Unlike the DPP, which promoted Taiwanese separatism, he voted for stronger economic and political relations between the island and the mainland. This was a position that the majority of Taiwanese seemed to support, as he won by 7.6 million votes over his opponent, Frank Hsieh of the DPP.

On the emotional level, the recent improvement of cross-strait ties became all the more evident when two giant pandas were flown (directly) from China to Taiwan as a goodwill gift. China had offered the pandas in 2006, but the former leader, Chen, had not accepted them—from his perspective, for a good reason. The names of the pandas are Tuan Tuan and Yuan Yuan. Together, they mean "reunion."

Instead of political posturing, the big story for some years has been the continuing economic integration of Taiwan and the mainland. It seems that mainland and island have moved from confrontation to negotiation and from political posturing to amicable cuddling.

Xiaowo and Dawo

Time and again, the truth shows different faces. In our search for the true face of China, its view on human rights plays a decisive role; and discussions and disputes about China's view are as emotional as the debates about the "three forbidden T's." We have written about the context of the tragedy at Tiananmen Square in the chapter on Pillar 2. What happened at Tiananmen Square is still casting clouds over China. And, as much sympathy as we have for China, it has not yet done enough to sweep those clouds way.

Human rights are the basic rights and freedoms to which all human beings are entitled. They include civil, political, social, economic, and cultural rights; rights to food; rights to work; and rights to education. The West and China look at the same Universal Declaration of Human Rights, adopted by the United Nations General Assembly in 1948, from different points of view, attributable to their different historic, political, economic, and cultural background.

Zhang Haihua, in her book *Think Like Chinese*, wrote, "While those in the West may believe we are all born equal, the Chinese believe we are all born connected. This belief means that one always lives as part of a network, or as a strand of a web."

Our friend Steve Rhinesmith—who served as a special U.S. ambassador to the Soviet Union and was coordinator of President Reagan's initiative encouraging exchanges between the people of the United States and the Soviet Union during the early days of glasnost—has put it to us this way: "Different interpretations of human rights between China and the United States and Europe can be traced to fundamental cultural differences. The Chinese, in the tradition of Confucianism, are a group-oriented society in which the relationships between individuals are always defined in the context of other people and to the group as a whole. In other words, Chinese think of themselves as part of a family, clan, village, province, ethnic group, and ultimately a state or nation.

"Americans and Europeans come from a tradition that dates back to ancient Greece, in which individuals come together to form a group, or a state. This was carried through John Locke, Rousseau, and other western philosophers as they wrote about the freedom of the individual from the group or state."

China did not have Heracleitus or Protagoras, the Renaissance, the Enlightenment, or the French Revolution; but it had Confucianism, Taoism, and Buddhism. The prevailing concept was loyalty to the country, and respect for and obedience to authorities, government, parents, senior relatives, and teachers. In Chinese, an individual is described as *xiaowo*— "small I." A group that a person belongs to is the *dawo*—the "big I."

Think Like Chinese explains that "it is common practice for Chinese to take up the professions or jobs because they were asked to by their parents or assigned by the country, the ultimate big I, even if they did not like it. When given orders by authorities, government, teacher, police officer, by parents or grandparents, Chinese always do as they are told."

Steve Rhinesmith: "If one begins with the assumption that all individuals are first and foremost members of a group and do not exist without relationships to one another, then one focuses on the group's obligation to provide the individual with social, economic, and cultural rights—the right to work, to be educated, to health, to housing, and to the arts. In return, the individual is loyal to the group in ways that are not readily understood in the West, where the freedom of the individual to leave one group and join another (when one's individual needs are no longer being met) is paramount.

"As a result, in the drafting of the Universal Declaration of Human Rights the Americans and other individualistic countries such as Great Britain were most concerned about political and civil rights and viewed economic, social, and cultural rights not as much as 'rights' as 'opportunities' for people to individually pursue (jobs, health, education). The Soviets, Chinese, and the rest of the world (since about 90 percent of the world has a "group-orientation") argued that it was more important for people to have economic, social, and cultural rights through the state provision of work, housing, education, and health care as basic human rights. Civil and political rights, in this scenario, might have to be sacrificed in order to ensure that the state could provide social, economic and cultural rights."

The Chinese position in trying to provide "human rights" to 1.3 billion people is strongly linked to paragraph three of the Human Rights Declaration: "Every person has the right for life, freedom, and security." To meet the basic needs of the people, to "bring down poverty and backwardness," was written into the constitution of China during the era of Deng Xiaoping, and is still in the version of October 10, 2007.

Rhinesmith: "The compromise between the two views in the Universal Declaration was to include both views of human rights—the individualistic view which became the Covenant on Civil and Political rights and the group view which became the Covenant on Social, Economic, and Cultural Rights. It did not specify, however, who (the individual or the group) was responsible for ensuring these rights.

"To this day, there continues to be a debate between the United States, Europe, and China on human rights, with the United States and Europe accusing the Chinese of violation of human rights because of the lack of civil and political rights and the Chinese accusing the United States of violation of human rights because of homelessness [and] the lack of health insurance and equal opportunity for education."

In some cases, we wrote, there is only one truth. In judging China the questions of what is good or bad and what serves the Chinese and what restrains them will lead to many answers. Personal views will remain, just as ours do, but they should be based on facts as much as possible.

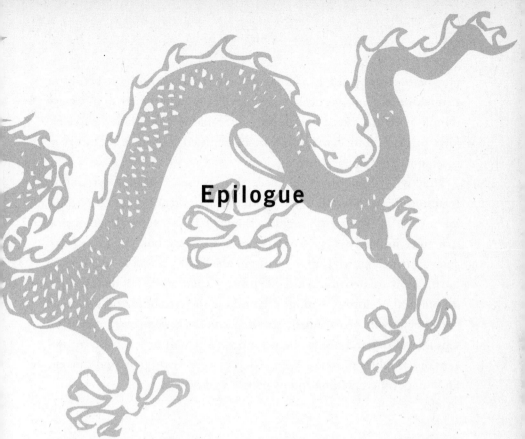

Epilogue

At the beginning of this book we posed a question. How did China succeed? We learned the answer in a conversation with a teenager. His father had been accused of being a revisionist during the Cultural Revolution and was still fighting to clear his name. "My father does not understand," the son said to us. "He is still thinking politics while we all are thinking realities."

Facing an oppressed, indigent, and poorly educated mass of more than 1 billion people with little or low self-esteem, Deng Xiaoping pledged China's Communist Party to switch its focus from politics to economics, from ideologies to growth strategies, and to set a different priority—to give the people what they needed most urgently: food, education, and hope.

In the years since then, China's people have matured. They are well educated; they have reached modest wealth on a huge scale; China has the luxury of concentrating on economics because it is not torn by election cycles and the accompanying conflicting views, goals, and solutions every four or five years. The gradual incorporation of its people into bottom-up decision-making processes is shaping the structure of China's developing vertical democracy. This new model of a society is built on trust. Instead of fighting to be reelected, the leaders make efforts to reach long-term goals. Being entitled to run the country is based on achievements, not elections.

How will China continue? Leadership, as the Chinese understand it, is authority, and it is still in the hands of the government and the Communist Party. The party decides. But in China's vertical democratic structure, authority is given top-down by the party but has to be earned and confirmed bottom-up to be sustainable. The criteria for bottom-up justification are becoming more expansive and the level of qualification for political positions is rising. That is how the system matures. China's self-esteem will grow larger, shaping a vertical democracy based on Chinese values and needs. To what degree it will match western perceptions troubles only the West. China has its own goals and dreams. How to get there, China and its people will decide.

A Note on Sources

As with the research for *Megatrends*, our conclusions in this book are based on the method of "content analysis," literally analyzing the changing content in local Chinese newspapers. Our staff at the Naisbitt China Institute in Tianjin and other associates monitored newspapers of all of China's provinces on the theory that what is happening locally—taken together—is what was happening in China. Uncounted articles about local events and activities—no opinions—were collected, translated into English, and incorporated into a database that was the foundation for this book. The following provincial newspapers were monitored in the research project.

Newspaper	City	Province	Population
Anhui Daily	Hefei	Anhui	62,199,000
Beijing Daily	Beijing	Beijing	12,850,000
Fujian Daily	Fuzhou	Fujian	22,121,000
Xiamen Daily	Xiamen	Fujian	
Gansu Daily	Lanzhou	Gansu	25,340,000

Newspaper	City	Province	Population
Guangzhou Daily	Guangzhou	Guangdong	71,580,000
Shenzen Special Zone Daily	Shenzen	Guangdong	
Zhuhai Daily	Zhuhai	Guangdong	
Guangxi Daily	Nanning	Guangxi	47,115,000
Guizhou Daily	Giuyang	Guizhou	36,631,000
Hebei Daily	Shijiazhuan	Hebei	66,283,000
Heilongjian Daily	Harbin	Heilongjian	38,108,000
Jiamusi Daily	Jiamusi	Heilongjian	
Henan Daily	Zhengzhou	Henan	93,916,000
Hubei Daily	Wuhan	Hubei	56,677,000
Xiangfan Daily	Xiangfan	Hubei	
Yichang Daily	Yichang	Hubei	
Hunan Daily	Changhsa	Hunan	65,670,000
Zhuzhou Daily	Zhuzhou	Hunan	
Xinhua Daily	Nanjing	Jiangsu	72,562,000
Wuxi Daily	Wuxi	Jiangsu	
Jiangxi Daily	Nanchang	Jiangxi	42,158,000
Jiujiang Daily	Jiujiang	Jiangxi	
Jilin Daily	Changchun	Jilin	26,697,000
Jiangcheng Daily	Jilin	Jilin	
Liaoning Daily	Shenyang	Liaoning	42,039,000
Dalian Daily	Dalian	Liaoning	
Inner Mongolia Daily	Hohhot	Neimongol	23,611,000
Ningxia Daily	Yinchuan	Ningxia	5,384,000
Qinghai Daily	Xining	Qinghai	5,035,000
Germu Daily	Germu	Qinghai	
Shaanxi Daily	Xian	Shaanxi	36,269,000
Dazhong Daily	Jinan	Shandong	89,178,000
Qingdao Daily	Qingdao	Shandong	
Weihai Daily	Weihai	Shandong	
Jie Fang Daily	Shanghai	Shanghai	14,913,000

Newspaper	City	Province	Population
Shanxi Daily	Taiyuan	Shanxi	31,908,000
Datong Daily	Datong	Shanxi	
Sichuan Daily	Chengdu	Sichuan	116,546,000
Panzhihua Daily	Panzhihua	Sichuan	
Mianyang Daily	Mianyang	Sichuan	
Tianjin Daily	Tianjin	Tianjin	9,678,000
Tibet Daily	Lhasa	Tibet	2,479,000
Xinjiang Daily	Urumqi	Xinjiang	17,453,000
Yilin Daily	Yilin	Xinjiang	
Yunnan Daily	Hunmin	Yunnan	41,589,000
Dali Daily	Dali	Yunnan	
Zhejiang Daily	Hangzhou	Zhejiang	45,051,000
Wenzhou	Wenzhou	Zhejiang	

Acknowledgments

The first person we must acknowledge is Wang Wei. During the last decade, China has been very much in our focus, but without Wang Wei, our dedication to finding out what is really going on in China would not have reached such depth and intensity. Since the beginning of our work in China, Wei has encouraged us in our efforts to analyze what China's megatrends will be. At every stage in our research and our founding of the Naisbitt China Institute, he connected us with people who added their insights, experience, and support. Wang Wei combines the cosmopolitan spirit of the new China with a love for his motherland. We are very grateful for Wei's initiative and stewardship. Jay Wang, his wife, and Lily, his bright and pretty daughter, always cheered up our time in China; they have become dear friends. Jay put a lot of time into the search for the children of Madam Sun Yat-sen's experimental school, and Lily helped us to gain a better understanding of China's adolescent generation, their hopes and dreams and the fresh view they have of China and the world.

Mr. Liu Ji, retired president for Ceibs (China European Business

School) and a longtime adviser to Mr. Jiang Zemin, hosted a speech in Shanghai, mentioning that *Megatrends* was one of the original sources for Jiang's vision in managing China. Former minister Zhao Qizheng, who had and has a strong share in shaping China, added his profound political and economic knowledge and experience in China's development. Madam Wu Wei, director of International Promotion and Planning Office, author and researcher herself, supported our work in every direction. The openness with which we could talk about China's challenges, worries, and problems helped the book greatly.

Vigi Ma, who is now assistant dean of the Asian Business School, served us so well as our executive assistant during the establishment of the Naisbitt China Institute.

For all the reasons we write about, we chose Tianjin to be our hometown in China. First we must thank Mayor Dai Xianglong for the warm welcome and early support in all our efforts. We appreciated the strong and continuing support of Vice Mayor Cui Jin Du, and we enjoyed his humor and openness. Very warm thanks to Deputy Secretary Chen Zongsheng for his early and strong support

We are grateful to the visionary leaders of Tianjin University of Finance and Economics who provided a splendid home and substantial help for the Naisbitt China Institute. We thank TUFE's president, Zhang Jia Xing, for his personal interest and support, and we are grateful to Wang Yu Ying, the chairperson of the university's Academic Council, for her spirited support. And special thanks to our liaison with the university, Huo Ying Yi, whose excellent English and ready assistance helped us tremendously in our work. We also extend warm thanks to our other university supporter in Tianjin, Nankai University, and its president, Rao Zihe, for their hospitality and early and continuing support.

We want to gratefully acknowledge and thank our Naisbitt China Institute colleagues at Tianjin University of Finance and Economics and Nankai University. First thanks go to our three codirectors of the *China's Megatrends* project: Dr. Wang Yukun and Drs. Zhou Yunbo and Wu Fan, both of Nankai University, all of whom had to deal not only with the challenge of the project but also with the translation of all the data collected. Wang Yukun added much more than his professional skills. In many conversations he helped us to gain a better understanding of China and its people; his personal story and his profound understanding of rural and urban China were of great help in forming the picture of the whole. Orchestrating the research team was not always easy, but Wu Fan and Zhou Yunbo always managed to build the bridge between our and the Chinese approach to research methods.

Many thanks to our team leaders: Wang Hankun, Li Yue, Zhang Xuan, Liu Kai, and Wang Miao. And warm thanks to staffers Wen Cao, Wei, Lin Zou, Wang Jingxin, Gong Yan, Xulan Niu, Cheng Lijuan, Zhang Xingwei, Li Guoqing, Liu Lei, Huang Wei, Huang Xiong, Zhang Kai, Huang Ling, Jia Sun, Cao Weili, Gong Yuan, Liu Hong, and Zhao Dorri.

While touring China we enjoyed the lively nightlong rooftop discussion in Chengdu with Professor Jiang Rongchang, head of the philosophy department at Sichuan University, and some of his colleagues. In Beijing, thanks to Yukun, we had a very instructive dialogue with the famous scholar Chen Ziming.

In all our conversations, studies, and travel, without the insights and advice from Haihua Zhang on the Chinese soul, and Geoff Baker's insights on Chinese business habits, we would have stumbled into numerous cultural traps. Haihua has also been an early reader of the manuscript, a highly valuable help in the translation into Chinese, and a link between us and our Beijing publisher and agent.

Our first outside-China reader was Stephen Rhinesmith, our friend for twenty-five years. Steve read and commented on all the early drafts. His extensive professional experience gave us solid guidance, and his wise counsel was invaluable in the process of writing this book. We will always be grateful for his contribution. We thank the Chinese representative of HarperCollins, our English-language publisher, Stella Chou, in Beijing, for her entrepreneurial verve and strong engagement in the project.

In Taiwan, very special thanks to our old friend Fred Li, whom we quote at length regarding Tibet. Importantly, Fred read the entire manuscript in English and furnished us with well-informed responses, and he also read and checked the translations of both simple and complex Chinese against our original.

We greatly appreciate the response and support of our longtime publisher in Taiwan, the Commonwealth Publishing Group, and its founder, Dr. Charles H. C. Kao, its publisher, Cora Wang, and its foreign rights director, Grace Chang. We very much value our continuing relationship with the Commonwealth team, which is not only professionally satisfying but also personally rewarding.

Martin Janik, program director of our German-language publisher, Hanser, has been an excellent editor and very early advocate of the book. His skills in Mandarin have been helpful along the way and in the combined efforts with the Chinese to present the book at the Frankfurt Book Fair. Wolfgang Stock, managing director of Spotlight Verlag, a good friend and publisher of several of John's books, edited the manuscript in the German translation and supported us with valuable comments. Tatjana Halek, cotranslator of the German edition, upgraded the language of the book with her outstanding literary skills. Daniel Schroeder saved us many times when technology was sabotaging our typing. Our Vienna assistant, Fabian Schroeder, who knows China firsthand and has traveled in Asia extensively, once again, as in *Mind Set!*, was a very thorough and cautious researcher.

Hollis Heimbouch, vice president and publisher of Harper Business at HarperCollins, who has traveled to China several times, showed strong interest in the manuscript before a line of it was written.

From the beginning of the project our agent, Jim Levine, stayed calm with the very tight schedule, the strong and early interest in the manuscript, and the short deadlines that created (great) pressure on all of us. As always, we are grateful to him.

Index